Summary of Contents

Appendices

*

Table of Contents

Appendices

*

Table of Cases

The principal cases are in bold type. Cases cited or discussed in the text are roman type. References are to pages. Cases cited in principal cases and within other quoted materials are not included.

*

THE ELEMENTS OF CONTRACT DRAFTING
WITH QUESTIONS AND CLAUSES FOR CONSIDERATION

*

INTRODUCTION

This book provides an overview of the issues and processes involved in drafting contracts and transactional documents. This should enable students to analyze the basic structure of contracts and other "deal documents" and develop the macro and micro techniques used to efficiently create those documents with precision and clarity. This book cannot cover every single form of contract or transactional document. It can, however, provide the principles necessary for an understanding of the common structures of transactional documents and their provisions that can then be applied to specific transactions.

Beyond structural drafting, this book also covers some of the substantive laws that may affect the contracts at issue. Contracts often govern on-going relationships. It is therefore important to understand how applicable law affects the parties' private dealings and what can be done to limit or expand this relationship. You should verify that the substantive laws referred to in the text are applicable in your jurisdiction and, if not, tailor your documents accordingly.

I have tried to be brief and to the point. These materials largely consist of declaratory statements, rules, and examples. A few noteworthy cases are included in the text or mentioned in the footnotes to illustrate the real world implications of good and bad drafting. Also included throughout the text and appendices are footnotes identifying or questioning various clauses, techniques, and statements. This presentation is intended to make the book easier to read and use while not substantially adding to its length.

The book has been influenced to a considerable degree by my practice experience and scholarly focus, which center on the restructuring of contracts and businesses faced with insolvency and failure. The result is an emphasis on "defensive" contract drafting and a critical evaluation of remedies and other contract provisions intended to protect one or more parties from down-side risk. This emphasis on defensive drafting seeks to avoid unintended consequences that arise because of the actions of others. It also shows that commercial transactional practice and commercial litigation practice are interrelated and are not as separate as they sometimes appear. The deal should be documented both to govern the upside and downside potential that the future holds for the parties. The deal of today may well be the litigation of tomorrow.

Transactional documents are an opportunity to attempt to prevent and plan for future litigation. You should think about how to integrate concepts from other courses and experiences into contracts. Transactional lawyers spend their time, in large part, drafting to fall within or to avoid the ambit of particular statutory or case law. For example, what contract remedies would be available under the common law if the contract makes no provision for them? How can this common law result be altered in the contract? What is the evidentiary significance of various parts of the contract in later litigation? What can be done to render these portions admissible evidence? How can they be drafted so that they are favorable evidence for either party? Contract drafting provides an opportunity to use and reinforce a full range of substantive legal skills.

Finally, every rule stated in this book is subject to exceptions, and legal drafting, like so many things, is subject to the whims of fashion. Reasonable minds may differ on many of these matters. As with all legal writing and drafting, the point is communication. Remember, it is easier to tailor the form of your message to your audience than to educate your audience to enjoy the form of your message. Use the rules, principles, and methods in this book as a default guide to contract drafting—but modify them to fit your audience and surroundings. Remain flexible at all times.

       Prof. George W. Kuney
       The University of Tennessee College of Law
       Knoxville, Tennessee
       January 2003

Chapter 1

FUNDAMENTAL CONSIDERATIONS
IN CONTRACT DRAFTING

This chapter discusses the context of transactional documents in terms of the "deal time line," a chain of events that characterizes most transactions, and then discusses the drafting process and its major, overarching components.

A. Context: The Deal Time Line: Big or Little, Deals Follow a Pattern.

A transaction generally follows a standard time line or chain of events. First, the parties make contact and negotiate. A preliminary agreement is reached and they contact their lawyers, if they have not done so already. Although the key business issues have probably been addressed by the parties, there will often be significant issues left open, some of which will only become apparent to the client after consultation with counsel.[1]

As the parties proceed with full, formal documentation, due diligence (detailed factual and legal investigation) begins, often with one party's production of documents and information relevant to representations and warranties that are being negotiated into the documentation.

The definitive transactional documents are finalized and signed, and further due diligence and other pre-closing activities take place. Then the "closing" occurs; this is the point at which the majority of the consideration changes hands. Payments or deliveries may be made directly, party-to-party, or through an escrow, the preferred route for all but the most basic transactions. Escrows provide the parties with the security of knowing that although they have parted with their consideration, often worth many thousands or millions of dollars, it will not be

---

1. If possible, it is helpful for clients to meet with counsel *prior* to negotiating the basic business deal to explore the possible issues and structures for the contemplated transaction. A well prepared client can then bargain for an issue or structure with the other party from the very beginning. This may result in key issues being resolved in your client's favor with little or no discussion or *quid pro quo*, which might not be the case if the opposing party was just as prepared, left the issue open, followed up with her own counsel, and then negotiated the point.

delivered to the other party until that party's deliveries are complete. In case of a dispute, the escrow agent can hold all consideration already delivered and maintain the status quo pending the dispute's resolution. There may be a post-closing adjustment period as well.

The Deal Time Line

For simple transactions, this time line is condensed and one or more steps may be omitted. On the other hand, in major business transactions, the time line can extend over a year or more. The middle ground of 30 to 90–120 days is represented by an average residential home purchase and sale transaction and is also a typical period in which a small to medium commercial lease or asset purchase transaction might take place.

Keep this time line in mind when drafting. Know where your transaction is and where it is going. Your relative position on this chain of events will affect the pace and the level of detail with which you draft.

Early in the process, have a frank, direct discussion with your client about your role in this process. Some clients prefer to have the lawyer take the lead in all negotiation, documentation and due diligence activities. Many prefer to take the lead in all matters and see the lawyer's role as one of a scrivener. Others fall in between these extremes. Clarify your client's expectations of your role early in the process to avoid confusion and client dissatisfaction. Both the costs and benefits of counsel's activities should be evaluated.

Contract negotiation and documentation is an exercise in *selling*. In the process, you are selling three things. You are:

(1) Selling the parties on executing the documents, now;

(2) Selling the parties on voluntary performance, after execution; and

(3) Selling a later court or other entity on enforcement, after voluntary performance has ceased.

These three sales goals undermine each other to some extent. Consider the tension between selling the parties on execution, which tends to imply vanilla documentation with few, if any, "teeth," on the one hand, and selling the parties later on voluntary performance, which is furthered by fairly detailed documents that contain both "carrot" and "stick" provisions tailored to the particular parties. Balanced documents that accomplish all three sales goals require careful consideration before and during the negotiating and drafting process.

B. The Drafting Process—Step by Step.

1. Investigate the facts (including related documents).

2. Investigate applicable law as needed.

3. Develop a contact list and task schedule according to deadline date and responsible party.

4. Check exemplars and other resources.

5. Prepare initial drafts.

6. Circulate drafts for comments—which may lead the drafter back to earlier steps in the process before moving ahead.

7. Negotiate and document the final, definitive documents.

8. Execution (signing) of the final, definitive documents.

9. Preparation for closing.

10. Closing.

11. Post–Closing Adjustments and Clean Up.

C. The Goal: Practical, *Precise* Documents.

The goal of the drafting process is to produce precise documents that are understandable to the legal and lay audience involved in the project. The words of the transactional document will govern the parties' relationship, rights, and duties. They will be considered to be the primary, and often only, evidence of the parties' intentions. Thus, precise documentation that clearly communicates its meaning to the parties, their counsel, and enforcing courts or other bodies is the goal of the drafting process.

As the discussion of plain English later in this chapter indicates, legal precision does not have to be sacrificed to achieve plain English. Avoid being a drafter that relies on less than plain language to achieve transactional ends. The plainer the language and the more clear the drafting organization and execution, the more likely it is that the parties will not have differing interpretations of their rights, duties, and remedies. This should minimize the potential for litigation, or at least the risk of loss in litigation caused by a court adopting a different interpretation.

Contractual precision has at least[2] four elements:

(1) It is *accurate,* meaning that it correctly expresses the deal.

(2) It is *complete,* meaning that all possibilities have been addressed. Look down the road, determine the range of different possible contingencies, and provide your client with rights and remedies to address contingencies when and if they occur. Focus on what could occur if one party fails to perform and is insolvent, injured,

---

2. This is an example of an inclusive, not exclusive, list, signaled by the use of "at least." Another triggering preamble word for inclusive lists is "including." As drafted, this sentence means there may be more than four elements to contractual precision. All you know is that the author has listed these four. In contrast, exclusive lists state all possibilities: It is either black, white, or grey.

or dead. Include protections for your client addressing these possibilities.

(3) It is *exact*, meaning it lacks both *vagueness* and *ambiguity*.[3]

(4) Finally, *it is able to withstand hostile, critical review. More likely than not, after the contract is executed, the next thorough review of its provisions is likely to be by someone trying to break the contract or sue over the transaction.* That person will focus on interpreting the document in a vacuum, ignoring any knowledge of the parties' intent not found in the four corners of the document. Edit your contract with an eye to identifying and fixing unclear pronoun references, modifiers that may relate to a series of terms or to only one in the series,[4] conjunctions that make a list conjunctive or disjunctive, introductions that make the list exclusive or inclusive, and classification or categorization systems that do not accurately reflect hierarchical relationships.

To address these elements, some drafters have tended to be long and wordy. They have used overlays of multiple synonyms, qualifying phrases and arcane or legalistic prose in an attempt to be accurate, complete, and exact. All too often, the work product collapses under the weight of these techniques. It becomes filled with ponderous, repetitious sentences, paragraphs, and sections. Rather than using as many words as possible—the "shotgun" approach—strive to find the right word or words. This will involve considering the level of detail and generality of the words involved as well as their potential multiple meanings and connotations.

Contractual precision is also achieved through good organization. Within a document, each section should address a specific subject or aspect of the transaction. Within each section, each subsection or paragraph should carry out one function or "job". Within each subsection, each sentence should perform one sub-task. Do not hesitate to subdivide sections, subsections, paragraphs, and sentences as needed to break them into meaningful, digestible chunks.

There are many rules of construction and interpretation and a host of equitable maxims, many of which you may have encountered in your contract law class. While lengthy discussion of these principles is possible, the key point, applicable to all of them, is that they are often used by courts to justify decisions that have been reached for other reasons.[5] Rather than taking comfort in the thought that an ambiguity in a document could be resolved in your client's favor under the doctrine of

---

3. Two different concepts. What is the difference?

4. *See* United States v. Ron Pair Enters., 489 U.S. 235, 109 S.Ct. 1026, 103 L.Ed.2d 290 (1989) (secured party's statutory entitlement to "interest on such claim, and any reasonable fees, costs or charges provided under the agreement under which such claim arose" construed to mean that an involuntary claim is entitled to interest but not fees, costs or charges, because "un-der the agreement ..." modifies only "fees, costs, or charges" not "interest on such claim"—placement of the comma after "claim" in the statute found to be dispositive).

5. For a wonderful tabulation of the contrary doctrines of interpretation, see Llewellyn, *Remarks on the Theory of Appellate Decision and How the Rules or Canons about How Statutes Are to be Construed*, 3 VAND. L REV. 395 (1950).

some such, realize that the ambiguity is more likely to allow a reviewing court to rearrange the parties' relationship according to its own perception of the correct outcome.[6]

Consider the following case involving ambiguity caused by two inconsistent clauses of a UCC security agreement and a variety of interpretive doctrines that can be brought to bear to resolve the ambiguity.

SHELBY COUNTY STATE BANK v. VAN DIEST SUPPLY COMPANY

United States Court of Appeals, Seventh Circuit, 2002.
303 F.3d 832.

DIANE P. WOOD, *Circuit Judge.*

Hennings Feed & Crop Care, Inc. (Hennings) filed a voluntary bankruptcy petition under Chapter 11 on August 23, 1999, after Van Diest Supply Co. (Van Diest), one of its creditors, filed a complaint against it in the Central District of Illinois. Shelby County State Bank (the Bank), another creditor of Hennings, brought this action in the bankruptcy proceeding against Van Diest and the Trustee for Hennings to assert the validity of the Bank's security interest in certain assets of Hennings. Van Diest was included as a defendant because the scope of Van Diest's security interest in Henning's assets affects the extent of the Bank's security interest. The Bank and Van Diest cross-moved for summary judgment, and the bankruptcy court granted the Bank's motion, finding that Van Diest's security interest was limited to the inventory it sold to Hennings (as opposed to the whole of Hennings's inventory). Van Diest appealed that order, and the district court reversed, finding that Van Diest's security interest extended to all of the inventory. Other claims that were at issue in those proceedings are not relevant to this appeal. The Bank now appeals. For the reasons set forth in this opinion, we reverse the decision of the district court and remand the case to the bankruptcy court.

I

Hennings, a corporation based in Iowa, was in the business of selling agricultural chemicals and products. As is customary, several of Hennings's suppliers extended credit to it from time to time to finance its business operations, and obtained liens or other security interests in Hennings's property and inventory to safeguard their advances.

The Bank is among Hennings's creditors. In December 1997, the Bank extended credit to Hennings for $500,000. In May 1998, the Bank increased this amount to a revolving line of credit of some $4,000,000.

---

6. *See* FARNSWORTH, CONTRACTS, §§ 7.11 at 496 (1982) ("none of these rules, however, has a validity beyond that of its underlying assumptions. Their use in judicial opinions is often more ceremonial (as being decora- tive rationalizations of decisions already reached on other grounds) than persuasive (as moving the court toward a decision not yet reached)").

Hennings in return granted the Bank a security interest in certain of its assets, including inventory and general intangibles. Van Diest, also a creditor, entered into several security agreements with Hennings and its predecessor over the years to protect its financing of materials supplied to Hennings. These agreements were covered by the Uniform Commercial Code, which Iowa has adopted (including the revised Article 9), *see* Iowa Code § § 554.9101–554.9507 (1999).

A financing statement entered into by Hennings and Van Diest on November 2, 1981, provided for a blanket lien in "all inventory, notes and accounts receivable, machinery and equipment now owned or hereafter acquired, including all replacements, substitutions and additions thereto." On August 29, 1983, Hennings and Van Diest entered into a new security agreement (the Security Agreement), the language of which is at the core of this dispute. The Security Agreement was based on a preprinted standard "Business Security Agreement" form. In the field for the description of collateral, the parties entered the following language, drafted by Van Diest, describing the security interest as being in:

> all inventory, including but not limited to agricultural chemicals, fertilizers, and fertilizer materials sold to Debtor by Van Diest Supply Co. whether now owned or hereafter acquired, including all replacements, substitutions and additions thereto, and the accounts, notes, and any other proceeds therefrom.

The Security Agreement contained a further preprinted clause providing:

> as additional collateral all additions to and replacements of all such collateral and all accessories, accessions, parts and equipment now or hereafter affixed thereto or used in connection with and the proceeds from all such collateral (including negotiable or nonnegotiable warehouse receipts now or hereafter issued for storage of collateral).

The bankruptcy court found that the language of the Security Agreement was ambiguous and susceptible on its face to two interpretations: under one, the security interest extended to all of Hennings's inventory; under the other, it was limited to inventory sold to Hennings by Van Diest. Proceeding under Iowa law, that court applied several canons of contract interpretation to resolve the ambiguity. The upshot was that the court rejected the use of parol evidence and concluded that the Security Agreement extended only to inventory sold to Hennings by Van Diest.

The district court disagreed. It found that the bankruptcy court had created an ambiguity out of thin air and that the language of the Security Agreement supported only the view that the collateral included all inventory. It relied on the presence of the "after-acquired clause," which provides for future inventory to be deemed part of the collateral. Such a clause ensures that an entity having an interest in inventory retains the interest even when the original goods have been sold and replaced in the course of business, given the natural turnaround of inventory. *See, e.g., Larsen v. Warrington*, 348 N.W.2d 637, 639 (Iowa 1984). To reach this conclusion, the district court found that the qualifier phrase mentioning specific items found in the first paragraph quoted above, while it concededly modified the term "inventory," was mere surplusage. Accordingly, it found that the description of "collateral" must have extended to "all inventory," and reversed the bankruptcy court's findings.

II

As this case requires the interpretation of a contract, which is a question of law, we review the district court's decision *de novo. In re Frain*, 230 F.3d 1014, 1017 (7th Cir.2000); *In re: Virtual Network Servs. Corp.*, 902 F.2d 1246, 1247 (7th Cir.1990). The facts underlying the contract interpretation are not disputed in this case.

In accordance with the Security Agreement's undisputed choice of law provision, we apply Iowa law.

A. Ambiguity of the "After–Acquired" Clause

In the process of divining the meaning of a contractual clause, a court must first establish whether the language in dispute supports more than one interpretation. The existence of such an ambiguity is a question of law, and under Iowa law, "the test for ambiguity is objective: whether the language is fairly susceptible to two interpretations." *DeJong v. Sioux Ctr., Iowa*, 168 F.3d 1115, 1119 (8th Cir.1999).

The description of the security interest in this case is a textbook example of ambiguous language: a term (all inventory) is followed by a qualifier (including all * * *) and then another (sold to Debtor by Van Diest). It is a basic rule of English syntax (of all syntax, in fact) that a modifier should be placed directly next to the element it aims to modify: placing two modifiers in a row leads to the question whether the latter one modifies only the first modifier, or modifies the entire term. In the first edition of his book on statutory interpretation, Sutherland described the "doctrine of the last antecedent" as providing that "relative and qualifying phrases, grammatically and legally, where no contrary intention appears, refer solely to the last antecedent." J.G. Sutherland, Statutes and Statutory Construction § 267, at 349 (1st ed. 1891).

The Supreme Court recognized the existence of the "last antecedent" rule as early as 1799 in *Sims Lessee v. Irvine*, 3 U.S. (3 U.S. 425, 3 Dall.) 425, 444, 1 L.Ed. 665 n. a (1799) ("The rule is, that 'such' applies to the last antecedent, unless the sense of the passage requires a different construction."). The Supreme Court of Iowa has also often endorsed resort to the doctrine in an attempt to resolve problems caused by ambiguously placed modifiers. *See, e.g., State v. Lohr*, 266 N.W.2d 1, 3 (Iowa 1978) (recognizing grammatical as well as legal origins of the rule); *In re Peterson's Will*, 166 N.W. 168, 170–71 (Iowa 1918). The rule is now thought to extend generally to the placement of all modifiers next to the term to be modified. See, *e.g.,* Bryan A. Garner, *Guidelines for*

Drafting and Editing Court Rules, 169 F.R.D. 176, 195 (1997) ("To avoid ambiguity, place a modifier next to the word or phrase it modifies.").

B.   Canons of Interpretation and Extrinsic Evidence

As a linguistic matter, therefore, the sentence is ambiguous. As both the Supreme Court and Iowa courts have recognized (and, indeed, as Sutherland himself pointed out) the rule is helpful in determining the existence of the ambiguity, but not in solving the puzzle when both readings are plausible. *See, e.g., Nobelman v. American Sav. Bank*, 508 U.S. 324, 330, 124 L.Ed.2d 228, 113 S.Ct. 2106 (1993); *In re: Kruse's Estate*, 250 N.W.2d 432, 433–34 (Iowa 1977). Unless one always followed a rigid formalistic approach, the rule would not cast light on which of the two interpretations should prevail. Instead, courts (including those in Iowa) turn to other canons of interpretation. Under Iowa law, those other canons should be used to resolve an ambiguity before parol evidence may be introduced. *See Kibbee v. State Farm & Cas. Co.*, 525 N.W.2d 866, 868 (Iowa 1994). The rules in Iowa are the familiar ones used in contract interpretation in United States courts: the contract must be construed as a whole; the court requires a fair and reasonable construction; avoid illegality; the interpretation must account for surrounding circumstances; and the parties' own practical construction is relevant. Iowa also applies the rule requiring the court to construe terms against the drafter of the instrument (still known to those fond of Latin phrases as the rule of *contra proferentem*); it favors specific terms over general terms; and it favors handwriting to typing and typing to printing.

Construing the contract before us as a whole leaves as many doubts as we had at the outset: nothing within it bears on the intended scope of the phrase "including but not limited to agricultural chemicals, fertilizers, and fertilizer materials sold to Debtor by Van Diest Supply Company." Van Diest could have acquired a security interest in everything that Hennings owned in inventory (as it had done, for instance, with the 1981 security agreement), or it could have limited its interest to the goods it supplied to Hennings. Without resort to other interpretive principles or to outside evidence, such as evidence of custom in the trade, it is impossible for a court to decide which reading the parties intended to adopt.

We do agree with the Bank's claim, however, that it would be bizarre as a commercial matter to claim a lien in everything, and then to describe in detail only a smaller part of that whole. This is not to say that there is no use for descriptive clauses of inclusion, so as to make clear the kind of entities that ought to be included. *See, e.g., National Cash Register Co. v. Firestone & Co., Inc.*, 346 Mass. 255, 191 N.E.2d 471 (Mass.1963). But if all goods of any kind are to be included, why mention only a few? A court required to give "reasonable and effective meaning to all terms," *AmerUs Bank v. Pinnacle Bank*, 51 F.Supp.2d 994, 999 (S.D.Iowa 1999), must shy away from finding that a significant phrase (like the lengthy description of chemicals and fertilizers we have here) is nothing but surplusage.

Iowa law permits courts to consider the parties' conduct, such as the prior security agreements that Van Diest entered into with Hennings, as one way of resolving the ambiguity. Those earlier agreements at times provided for a blanket security with collateral in all inventory. This, too, is not terribly helpful here. On the one hand, the prior use of a general claim for all inventory demonstrates the availability in the trade of such a term and the willingness of Hennings, on occasion at least, to enter into such broad lien grants. On the other hand, it tends to show that the parties knew how to achieve such a result if they wanted to. There must be a reason why the historically used "all inventory," was modified in this case.

More useful is the parties' own practical construction of this particular agreement—a source that Iowa courts agree may be consulted without opening the door entirely to parol evidence. See *Ackerman v. Lauver*, 242 N.W.2d 342, 347 (Iowa 1976). After the Security Agreement was executed, Van Diest sent to other lenders notices of its interest thereunder. In all the notices, it claimed a "purchase money security interest" only in the inventory it sold to Hennings. In a July 1993 letter to the Bank, for instance, Van Diest described its security interest as being in "all of Debtor's property (including without limitation all inventory of agricultural chemicals and additives thereto) purchased or otherwise acquired from the Secured Party.* * * " In the parenthetical, Van Diest then construed its own interest as being limited to the goods it sold to Hennings—not to the whole of Hennings's inventory, as it now claims.

It is true that this canon of construction treads remarkably close to the ground covered by extrinsic evidence. Furthermore, the course of dealing between principal parties A and B is not likely to shed light on the way that third party C should have understood an agreement. Where a third party disputes a reading of a contract, it is not in a good position to use course of dealing or other extrinsic evidence to support its position. It was not a part of the negotiations and does not have the access that we otherwise presume of both parties to outside materials relating to the contract.

The Bank also argues that contractual terms must be interpreted in a "commercially reasonable" fashion, even though the Bank has not supported this specific proposition with references to Iowa law. Nevertheless, the somewhat broader requirement of a generally fair and reasonable construction is amply recognized in Iowa. *See Dental Prosthetic Servs., Inc. v. Hurst*, 463 N.W.2d 36, 38–39 (Iowa 1990). Of two plausible interpretations, we should assume the parties meant one that was fair and reasonable. The problem once again is that there is nothing inherently commercially unreasonable about either of the two possible readings. Under the circumstances, it would have been quite reasonable for Van Diest to get as much security from Hennings as it could, as the latter managed to ratchet up millions of dollars in debt before it went bust (it owes the Bank some $1,412,233.10; Van Diest had, at the time of the petition, some $2,890,288.75 in unpaid invoices; countless other creditors have lined up). On the other hand, it might have been unreasonable for Hennings to commit all of its potential collateral to Van Diest, if so doing might have made it more difficult for the company to obtain credit from others.

C. *Contra Proferentem*

As between the two parties to a contract, there is another doctrine that often resolves ambiguities: it is the rule requiring that ambiguous language must be construed against its drafter. Not only should the drafter be penalized by bearing the costs *ex post* of having cut corners *ex ante*, the penalty of interpretation against the drafter also aims to avoid overbearing behavior between contracting parties where the drafter, often the one in the better bargaining position, tries to pull a fast one over the party who can merely accept or reject the contract as a whole. Although this doctrine of *contra proferentem* is perhaps on the wane in some jurisdictions, it is alive and well in Iowa, *e.g., DeJong*, 168 F.3d at 1121 (applying Iowa law), *Continental Ins. Co. v. Bones*, 596 N.W.2d 552, 558 (Iowa 1999), and in many interpretive contexts, see *DeGeare v. Alpha Portland Indus., Inc.*, 837 F.2d 812, 816 (8th Cir.1988) (recognizing *contra proferentem* rule as a matter of federal common law).

Unlike many jurisdictions that relegate the *contra proferentem* rule to the status of "tie-breaker," *see, e.g., Baker v. America's Mortgage Servicing, Inc.*, 58 F.3d 321, 327 (7th Cir.1995) (Illinois law), Iowa takes a strong view of the rule, holding that ambiguous language is to be "strictly construed against the drafter." *Iowa Fuel & Minerals Co., Inc. v. Iowa State Bd. of Regents*, 471 N.W. 2d 859, 863 (Iowa 1991); see also *Village Supply Co. v. Iowa Fund, Inc.*, 312 N.W.2d 551, 555 (Iowa 1981); *Fashion Fabrics of Iowa, Inc. v. Retail Investors Corp.*, 266 N.W.2d 22, 27 (Iowa 1978). *Cf.* RESTATEMENT (SECOND) OF CONTRACTS § 206 (1981) ("In choosing among the reasonable meanings ... that meaning is generally preferred which operates against the party who supplies the words.").

Here, the drafting party was Van Diest. It was Van Diest that was trying to obtain a security interest in certain property of Hennings, in order to protect its advances to the latter. At least if this were a case against Hennings, the use of the *contra proferentem* rule would provide a way out of the ambiguity in the key contractual language: construing it against Van Diest, the security interest extends only to the products Van Diest sold to Hennings, not to "all inventory." It is not such a case, however, and so we turn to the final consideration that persuades us that the Bank must prevail.

D.   Third–Party Interests

The most compelling reason to construe the language of this agreement against Van Diest is the fact that it was Van Diest that drafted the security agreement, and that the language of that agreement plays an important part for third-party creditors. Those creditors have no way of knowing what transpired between the parties; there is no parol evidence to which they may turn; and they have no way to resolve ambiguities internal to a contract. Here, we are not facing a garden-variety breach of contract action between the two contracting parties, both of whom were present during the negotiations. Instead, this case involves the effect of a contract between two parties (Hennings and Van Diest) on a third party (the Bank). The Bank, as we have already mentioned, is a stranger to the agreement, albeit one whose rights are affected by it. As the Bank could not have invested resources *ex ante* to avoid problems arising from ambiguous language, while Van Diest could have, it should be Van Diest who pays the price *ex post*.

A security agreement is a special kind of contract for which an important audience is third parties who need to know how much collateral has become encumbered. A potential creditor's decision whether to provide credit to Hennings (or anyone else), is contingent on the creditor's understanding of the extent of pre-existing security interests. An unclear statement of that extent should be avoided at all costs: if the creditor reads it reasonably, but too narrowly, when extending credit, it will be out of luck when the debtor defaults. If the potential creditor on the other hand takes a more conservative position and, fearful of the ambiguity, decides not to extend credit, the party seeking that credit is penalized in its access to capital by the shoddy work of its prior creditor—another result to be avoided.

By perfecting its security interest, Van Diest purported to give prospective creditors of Hennings notice of Van Diest's existing interest in Hennings's goods. A prospective creditor should have been able to look at Van Diest's filing and determine on that basis whether to extend credit to Hennings. Here, the Bank presumably did so, especially when it received Van Diest's letter in July 1993 telling it that the Van Diest security interest covered only goods bought from Van Diest. Whether this statement alone would have justified reliance on the Bank's part is debatable; but coupled with the language in the perfected Security Agreement that was susceptible to this interpretation, reliance was certainly reasonable.

The Supreme Court has also noted the special position that third parties occupy, given their limited ways of learning about the existence or the precise extent of a security interest. In *United States v. McDermott*, 507 U.S. 447, 123 L.Ed. 2d 128, 113 S.Ct. 1526 (1993), the Court expressed concern over the possibility that an after-acquired security interest clause might prevent the Government from asserting its interests. Like the Bank, the Government could not have protected itself by contracting with the parties or by analyzing the terms of the clause. The underlying rationale for the decision is equally applicable here: for the notice requirement to be a valid instrument of protection for potential creditors, that notice must be clearly expressed, and it must be such as is needed to inform the behavior of the potential creditor. "When two private lenders both exact from the same debtor security agreements with after-acquired-property clauses, the second lender knows, by reason of the earlier recording, that that category of property will be subject to another claim, and if the remaining security is inadequate he may avoid the difficulty by declining to extend credit." *Id. at 454.* When the earlier recording is ambiguous, the "second lender" does not know what collateral will be at its disposal.

In a broad sense, the problem of later creditors is similar to the problem of any third-party beneficiary. In the context of pension or welfare funds, which might be third-party beneficiaries to agreements between unions and multi-employer bargaining units, this court has held that the language of the collective bargaining agreement must stand on its own; it cannot be altered by oral agreements. *See Central States, Southeast and Southwest Areas Pension Fund v. Gerber Truck Serv., Inc.,* 870 F.2d 1148, 1154 (7th Cir.1989) (en banc). Similarly, security agreements should be construed if at all possible without resort to external evidence, and they should be construed in a way that recognizes the important role they play for third-party creditors. Doing so here leads to the same result we have already reached: Van Diest's security interest extend only to the inventory it furnished. The limiting clause modifies the term "all inventory," and it is not surplusage.

For these reasons, we REVERSE the judgment of the district court and REMAND the case to the bankruptcy court for the entry of judgment in favor of the Bank.

* * *

Shelby County State Bank's security interest was saved by the 7th Circuit, which essentially reinstated the decision of the bankruptcy court that the district court had overturned. Three costly levels of judicial review were necessary to construe this ambiguous contract. All this litigation might have been avoided had the descriptions of collateral in the financing statement and the security agreement—both form documents with little to fill in apart from the parties names and the description of the collateral—matched.

One often used technique that greatly increases clarity, precision, and overall readability is a "tabulated" or "tabular" form, which uses indented sub-paragraphs to format lists and set out items and terms. Here is an example of the tabular form used for part of an indemnification provision:

9.12 *Participating in or Assuming the Defense*

The indemnifying party may participate in the defense at any time. Or it may assume the defense by giving notice to the other party. After assuming the defense, the indemnifying party:

    (1) must select an attorney that is satisfactory to the other party;

    (2) is not liable to the other party for any later attorney's fees or for any other later expenses that the other party incurs, except for reasonable investigation costs;

    (3) must not compromise or settle the action without the other party's consent (but the other party must not unreasonably withhold its consent); and

    (4) is not liable for any compromise or settlement made without its consent.

For tabular form to be effective, all items in each level of subparagraphs, indicated by successive indents, must be part of the same hierarchical rank or class. Each item in the list also must be structured so that, if read immediately after the introductory language, it would be grammatically correct. This also means that each of the list's items must be grammatically similar or "parallel." The same is true for sentences that continue beyond the list.

    Finally, either:[7]

    (A) each item in the list should be followed by the appropriate conjunction,[8] or

    (B) the second to last item should be followed by the appropriate conjunction,

which is applicable to the whole list. Form "B"—used in the indemnification provision above—is most common.

    Remember how important it is to listen to what your client says is desired, then translate this into legal terms and discuss or "mirror" your understanding back to her until both of you are satisfied. Do this first, before putting ink on a page, or fingers to keyboard, to avoid wasting your time or your client's money.

D. Plain English & Clear and Conspicuous Drafting.

    The Securities and Exchange Commission ("SEC") has issued plain English guidelines for disclosure documents filed under the Securities Exchange Act of 1933,[9] and, since October 1, 1998, companies filing registration statements under the Securities Act of 1933 must:

- write the forepart of these registration statements in plain English;

- write the remaining portions of these registration statements in a clear, understandable manner; and

- design these registration statements to be visually inviting and easy to read.

The principles of the SEC's plain English rule can and should be applied to almost any legal document. Plain English is characterized by:

---

7. Is the word "either" really needed here in light of the tabular use of the conjunction "or"?

8. "And" or "or" are most common.

9. Brief Description of the New Plain English Rule and Amendments Securities and Exchange Commission, Division of Corporation Finance: Updated Staff Legal Bulletin No. 7, "Plain English Disclosure" June 7, 1999.

Characteristics of Plain English

1. Short sentences.[10]

2. Definite, concrete, everyday language.

3. The active voice.

4. Tabular presentation of complex or multi-factor information.

5. Separate paragraphs and sections, with headings, for separate concepts.

6. The absence of highly legal jargon or highly technical business terminology and use of Latin or other foreign terms.

7. The absence of double or multiple negatives.

8. The use of multiple columns of text if the font is small.

Closely related to the virtues of plain English is the problem of how to draft provisions that are clear and conspicuous to non-lawyers. Consider the following case.

AMERICAN GENERAL FINANCE, INC. v. BASSETT (IN RE BASSET)

United States Court of Appeals, Ninth Circuit, 2002.
285 F.3d 882.

KOZINSKI, Circuit Judge:

Darlene Bassett bought two chairs and two ottomans, and financed the purchase with a secured loan from American General Finance, Inc. (Finance). Months later, Bassett filed a voluntary Chapter 7 bankruptcy petition. Before receiving a discharge, Bassett signed a reaffirmation agreement with Finance. Bassett kept up with her payments to Finance for a few months but eventually stopped. Finance sent a series of letters, first friendly and later pointed, asking to be paid. Bassett responded by moving to reopen her bankruptcy so that she could bring this putative class action lawsuit. Bassett argues that the reaffirmation agreement she signed is unenforceable and that Finance's collection letters were therefore illegal. Under a number of theories, she seeks damages and a declaration that the reaffirmation agreement is unenforceable.

The bankruptcy court concluded that the agreement is enforceable and granted Finance's motion for judgment on the pleadings. The Bankruptcy Appellate Panel reversed, concluding that the reaffirmation agreement is not enforceable and that Finance's attempted collection of the debt violated Bassett's discharge. The BAP remanded so that Bassett could proceed with claims for civil contempt and violation of the automatic bankruptcy stay. *See Bassett v. Am. Gen. Fin., Inc. (In re Bassett),*

---

10. Remember the "one breath test": if the sentence is too long to be said without pausing to draw a breath, it is too long. Remember also that this is a test for *maximum* length. Brevity is generally a blessing.

255 B.R. 747, 760 (B.A.P. 9th Cir.2000). Finance appeals and Bassett cross-appeals the BAP's affirmance of the dismissal of a implied cause of action under 11 U.S.C. §§ 524, and of her state law and Truth in Lending Act claims.

1. Bassett argues that the reaffirmation agreement is unenforceable because it fails to comply with 11 U.S.C. §§ 524(c)(2)(A), which requires the agreement to have a "clear and conspicuous" statement that "advises the debtor that the agreement may be rescinded at any time prior to discharge or within sixty days after such agreement is filed with the court." 11 U.S.C. §§ 524(c)(2)(A). Bassett does not dispute that the agreement contains this "right-to-rescind" statement; she argues that the statement is not "clear and conspicuous."

The bankruptcy code doesn't define "clear and conspicuous." Other courts considering this question have defined the term by borrowing the state law definition of "conspicuous" found in section 1–201(10) of the Uniform Commercial Code. *See, e.g., In re Noble,* 182 B.R. 854, 858 (Bankr.W.D.Wash.1995); *In re Roberts,* 154 B.R. 967, 969–70 (Bankr. D.Neb.1993). We see no reason to depart. When a federal statute leaves terms undefined or otherwise has a "gap," we often borrow from state law in creating a federal common law rule. *See PM Group Life Ins. Co. v. W. Growers Assurance Trust,* 953 F.2d 543, 546 (9th Cir.1992); *De Sylva v. Ballentine,* 351 U.S. 570, 580–81 (1956) (borrowing a state law definition of "children" for purposes of the Copyright Act). The UCC's definition of "conspicuous" is an obvious choice, because it, like section 524(c)(2), is concerned with making contract language readily accessible to unsophisticated parties.

Hence,

> [a] term or clause is conspicuous when it is so written that a reasonable person against whom it is to operate ought to have noticed it. A printed heading in capitals (as: Non–Negotiable Bill of Lading) is conspicuous. Language in the body of a form is "conspicuous" if it is in larger or other contrasting type or color. But in a telegram any stated term is "conspicuous". Whether a term or clause is "conspicuous" or not is for decision by the court.

U.C.C. §§ 1–201(10), 1 U.L.A. 64 (1977).

The BAP also borrowed the UCC's definition of "conspicuous," but looked to caselaw from the District of South Carolina to interpret it. *See Bassett,* 255 B.R. at 751–52 (citing *Myrtle Beach Pipeline Corp. v. Emerson Elec. Co.,* 843 F.Supp. 1027, 1038 (D.S.C.1993)). It needn't have reached quite so far. Interpreting Nevada's version of the UCC, we held that a term is conspicuous if "a reasonable person in the buyer's position would not have been surprised to find the [term] in the contract." *Sierra Diesel Injection Serv., Inc. v. Burroughs Corp.,* 890 F.2d 108, 114 (9th Cir.1989).

We decide conspicuousness as a matter of law. This is not because judges are experts at graphic design, but because subjecting conspicuousness to fact-finding would introduce too much uncertainty into the drafting process. *See Smith v. Check–N–Go of Illinois, Inc.*, 200 F.3d 511, 515 (7th Cir.1999) ("No matter *what* a lender did, a borrower could say that to his eyes the combination of color, typeface, spacing, size, style, underlining, capitalization, border, and placement ... emphasized one disclosure over another."); U.C.C. §§ 1–201(10).

Bassett's reaffirmation agreement is two pages long. Roughly three-fourths of the top of the first page contains instructions and spaces for such information as Bassett's name and the loan's principal amount and interest rate. Much of this is white space. Just three sentences appear below these blanks:

> The parties understand that this agreement is purely voluntary and that the debtor may rescind the agreement at any time prior to discharge or within 60 days after such agreement is filed with the court, whichever occurs later, by giving notice of rescission to the creditor. Rescission of the Reaffirmation Agreement shall be considered default under the terms and conditions of the Installment Agreement referred to above.

> THE DEBTOR UNDERSTANDS THAT THIS AGREEMENT IS NOT REQUIRED UNDER THE UNITED STATES BANKRUPTCY CODE TITLE 11 U.S.C. AND NOT REQUIRED UNDER NON BANKRUPTCY LAW OR ANY AGREEMENT NOT IN ACCORDANCE WITH THE PROVISION OF 11 U.S.C. SECTION 524(C).

The signature line appears just below, as the very last item in the agreement proper.

The second page of the reaffirmation agreement contains a space for the attorney's declaration required by 11 U.S.C. §§ 524(c)(3), the motion for court approval and the court order. The attorney declaration affirms that the debtor is fully advised of the agreement's consequences, and that the agreement does not impose an undue burden on the debtor.

The BAP held that Finance's right-to-rescind statement is not "conspicuous" because it is in lower case, and near a sentence that is in capitals. This, the panel concluded, "has the effect of deemphasizing the right-to-rescind language." *Bassett*, 255 B.R. at 752. Additionally, the BAP found that the right-to-rescind statement is "rendered visually less prominent" because it is next to a sentence stating that the rescission constitutes a default. *Id.* The BAP insisted that it was not making a hard-and-fast rule about whether section 524(c)(2) requires any particular formatting; instead, "[o]n this particular form, the combined effect of printing the right-to-rescind language in lower-case type, of including unnecessary language in the same paragraph, and of printing nearby language in upper-case type renders the present reaffirmation agreement unenforceable." *Id.*

None of these factors justify holding that the right-to-rescind statement is not clear and conspicuous. Including "unnecessary language" in the same paragraph as the right-to-rescind statement has only a minor impact. The "unnecessary language" the BAP identifies is a single sentence that takes up about two lines of text. While it's possible that the statement would be marginally more visible with an entire paragraph to itself, the encroachment of a few extra words hardly matters.

The BAP was troubled that the right-to-rescind statement is in lower case, but there is nothing magical about capitals. True, the UCC specifies that "[a] printed *heading* in capitals" is normally conspicuous. U.C.C. §§ 1–201(10) (emphasis added). This has given rise to the canard that all language in capitals is automatically conspicuous, and the fallacy that language not in capitals isn't conspicuous. One leading sales law treatise goes farther and advises readers to use "bold-face capitals of a contrasting color" to be conspicuous. 1 James J. White & Robert S. Summers, *Uniform Commercial Code* §§ 12–5 at 637 (4th ed. 1995). The use of capitals as a talisman of conspicuousness has survived intact despite decades of improved literacy and technology. Even some web page "click-through" agreements have clauses written in capitals, though there are better ways of making text stand out in a web browser window. *See, e.g., Specht v. Netscape Communications Corp.*, 150 F.Supp.2d 585, 588–89 (S.D.N.Y.2001).

Lawyers who think their caps lock keys are instant "make conspicuous" buttons are deluded. In determining whether a term is conspicuous, we look at more than formatting. A term that appears in capitals can still be inconspicuous if it is hidden on the back of a contract in small type. *See, e.g., Sierra Diesel*, 890 F.2d at 114. Terms that are in capitals but also appear in hard-to-read type may flunk the conspicuous-ness test. *See, e.g., id.; Lupa v. Jock's*, 500 N.Y.S.2d 962, 965 (N.Y.City Ct.1986). A sentence in capitals, buried deep within a long paragraph in capitals will probably not be deemed conspicuous. Formatting does matter, but conspicuousness ultimately turns on the likelihood that a reasonable person would actually see a term in an agreement. Thus, it is entirely possible for text to be conspicuous without being in capitals.

The BAP suggested that the right-to-rescind statement is inconspicuous because a nearby sentence in capitals "deemphasiz[es]" it. Formatting does have the potential to distract: A bold, red, 24–point gothic-font sentence etched holographically onto a page might steal the spotlight from neighboring sentences. Some purists insist that using emphasis "as a guarantee that some portion of what one has written is really worth attending to is a miserable confession that the rest is negligible." H. W. Fowler, *A Dictionary of Modern English Usage* 305–06 (Crown Publishers 1983). But this problem arises only when formatting highlights a sentence by making it stand out from a surrounding sea of text. When an agreement is three sentences long, this isn't an issue.

Finance's reaffirmation agreement demonstrates the short-comings of any conspicuousness test that turns on contrasting formatting. Section 524 requires two "clear and conspicuous" statements. Aside from the right-to-rescind statement, the agreement must also have a "clear and conspicuous" notification to the debtor that the law does not require him to enter into a rescission agreement. *See* 11 U.S.C. §§ 524(c)(2)(B). Finance's form puts this notification in capitals. If Finance had also put the right-to-rescind statement in capitals, that would have left a single sentence in lower case. Normally statements in capitals stand out; but if every sentence *except* one is in capitals, then only that (supposedly inconspicuous) sentence contrasts with the others. Of course, had Finance deleted that odd lower-case sentence, the entire agreement would have been in capitals.

Brevity promotes conspicuousness. Bassett's rescission agreement takes up significantly less than one side of a page. The right-to-rescind statement is the first sentence in the agreement, making it even more conspicuous—even the least attentive reader is likely to see it. No aspect of the formatting or appearance of the statement makes it less visible or difficult to read. A reasonable person "would not have been surprised to find" the agreement's right-to-rescind statement. *Sierra Diesel*, 890 F.2d at 114.

2.   Bassett also argues that the reaffirmation agreement is unenforceable because it contains a misleading (and hence not "clear") statement. Bassett faults the agreement's second sentence: "Rescission of the Reaffirmation Agreement shall be considered default under the terms and conditions of the Installment Agreement referred to above."

3.   We conclude that the right-to-rescind statement is clear and conspicuous as required by 11 U.S.C. §§ 524, and that Bassett's reaffirmation agreement is therefore enforceable. Bassett's claims for violation of the post-discharge injunction, civil contempt, violation of the Washington Consumer Protection Act, unjust enrichment, and violation of the Truth in Lending Act all require a finding that the reaffirmation agreement is unenforceable. Thus, they all fail.

. . . . .

[the portion of the opinion dealing with Bassett's claim for a willful violation of the automatic stay of 11 U.S.C. § 362 is omitted]

* * *

Although the Ninth Circuit panel saved American General Finance's reaffirmation agreement from Bassett's clear and conspicuous challenge, reasonable minds can certainly differ on the subject. This is demonstrated by the result below in the Bankruptcy Appellate Panel and in the length of Judge Kozinski's opinion. Being clear and conspicuous can obviously take some thought and involves skills beyond mere substantive legal knowledge, such as layout design.[11]

11.   A delightfully radical approach to clear and conspicuous drafting, among other things, is taken by experienced business attorney and writer on contract drafting Howard Darmstadter in his contrarian guide to legal drafting "Hereof, Thereof, and Everywhereof" (ABA 2002). Mr. Darmstadter recommends that lawyers take their cue from the publishing industry and create documents that feature formatting similar to that found in magazines such as the *Atlantic Monthly*. Although this author agrees with many of Mr. Darmstadter's observations and prescriptions for better

QUESTIONS & CLAUSES FOR CONSIDERATION

1. Do you agree with Judge Kozinski or with the BAP?

2. What do you think about the different formatting of the two statements that are required to be clear and conspicuous?

3. What about Judge Kozinski's conclusion that because Bassett had a lawyer she cannot claim the language was not clear although the statute requires *both* clear and conspicuous language *and* the attorney declaration?

E. Attention to Detail; Pride in Your Work; Neatness Counts.

Lawyers are word people. Words, phrases, sentences, paragraphs, sections, contracts, and briefs are their stock in trade. The contracts that you draft must be clear, practical, and precise so that they work by guiding the course of performance or providing the foundation for a successful lawsuit. All that is for your client's sake.

Beyond the client, however, aspiring lawyers need to pay close attention to detail and take pride in *all* their written work product for their *own* sake. Each document you create—your work product—is your calling card. It is on this that you will be evaluated by your colleagues, clients, opponents, and others. Documents, including correspondence, that contain typos or substantive errors, that are badly formatted, or that do not convey an appearance of well-thought-out precision and accuracy will be held against you in the court of professional reputation. All documents that go out over your name should be proofed, spell-checked, substantively correct, neat, and well organized. This requires a level of attention to detail that few people other than lawyers, accountants, and serious editors and publishers give to writing. Each error that slips out can have a damaging effect upon the way others judge your professional competence, prudence, and attention to the matter at hand. The effect is cumulative. At some point—reached fairly quickly—mistakes add up to the reader, who assumes that the author is (a) not very smart, (b) not very careful, or (c) not paying attention. None of these impressions will advance your legal career.

transactional documents, if the survival of form contracts studded with "know all men by these presents," "wherefore" and other archaic phrases is any indication, these prescriptions may take some time to be accepted by the mainstream business bar. As a result, many of Mr. Darmstadter's suggestions are not adopted in this text, which is meant as a first level primer on contract drafting. Interested or more advanced readers should read Mr. Darmstadter's book and adopt his common-sense techniques to improve clarity and readabililty as appropriate (or as much as they can get away with).

I take specific issue with only one of Mr. Darmstadter's points. He believes that the convention of using two spaces at the end of a sentence is no longer justified as the typewriter has been all by replaced by the word processor. I disagree and find that the two space rule allows the eye to quickly and easily find the end of the sentence (or, more to the point, the beginning of the next sentence), speeding the process of skimming or quickly reviewing a standard, left-justified document. The two space rule should be retained.

QUESTIONS & CLAUSES FOR CONSIDERATION

1. The following is a section of an "Application of Deductibles" clause from an insurance policy:[12]

> A series of losses arising from the same event shall be treated as a single loss in the application of the deductibles. However, notwithstanding the foregoing, in the event of losses to property arising out of which separate deductibles are applicable, then such deductibles will be applicable by class of property as if the losses had occurred separately.

How do you interpret this provision? Rewrite it so that it clearly states your interpretation.

2. Here is an example of a provision written in less than plain English in the non-recourse provision[13] of a loan agreement:

> Section 2.10. *Nonrecourse Obligation*. Without releasing, impairing, forgiving or waiving in any manner or amount the obligations or promises of the Borrower or any other party contained, referred to or defined in the Loan Agreement or the Financing Documents, and without releasing, impairing, forgiving or waiving the right to foreclosure of the Mortgage for the full amount of all indebtedness evidenced by the Loan Agreement and by the Mortgage, which right of foreclosure, by any lawful means, as to real and personal property described or referred to therein, is specifically reserved by the Loan Agreement, the covenants and agreements of Borrower to make the payments required under the Loan Agreement and under the Financing Documents shall be without recourse to any partner of Borrower, or any officer, director, employee or agent of any partner of Borrower. Upon the occurrence of an Event of Default, neither the Trustee, the Issuer nor the Bondholders shall take any action against the partners of the Borrower except such action as may be necessary to exercise any and all rights and interests the Trustee or the Issuer may have in and to any and all collateral securing such indebtedness and to subject such collateral to the satisfaction of such indebtedness. The provisions of this Section 2.10 shall not apply to the Borrower's indemnification obligations under Section 4.1 hereof.

Describe, in outline form, what the provision means, referring only to the text above and your general knowledge. Redraft this provision in

---

12. This clause was litigated in Puerto Rico Elec. Power Auth. v. Philipps, 645 F.Supp. 770 (D.P.R.1986).

13. A non-recourse provision in a loan agreement limits a lender's remedies to foreclosure and sale of its collateral in case of default. It bars the lender from recovering any deficiency (the difference between the total owed and the amount the lender recovers through foreclosure on the collateral) from the borrower or the borrower's other assets.

plain English while retaining its meaning. Then describe the process and techniques that you used to accomplish this rewrite.

3. Redraft the following provision from a commercial lease in plain English.

Article XI

Assignment or Subletting

The Lessee shall not assign nor permit any assignment by mortgage, operation of law or otherwise of this Lease, nor underlet any portion of the premises nor permit the occupation of the whole or any part thereof by another by license or otherwise without, on each occasion, first obtaining the Lessor's approval in writing, which approval shall not be unreasonably withheld or delayed subject to the approval of any Mortgagee of the premises or the Land or Building including the premises, provided, however, that (except in the case of a sale of the entire business [whether by sale of stock or assets] of Lessee or of substantially all of the tangible assets of either the industrial or clock business, as a result of which the entire premises or the portion thereof attributable to such clock or industrial business is subleased to the purchaser) it shall be a condition to such approval that Lessor shall be entitled to receive, monthly as rent is paid to Lessee under any such sublease or assignment, one half of the excess (if any) of the annual base rent payable under such sublease or assignment over the Annual Base Rent hereunder, on a per square foot basis, provided, however that Lessee shall first be entitled to deduct from such excess as received the cost of a initial improvements required to sublease such space. It shall not be reasonable for the Lessor or Mortgagee to withhold consent to any proposed assignment or subletting to an affiliate of Lessee or to any other reasonably creditworthy proposed assignee or subtenant. No consent by the Lessor to an assignment, sublease or other indulgence or favor at any time granted by the Lessor to Lessee or to anyone claiming under the Lessee, nor acceptance of rent form, or otherwise dealing with, anyone claiming under the Lessee, shall be deemed to constitute any consent to any further assignment of Lessee's entire interest in this Lease. The Lessee and all persons claiming under the Lessee shall be deemed to have waived any and all suretyship defenses. It shall be a condition of the validity of any such assignment or underletting, that the assignee or sublessee agrees directly with Lessor, by written instrument in form satisfactory to Lessor, to be bound by all the obligations of the Lessee hereunder, including, without limitation, the obligation to pay rent and other amounts provided for under this Lease and the covenant against further assignment and subletting.

*

Chapter 2

THE FORM OF TRANSACTIONAL DOCUMENTS[1]

This chapter discusses "macro" issues relating to the form of transactional documents and includes some overall rules for successful structuring and drafting. You should refer to the contracts in the appendices for examples of these concepts as needed.

A. General Outline.

1. Title.

2. Introductory paragraph, including the parties and the date of agreement.

3. Recitals or a Statement of Background Facts.

4. Definitions.

5. Core substantive provisions, including consideration, conditions, closing.

6. Representations, warranties, covenants, indemnities, guaranties, releases.

7. Events of default and remedies.

8. "Boilerplate."

9. Signature Blocks.

10. Exhibits and Attachments.

The overall organization of a transactional document or group of transactional documents follows a group of rules:

- General provisions before specific ones.
- Important, central provisions before others.
- Rules before exceptions.
- Separate provisions or sub-sections for each concept.

1. The sample transactional documents in the appendices illustrate many of these points.

- Technical, boilerplate, housekeeping, and miscellaneous provisions located last, before the signature blocks.

B.   Transactional Documents Memorialize a Deal.[2]

They are documents that speak as of one particular time (in the case of most, the date of their execution). This means that they are intended to capture the agreements of the parties, and their respective rights and obligations, and to establish a set of rules that will govern future dealings. They must provide for substantially all the details of the parties' future dealings or they fail in their job.

C.   The Document's Title and Introduction.

Generally, begin the first page of any transactional document with a title in ALL CAPS, centered, and underlined. The title should identify the type of contract using a generic term, such as "Lease," "Prenuptial Agreement" or "Asset Purchase Agreement."

The introduction paragraph is not numbered. It should be in the form:[3]

> This [Agreement, Lease, etc. as appropriate] ("[Defined Term]") dated [as of] _____, 20xx, is between ___, [a _____ Corporation, Limited Liability Company, General Partnership, an Individual, etc., as appropriate] ("[Defined Term]")[4] and ___, [a _____ Corporation, Limited Liability Company, General Partnership, an Individual, etc., as appropriate] ("[Defined Term]") [add additional parties as needed].

For example:

> This asset purchase agreement ("APA") dated September 21, 2003, is between Mayfield & Associates, LLC, a Delaware limited liability company ("Buyer") and Bronson Construction, Inc., a California Corporation ("Seller").

The first paragraph of the agreement identifies the parties and the type of transaction they are documenting, establishes defined terms for the parties, and provides a reference date for the document. Ensure that all parties' names and other information (such as state of incorporation) are correct—using defined terms means they will not come up again until the signature blocks. Beyond these

---

2. Remember the Deal Timeline from Chapter 1: parties meet, negotiate, prepare preliminary documentation, conduct due diligence and prepare final transactional documents, conduct further due diligence, participate in the closing, make post closing adjustments, and clean up.

3. Bracketed—[_____]—text in examples is optional language or language needing replacement when drafting a specific provision. Brackets should be deleted when using these provisions.

4. Note the form used to define a term. It should be used consistently throughout the document. For ease of future use of this agreement as an exemplar for future transactions, choose generic defined terms like "Buyer," "Seller," "Landlord," "Tenant," etc. This allows a change of party name in the first paragraph to ripple or flow through the document automatically when the document is used as an exemplar in a subsequent matter.

items there is no need for further detail. Leave that for the recitals and the body of the contract.

D. Preambles/Recitals and Transitioning into the Agreement.

Preambles or recitals set the context for the agreement and are useful in later interpretation. They also provide a place to list related transactional documents and other things that may be part of the transaction as a whole but are otherwise not referenced in the particular agreement itself. Preambles or recitals do not need to be preceded by the word "whereas" and it is not necessary to title the section "Recitals," although you will no doubt run into those forms (and those who aggressively adhere to them) in practice.

Each recital should be written in plain English, and should be preceded by a capital letter "numbering" or "ordinal" system (just like this section of this text). In the recitals, include facts that will help a later reader grasp the nature, purpose and basis for the agreement. Examples of appropriate facts for recitals include: (i) the relationship and goals of the parties, (ii) the nature of the transaction, and (iii) other transactional documents and things associated with the transaction. Take care to be accurate and not to include unnecessary facts in the recitals—they may be used later in litigation to prove that which they state.[5] When in doubt be more general than specific in the recitals and avoid the temptation to recite everything.

Immediately after the recitals, you will want to draft a transition to begin the substantive portions of the agreement. One useful formulation is:

> *The parties agree [as follows]:*

It is not necessary or desirable to draft a lengthy transition using archaic phrases, such as:

> *Know all men by these presents: Now, THEREFORE, and in consideration of the premises and the mutual promises, terms and conditions stated herein, the parties do now AGREE as follows:*

If your recitals are stated prior to a section of the document that is labeled "agreement" or could be construed as the "real" agreement, as distinct from the "mere" recitals, then the accuracy of the recitals should be addressed in the "real" agreement section. This can be done by including a provision stating that the parties represent and warrant to one another that the recitals are accurate, perhaps with a "to the best of their knowledge" limitation.[6] Alternatively, one or both of the parties may desire to disclaim any implication that they are representing or

---

5. Barbara Child, Drafting Legal Documents, Principles and Practices 125 (West 1992); *see also* Fed. R. Evid. 801(d) (defining as non-hearsay both prior statements by a witness and admissions of party-opponents).

6. Representations, warranties, and limitations are discussed in Chapter 7.

warranting that the recitals are accurate. This can be accomplished by introducing the subject recital with *"[specify party] asserts that [state recital]."* In either case, a provision regarding the accuracy of the recitals should be expressed clearly in the main "agreement" section of the document to avoid any implication that the recitals are not part of the agreement.

E. Definitions/Defined Terms: A Powerful Technique to Enhance Meaning and Readability Simultaneously.

When an agreement's definitions are numerous or complicated, the defined terms should be set out alphabetically in a separate section located near the beginning or end of the agreement.[7] If the document is a short one, if definitions are not numerous, or if it makes sense for some other reason, definitions can be introduced "on the fly" in the first place they occur, including in the preamble or introductory paragraph or the recitals. For example:

> This *ASSET PURCHASE AGREEMENT AND ESCROW INSTRUCTIONS (the "Agreement") is entered into and effective as of [date], at [city], [state], by and between _____ (the "Seller"), and _____ ("Buyer"), on the basis of the following facts and constitutes (i) a contract of purchase and sale between the parties, and (ii) escrow instructions to _____ ("Escrow Agent"), the consent of whom appears at the end of the Agreement.*

—or—

> *THIS LEASE, made at _____, _____, on the ___ day of _____, 20___, between _____ a _____ _____ (the "Landlord"), and _____, a _____ (the "Tenant").*
>
> *1. Premises. Landlord hereby leases to Tenant, and Tenant hereby hires and takes from Landlord, upon the terms and conditions below, the premises containing approximately _____ square feet located in _____ and outlined in red on Exhibit "A" attached hereto, which are located on the _____ _____ floor(s) of the building (the "Building") located at _____.*
>
> *2. Term. The term of this lease shall be for _____ _____ (_____) years and shall commence on the _____ day of_____, 20___ (the "Commencement Date"), and end on the _____ day of_____ _____ _____, 20___, (the "Termination Date").*

Defined terms used in only one section or subsection may be defined when used. If defined when used and a definitions section is included, the term should be included in the definition section as well, stating "defined as stated in section ___" for its definition. The idea is to ensure that, if the definition is changed, the change will "ripple" through the

---

7. If defined terms are used in the recitals, the definitions section most commonly   follows the recitals.

document automatically to avoid ambiguity that could be caused by revising one appearance of the definition and not another.

Defined terms are a powerful tool that can decrease the length and increase the readability of substantive provisions. They are the solution that allows you to draft to avoid leaving out a concept while not cluttering your provisions with litanies of near-synonymous terms. They enable you to retain the list of terms that can not be done without while, at the same time, increasing the readability of your document by "unpacking" your provisions. In the same way that nick-names can make it easier to refer to a person, defined terms simplify references to longer, more detailed concepts, people, places, and things.

For example, one definition of the word "claim" might be: "Any to right payment, whether or not such right is reduced to judgement, or is liquidated, unliquidated, fixed, contingent, matured, unmatured, disputed, undisputed, legal, equitable, secured or unsecured, or a right to an equitable remedy for breach of performance whether or not such right to an equitable remedy is reduced to judgment, fixed, contingent, matured, unmatured, disputed, undisputed, secured or unsecured."[8] If this definition is provided for separately in the document, the single word "Claim" can be used when needed in the contract's substantive provisions and its broad meaning is included without need for the litany.

Beware: Defined terms can also be used to intentionally cloud meaning. The less than careful reader will often assume that a term has its ordinary, lay meaning and will not refer to a definitions section for clarification. Consider a contract that provides that refund claims submitted to a local company "will be Paid In Full within 90 days of Receipt" and where the initial-capped terms are defined, many pages away, as meaning "compensated in lawful money of [name of non-domestic country or state], calculated at the then prevalent exchange rate" and "when received by the Claims Processor [itself defined as a company in China]," respectively. Consider the ethical implications of using defined terms to obfuscate or mislead. Does it matter to these considerations if the contract is a form, once prepared by a team of lawyers, that is distributed by non-lawyers to commercial clients? To consumers? Beyond ethics, what about the morality of that conduct? Is there a standard to judge when elegant, persuasive drafting of a contract crosses a line and is criminal, tortious, unethical or immoral? What is that standard?

But be careful—if you define a term, it must *only* be used in the defined sense in the document. If not, ambiguity crops up. This is closely related to the practice of "elegant variation" from English composition classes. Those courses often encourage the use of different words for the

---

8. 11 U.S.C. § 101(5) (bankruptcy code definition of "claim"). If there is a body of law that covers the concept you are trying to express, consider incorporating this law into your contract. In doing so, consider the effects of future amendments or repeals of the statute when deciding whether to define by reference to the citation of the statute alone or to quote the current statutory definition, and, if the latter, whether to include the phrase "as it may be amended from time to time" or not.

same concept to avoid repetitive prose. *The rule is different in legal drafting. Consistently use the same words for the same meanings every time!*

To protect against inadvertent use of defined terms that may create ambiguity, many drafters adopt a standard form of defined term that varies the normal rules of format, capitalization, and the like. Examples include: Initial Caps,[9] ALL CAPS, *italics*, **boldface**, or underlining.[10]

Initial capitalization drapes the defined term in the mantle of a proper noun, such as "France." This is appropriate as, within the document, the term essentially becomes a proper noun.[11] This book places the defined term in parentheses and quotes when it is defined, with an appropriate article, if any, outside the quotes but inside the parentheses, *e.g.*:

.... June 7, 2005 (the "Due Date").

When the defined term is later used, it is in initial capitals (also known as "Initial Caps"), but without quotes, *e.g.*

" . . . on the Due Date, the Payer shall...."

This is not a perfect solution, as it really moves the problem from (a) using the defined term in its defined sense every time to avoid elegant variation to (b) ensuring that defined terms are initial capped every time they are used. It is, however, the dominant solution in practice.

Finally, take care to make the definition either inclusive or exclusive. Consider, for example, whether trade secrets constitute Intellectual Property under each of the following definitions:

Inclusive: *"Intellectual Property" means intellectual property as that term is generally used and includes all patents, copyrights, and trademarks. (Yes).*

Exclusive: *"Intellectual Property" means patents, copyrights, and trademarks. (No).*

Ambiguous: *"Intellectual Property" means and includes patents, copyrights, and trademarks. (Maybe?).*

---

9. Not only does capitalization emphasize a defined term, it helps distinguish whether a word is used as a defined term or as a common word (in its "ordinary sense") in the document. For example, a contract may refer to a party with the defined term "Developer"; however, the contract may also make a reference to a photo developer, in which case the generic use of the word "developer" is distinguished by using lower case. Bryan A. Garner, the Red Book, A Manual on Legal Style § 2.9 p. 50 (West 2002) ("Garner"). The author and the attorneys and firms he practices with generally prefer using initial capitalization to indicate a defined term, but there is great variety across the country, between fields of practice, and so on.

10. In the age of word processing, italics is the preferred method of emphasis over underlining. "Underlining is a holdover from the typewriter era and should be avoided altogether," according to Garner. Garner does note, however, that underlining may be useful in a passage already fraught with italics. When more italics just will not stand out, underlining may be used. Garner § 3.2, p. 59.

11. *See* Webster's Third New International Dictionary (Unabridged) 1818 (1986) ("proper noun *n*: a noun that designates a particular being or thing, does not take a limiting modifier, and is usu[ally] capitalized in English").

F. Information Schedules.

Certain sections of agreements are designed to elicit information from the parties to the agreement, such as lists of existing indebtedness, contracts, subsidiaries, etc. Those items should be included as a schedule to the agreement or identified as having been delivered under the agreement. Identification of the schedules can be by sequential numbering or lettering, or may correspond to the section numbers addressing this information in the agreement. Rather than leaving the form of schedules as an open issue to be resolved after the parties have signed the main transactional documents, negotiate and agree to them up front to avoid later disputes when one party or the other will have gained or lost negotiating leverage. This clarifies that everyone knows what is expected and helps to avoid later, disruptive disputes.

G. Informational Documents.

Where an agreement requires the delivery of *existing* documents or certificates, copies of the documents do not need to be attached to the agreement as long as it states that the documents have been or will be delivered prior to closing. Often, the attorney will also want the representations and warranties of the party to apply to these documents, in which case the documents should be accurately identified and incorporated into the agreement with a specific reference in the representations or warranty section.

H. Supplemental Documents.

Where an agreement calls for the execution and delivery of other, related documents (notes, employment agreements, security documents, etc.), consider attaching forms of these documents as consecutively numbered or lettered exhibits ("... in substantially the form of Exhibit A to this Agreement.")[12] As with schedules to an agreement, it is the best practice to negotiate the form of supplemental documents up front rather than leaving them for negotiation and preparation after execution of the main agreement. Among other things, this will force the parties and counsel to really think through all aspects of the deal and make appropriate arrangements for all foreseeable contingencies. This practice can make for bulky documents, but its benefits generally outweigh the extra work and paper expended on the front end to prevent disputes later.

I. Substantive Provisions as Exhibits.

Consider including complicated provisions dealing with special aspects of the transaction (complex valuation or pricing formulas, for example) as exhibits. This is common practice in real estate transactions, where a "meets and bounds" description of property can be long and cumbersome, and it is often used in purchase contracts, where pricing

---

12. *See* Appendix 2, a sample asset purchase and sale agreement with exemplary exhibits.

formulas and worksheets can be complex, but its use can be expanded into many other areas of practice.

J.   The Table of Contents.

Include a table of contents listing all major sections and all schedules and exhibits in any agreement of more than ten pages; consider doing so even with shorter documents.

K.   Cross-references and Section/Paragraph References.

Cross-referencing can help in cutting down on otherwise repetitive provisions. It is generally better to cross-reference to articles, sections, and paragraphs rather than pages, as pages change in the drafting process. A good general rule is to use the word "section" to refer to separate provisions of a formal agreement and the word "paragraph" to refer to separate provisions of an informal letter or letter agreement. The key is to be specific and consistent. Remember to proofread cross-references at the very end of the drafting process to make sure they remain accurate. Some drafters prefer to leave the section or paragraph reference blank until the last draft, *e.g.,* "section ____", essentially forcing themselves to proof the cross-references at this last junction.

L.   Substantive Numbers.

It is common practice that numbers used in legal agreements are both spelled and represented in numerals to avoid confusion, ease proofreading, and make later alteration more difficult. For example, "the sum of five-thousand, five hundred dollars ($5,500) will be paid at closing." The only justification professed for this practice that makes any sense today is that it makes later alteration—forgery—more difficult. Using the written-out and numerical format makes it harder to slip in an extra zero—or delete one—as one must adjust text, also.

Recognizing that large numbers are difficult to read when expressed in words, drafters long ago began placing numbers in parentheticals to aid the reader—like a pronunciation annotation accompanying a new or unfamiliar word in an article or magazine. This makes reading easier, and the form has stuck. Because drafters continued also to express the number in words, however, eventually discrepancies between the two occurred. This made it necessary to develop rules governing how to resolve the ambiguity.[13] Now, for over 50 years, leading commentators on modern formal use of English disfavor writing out numbers in words.[14] Unless concerns about alteration of the document are strong, drop the double form of expression and use numerals exclusively. They are easier to proofread and will not have words to conflict with, eliminating

---

13.   *See, e.g.,* U.C.C. § 3–114 (contradictory terms; typewritten terms prevail over printed terms, handwritten terms prevail over typewritten or printed terms, and words prevail over numbers).

14.   *See* William Strunk, Jr. & E.B.White, the Elements of Style 35 (3d ed. 1979) ("do not spell out dates or other serial numbers. Write them in figures . . .").

another source of ambiguity.[15] Where concerns regarding alteration of the document are strong, use the double format, as in the case of checks and other negotiable instruments. Read and proof substantive numbers carefully—mistakes can be costly to fix.[16]

M. Exemplar Considerations.[17]

In order to save time and expense, it is generally best to maintain exemplars from prior deals so that they can be accessed and tailored for a new transaction quickly and with a minimum of revisions. This is most easily accomplished by maintaining files in word processing format in separate folders in your computer system along with an index listing file names, document title, and comments (*e.g.* "LeaseLL.wpd, Lease of Real Property, Landlord Oriented"). Then, when a similar matter arises, you will be able to consult the index, pull up the exemplar, and proceed to tailor the document to the specifics of the new deal. This technique will greatly speed your revision of the document if your agreements use generic defined terms for parties and other deal specifics, and you can then change these items in the preamble and definitions sections, and proceed to review and modify the substantive provisions. Remember, laws and practices change, exemplars do not. Always understand what substantive provisions and legal phrases mean; don't simply parrot a document. It may be outdated.[18]

---

15. As with other matters of style, be sensitive to your audience. If that audience is willing to embrace modern plain English drafting styles, use them. If, however, your client or supervisor expects numerals *and* words to be used to express numbers, by all means take that into account. Whatever you do, be consistent.

16. *See, e.g.*, Prudential Ins. Co. v. S.S. Am. Aquarius, 870 F.2d 867 (2d Cir.1989) (circuit court of appeals saves Prudential— and its counsel, one would think—from the adverse effects of a multi-million dollar typographical error that stated an amount due of $92,855.00 rather than $92,885,000.00 as the parties originally intended). As the *Prudential* case demonstrates, courts may save a client from the inequitable results of sloppy drafting. The journey to the circuit courts of appeal, however, is likely to be both expensive and unsettling for the clients and counsel involved.

17. The term "exemplar" rather than the word "form" is used because, except for the most basic documents, there are no real "forms" in the sense of "fill in the blanks and it is done." Most true forms will be more cost-effectively prepared by counsel's assistant or paralegal. Counsel should think of the documents used as precedent for new documents as examples, models, of what was done in the last, similar deal, and proceed to modify the *entire* document to fit the new transaction. Thus, "exemplar". You may also describe exemplars as "precedent documents"—a formulation that highlights their use in prior, somewhat analogous transactions, and the need to apply precedent to the new and different matter at hand. When using an exemplar, analyze each provision and whether it is appropriate for the current transaction. Do not include unnecessary provisions or ones that you do not understand just because they are in the exemplar.

18. *See, e.g.*, Howard Darmstadter, *Legal-ease: In the Petrified Forest, Business Law Today* 40, 41 (ABA, March/April 2002) (reflecting on form guaranty featuring outdated "waiver of notice, presentment and demand" rather than post–1990 UCC Article 3 "waiver of defenses based on suretyship or impairment of collateral" and observing "there have been a few developments in commercial law since 1980").

*

Chapter 3

DRAFTING RULES

This section presents a detailed list of generally applicable rules—basically a series of Do's and Don'ts—for contract drafting. In contrast to the prior chapter, these rules focus on the "micro" level of the contract or transactional document—the sentence and word level. Skim the list and use it as a reference on points where guidance is needed.

A. The Active Voice—Who does What to Whom/What, When.

The "Active Voice" of English grammar is characterized by a sentence structure in which an actor (the subject) performs an action (the verb) on or in relation to another thing (the object). *Contract clauses should be drafted in the active voice whenever possible.* Test your clauses by looking for the Subject–Verb–Object (SVO) structure.[1] Each clause should specify "who" is doing "what" to "whom" or "what,""when" in order to be complete.

B. Herein.

If you are trying to say "in this document," say that—name the document (using a defined term—this Agreement, this Lease, etc.—can be helpful here). If you are trying to say "in this paragraph/section/etc.," just say it.

The same applies to all the here-, there-and-said words like hereby, hereinbefore, hereinafter, thereon, therefrom, therefor, therein, aforesaid, aftersaid, etc. Similarly, "same," and "such" should be avoided if at all possible. They are weak substitutes for proper pronouns and good defined terms. They can also create ambiguous references.

---

1. Passive voice, on the other hand, is formed with a *"be-verb."* To spot passive construction, look for or read in a "by" prepositional phrase following the verb. Since the subject of a passive construct has the action done *to* it (as opposed to *doing* the action itself in the active voice), a reader should be able to determine "by whom" or "by what" the action was done. For example, the sentence "the conviction could be overturned on appeal" is passive voice; the writer could have included additional information and written "the conviction could be overturned by ____ on appeal." Garner at § 10.27, p. 143.

C. And/Or—Ambiguity Alert.

"And" is generally inclusive. To draw on tort language, it is "joint and several" (meaning A and B, together (jointly) and each separate and apart (severally)). But there are times when "and" needs to be restricted to its joint sense (when "A and B" means only both together). "Or" can also be exclusive (A or B but not both) *or* inclusive.[2]

A partial solution may be the use of "and" only jointly, "or" only severally, and "and/or" to indicate joint and several relationships. This could be accomplished by use of a provision defining the terms. This would require one to carefully and consistently use the defined terms appropriately. Because 100% consistency is the exception rather than the rule, this may be unworkable in the rigors of actual practice. Many commentators recommend strongly against the use of "and/or," finding it ambiguous and/or a sign of hasty, sloppy drafting.[3] One can also use constructions such as "A or B or both," "A or B but not both," or "A and B together but not separately" and the like. Confront this issue, adopt a workable solution, and apply it uniformly to your drafting.

D. Shall, Will, Must and May.

1. The key problem here is that "shall" is commonly (mis)used for all four words, causing ambiguity.

2. "May" is permissive—meaning the actor has an *option* of taking an action or receiving a benefit—it expresses a *right*. "Shall," on the other hand, means the actor has no choice, he has a *duty*.

   At or before the closing, the Seller shall *deliver the Purchase Price to the Escrow Agent.*

   Buyer may *waive any of the conditions to Buyer's performance in its sole and absolute discretion.*

3. Differentiate between rights (permissive) and duties (mandatory). Rights are "may" phrases (tenants *may* landscape the area adjacent[4] to the patio); duties are "shall" phrases (tenants *shall* clean and maintain the area around their front doors in good repair). If the word "must" could be substituted, "shall" is appropriate.[5]

2. *See* Am. Surety Co. v. Marotta, 287 U.S. 513, 53 S.Ct. 260, 77 L.Ed. 466 (1933) (holding that "or" includes "and"); 11 U.S.C. § 102(5) (accord).

3. *See* SCOTT J. BURNHAM, DRAFTING CONTRACTS §§ 7.4.2 (2d ed. 1993)

4. Vagueness alert. What does "adjacent" mean here? Couldn't a better description be used?

5. You may be tempted to just use "must" in place of "shall"—and this author and others would have no objection. *See* Joseph Kimble, *The Great Myth that Plain Language is Not Precise*, BUS. LAW TODAY 48, 50 (ABA, July/August 2000). However this is not standard in United States practice and opposing counsel and colleagues may object. *See also* Geoffrey Nunberg, *The Last Word in Shall*, CAL. LAW. 23 (March 2001) (describing Australia's effort to rewrite its statutes in plain language, including the use of "must" in place of "shall" to indicate a mandatory duty, and observing that "*shall* means *must* except when it means *may, should* or *will.*").

4. "Will" is predictive but is otherwise similar to "shall," as it may refer to a duty. When indicating a duty, it is best to stick to "shall" (or "must") and eliminate "will" to avoid the implication of different meanings.[6] "Will," however, being predictive, is appropriate when speaking of future events.

    If the bill passes as it is, the President will *veto it.*

    At the end of this session, the Legislation will adjourn. At that time, Contractor shall begin installation of new carpet in the Assembly Chamber.

5. If the name of a party or other actor (such as an agent or third party beneficiary) does not appear before the word "shall" in an apparent shall/duty clause, it is probably incorrect use of the imperative tense. For example, agreements often state that they "shall" be governed by the law of a particular state. This is incorrect. Rather, the agreement should state the choice of law clause as a present tense actual circumstance, i.e. using "is."

    This agreement is governed by the laws of [state].

    If the provision is a declaration of a future fact, use "will" in its predictive sense instead of "shall."

    Final approval or disapproval will occur no later than June 1, 2004.

    Note, however, that this same phrase, cast in the active voice to identify the actor, becomes a "shall clause":

    The Buyer shall approve or disapprove performance no later than June 1, 2004.

E. Doublets, Triplets, and Other Forms of Synonymous Repetition. . . .

Avoid legal "doublets" (and "triplets," etc.).

These are those famous repetitious chains of words that are part of the hoary legal chant that has come down through the ages. Examples: null and void; settlement and compromise; swear and affirm; right, title and interest; etc. Ask yourself, do I really need each of these terms? Will fewer do? Will listing these terms leave the provision vulnerable to the doctrine of *expressio unis et exclusio alterius* (expressing one thing excludes all other things not expressed)?[7] If so, consider using a more general term that contains within its meaning all desired alternatives.

---

6. Even courts make mistakes in this area. *See, e.g.,* Ashlodge, Ltd. v. Hauser, 163 F.3d 681 (2d Cir.1998) (district court abused its discretion when it imposed sanctions for an attorney's failure to comply with the court's order to file a document by a date certain; court used word "should" rather than "shall" in the order, creating ambiguity as to whether the filing was a mandatory duty).

7. It may be tempting to think that a proper interpretive doctrine or equitable maxim will assist in correcting any ambigu-

Further, tucking a general reference such as "etc." or "and the like" at the end of a list to cure the *expressio unis* problem may invoke the dangers of the doctrine of *ejusdem generis* (of the same kind). When using a general reference like this, look back at the specific examples previously given as they establish the scope of the general reference, limiting its effectiveness in expanding the scope of the list.[8]

Examine lists of synonymous terms and rank them in a hierarchy. Are they all of the same rank? If not, this is an indicator that *expressio unis* and *ejusdem generis* problems may be lurking in the list. Consider eliminating lower rank words and using fewer words of a higher rank. For example: Consider the list "carrots, peas and other vegetables." Why not replace all three words with one, "vegetables." Similarly, the list "tigers, lions, and other animals" can be reduced to "animals." Legal terms can be similarly arranged and the term or terms at the correct hierarchical level can be chosen.

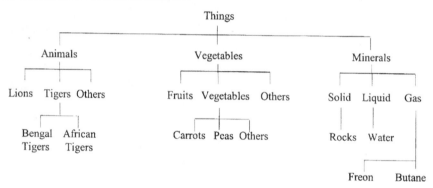

In all cases, reduction and clarification of the list is accomplished by "moving up a level," such as from "Lions, Tigers and other animals" to "Animals." Legal lists are no different and can also be charted. Consider:

---

ity in documents that you draft. The problem is that for every doctrine or maxim that would favor one interpretation, there is another that will defeat it. These principles are largely ceremonial support for reaching the result that the court has determined is just rather than the reasoning that leads to that determination. FARNSWORTH, CONTRACTS § 7.11 at 496 (1982).

8. This discussion illustrates the contradictions within the canons of construction and the equitable maxims. There is usually a canon or maxim that counters another canon or maxim. *See* Chapter 1, note 5.

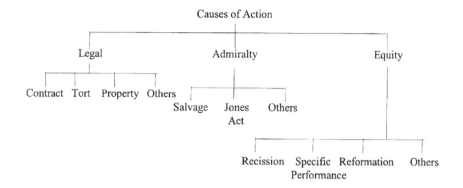

F. Omit Needless Words.

The statements made in this section are, by nature, general ones, and you *must* evaluate, in each instance, whether or not the general advice should be followed. In drafting agreements and other transactional documents, concentrate especially on whether or not your chosen word has the correct level of generality or specificity. Underlying these rules is the belief that *overdressing one's writing makes it harder to read and does not demonstrate education or sophistication. Rather, education and sophistication are shown by elegant drafting that makes its meaning clear with little effort on the reader's part.* Of course, reasonable minds can differ on matters such as word choice. Use the following suggestions as a guide but, as with most legal drafting, it is best for you to make up your own mind as to what is appropriate under particular circumstances.

Avoid compound prepositions:

Avoid	Using Instead
the question as to whether	whether (the question whether)
all of the issues	all the issues
at that point in time	then
in the nature of	like

Avoid overly showy words:

Avoid	Using Instead
additionally	also
adequate number of	enough, sufficient
adjacent	next to (specify distance?)
aforesaid	previous, prior

<u>Avoid</u>	<u>Using Instead</u>
any and all	any
at the time	when
approximately	about
at [the] present [time]	now
by means of	by
cease and desist	stop or cease
circumstances in which	when or where
commence	begin
contained in	in
contiguous	next to
due [to the fact that]	because
eventuates	occurs, happens
facilitate	help, assist
has a negative impact	harms
including but not limited to	including
inquire	ask
null and void	void
notify	tell or inform
permit	let or allow
penultimate	second to last
request	ask
retain	keep
ultimate (in the since of last)	last
utilize	use (unless this will imply oppressive exploitation in the sense of "using" someone)

G. Keep Related Words Together.

1. Avoid inserting clauses between the subject and the verb, particularly if the clause can be transferred to the beginning or end of the sentence.

Avoid	Using
The borrower, in its notice of borrowing, should specify the method for computing interest.	*The borrower should specify the method for computing interest in its notice of borrowing.*

2. Keep modifiers next to the word they modify.

Avoid	Using
The weak lawyer's contract.	*The lawyer's weak contract.*

Assuming that "weak" is intended to modify the "contract," not "the lawyer."

3. Do not insert adverbs between the component parts of verbs unless done for emphasis.[9] This is particularly true for infinitives ("to clearly write"). Keep objects close to verbs.

Avoid	Using
The local court has repeatedly interpreted incorrectly that line of cases.	*The local court has misinterpreted that line of cases repeatedly.*

H. Use Familiar and Concrete Words; Avoid Lawyerisms.

"Witnesseth,"[10] "Now, Therefore," "Know all men by these presents," "Based on the above premises" and "in consideration of the following covenants and conditions" and the like can all be eliminated. Use common English in their place:

Accordingly, the parties agree:

I. Use Normal Word Order and Inversions for Emphasis.

The normal, active-voice word order in English is *subject, verb,* and *object.* If you wish to change this order for emphasis, remember that the strongest places in the sentence are the beginning and the end. Generally, stick to subject, verb, object (SVO) order. The best

---

9. The "unless done for emphasis" exception is more widely accepted now than in the past, but take care to know what your audience prefers. A split infinitive can *really* bother traditionalists.

10. "Witnesseth" in particular, and "Now, Therefore" and "Know all men by these presents" reflect what contract drafting is all about: providing an accurate, objective written record of a transaction that can be referred to by the parties or others, now or later. It is "making a record" of the deal struck, to borrow a phrase from litigation practice. These terms thus make historical sense, but they can safely be avoided when drafting modern transactional documents.

contract clauses follow this order and tell the reader *who* is to do *what* to *what or whom, when*.

J. Hyphens.

Limit your use of hyphens.[11]

1. Generally, hyphens should be used to form compound adjectives:

    The short-term loan agreement contained a cross-default clause.

    There are, however, exceptions. Nonpayment, intercompany, and pro rata should all be written without hyphens.

2. In some cases hyphens are helpful in distinguishing use of a word as a verb (no-hyphen) or a noun (hyphen). Verb: "*. . . the bank is entitled to set off any deposit. . . .*" Noun: "*. . . the bank is entitled to a set-off in the event. . . .*" But the same effect can be generated with the use of an article to indicate the noun, as is also done in this example with the indefinite article "a."

3. When in doubt as to the use of a hyphen, write the word as one unit without one.

K. Parentheses.[12]

A sentence containing a parenthetical expression is punctuated outside the parenthesis exactly as if the parenthetical expression were absent. The parenthetical expression itself is punctuated as if it stood by itself, except that the final or "terminal" punctuation mark is omitted unless it is a question mark or an exclamation point:

> *Payments of interest should be made quarterly*
>
> *(on the first business day of each quarter), but will be compounded daily.*
>
> *The defendant protested (and why should we doubt his word?) that he had delivered the goods as specified.*

(When a wholly detached expression or sentence is contained in parentheses, the final punctuation comes before the closing of the parenthesis, as here.)

---

11. Even if omitting a hyphen results in a double letter, a hyphen should generally not be used to attach a prefix to a word. However, if the result would cause confusion or mispronunciation (such as in the case of co-op or re-lease), a hyphen is justified. Garner at § 1.61, p. 36.

12. Garner reminds writers that "[i]f the writer's purpose is to make the parenthetical content stand out rather than hide, a pair of . . . dashes is probably the better tool." Garner at § 1.33 p. 21.

L.   Some Basic Rules of Grammar Relevant to Drafting Contracts.

1.   *Forming the possessive.*

   a.   Form the possessive singular of nouns by adding " 's" even if the singular noun ends in "s."

   James's case. The judge's ruling.

Note the possessive is *not* used when specifying a time period, such as a for notice period. For example it is "20–days notice" (compound adjective form) rather than "20 days' notice" or, worse, "20 day's notice" (incorrect possessive forms).[13]

   b.   Form the possessive plural by adding an apostrophe " '".

   The lawyers' presentations.

   c.   Note re: its, it's, his and hers.

"Its" is the possessive singular of "it."

"It's" is a contraction for "it is."

"His" and "hers" are already possessive and take no apostrophe.

2.   *Use of the semicolon vs. the colon.*

   a.   The Semicolon.

When joining two or more grammatically complete (independent) clauses without a conjunction, use a semicolon.

   The attorney's argument was compelling; he persuaded the jury.

Apart from being used to separate items in a list that are themselves long or compound, this punctuation mark has limited relevance to contracts and transactional documents. If you find that you are using semi-colons in transactional documents other than as part of a list, examine your use carefully and critically.

   b.   The Colon.

A colon directs the reader to what follows. It usually follows an independent clause and can be used to introduce a variety of related statements: a list of particulars, a quotation, an appositive, an illustration, or an amplification. Even two independent clauses can be joined with a colon if the second interprets or amplifies the first.

Incidentally, a list can be a list of one, i.e., a list can have only one item.

It is not necessary to use a colon every time a list is introduced. For example, "The model you like is available in red, blue, white,

---

13.   An apostrophe followed by an "s" is often used to form the plural of letters, single-digit numbers, and symbols. While this form looks like possessive form, it is merely plural. It is incorrect to pluralize names with an apostrophe followed by "s". For example, "the Brown's" is the incorrect plural form. The correct plural form is "the Browns" with no apostrophe. Garner at § 1.79 p. 42.

and ochre" takes no colon. Over use of a colon with lists is cumbersome.

The first letter of the word that follows a colon is capitalized unless that word is the first in a list of multiple items, in which case each item begins with a lower case letter.[14]

c. Slashes.

The slash should not be used in legal writing because of the ambiguity involved. The slash could indicate "and" (conjunctive) or "or" (disjunctive), thus creating unnecessary ambiguity. The only acceptable use for a slash in legal writing is for dates and fractions.[15]

3. *The series comma and semi-colon.*

    a. In a compound sentence composed of a series of short independent clauses the last two of which are joined by a conjunction, commas should be placed between the clauses and before the conjunction:

        The attorney presented his closing argument, the judge instructed the jury, and the jury retired to consider the case.

    b. In a series consisting of three or more elements, the elements are separated by commas. When a conjunction joins the last two elements in a series, a comma is used before the conjunction:

        Small, Nelson, and Lee attended the conference.

        The owner, the agent, and the tenant were having an acrimonious discussion.

    c. Although not technically correct, increasingly, writers often delete the last comma in the series: "Payments should be made to the bank, the payee[,] or the agent." The technically correct method is to include that last comma. Using the last comma will never be wrong, but omitting it may cause confusion.[16] Whichever method is chosen, be consistent throughout the document and examine your result carefully to ensure your intended meaning is clear and legally precise.

    d. In a series consisting of three or more elements that are themselves either clauses or sub-series, use a semi-colon in place of a comma for the highest level of the list. For example, "the available color combinations are red, white, and blue; yellow, green, and tan; gold, red, and purple."

4. *Subject and verb must agree in number.*

---

14. Garner takes a different stance on this matter. He leans toward not capitalizing the first letter of the word that follows a colon. *See* Garner at § 1.22, p. 14. In any event, Garner agrees with the author and these materials when he states "be consistent in your decision about whether to capitalize the first word" following a colon. *See id.*

15. *Accord* Garner at § 1.80, 1.81 p. 43.

16. *See* Garner at § 1.3, p.4.

a. The number of the subject determines the number of the verb. This is true even if other nouns are connected to it by "with," or "no less than."

The statute as well as the regulation favors a strict construction.

The statutes favor a strict construction.

b. Plural vs. singular nouns.

A. When none means "no one" or "not one" use a singular verb. If none suggests more than one thing or person use a plural verb:

B. Remember—forum, memorandum, datum, and criterion are singular; fora, memoranda, data, and criteria are plural.

C. Singular verbs should be used with "either" and "any" and, in its usual form, "neither . . . nor."

M.   Misused and Abused Words and Expressions.

1. Between and Among. Number is not the only distinction between "between" and "among." A contract is made *between* three parties, not *among* them.[17] Essentially, "between" indicates a direct relationship from each party to each party. "Among" is less specific and may connote an arrangement where some parties are directly connected and some are not.

2. Effect/Affect. *Effect* as a noun means "result" or "appearance." As a verb it means "to bring about" or "to accomplish." *Affect*, a verb, means "to influence" or "to simulate."

3. Farther and Further. Use *farther* when distance is involved and *further* when referring to time or quantities. My dog chases balls *farther* than other dogs. Attorneys often pursue a subject *further* than others.

4. Fortuitous. Refers to something that happens by chance and is not limited to fortunate or lucky happenings.

5. In regard to. Often incorrectly written *in regards to. As regards* is correct, and means the same thing. Even better is the use of *regarding.*

6. Irregardless. Should be *regardless.*

7. Fewer/Less. *Fewer* refers to number; *less* refers to quantity.

---

17. H.W. Fowler in Modern English Usage 57 (1965) (". . . we should not say *the space lying among the three points* or *a treaty among three Powers.* But the superstition dies hard.").

My troubles are less *than Rebecca's because she has* fewer *clients.*

8. <u>Like.</u> Often incorrectly used for the conjunction *as. Like* is a preposition that compares nouns and pronouns; *as* is a conjunction used to introduce subordinate clauses (which generally contain a verb). This distinction has seen some erosion in recent years but is still drawn by purists.

<u>Wrong</u>	<u>Right</u>
He addressed the jury like an expert.	*He addressed the jury as an expert would.*

9. <u>Loan.</u> A noun. *Lend* is the verb, as in "I shall lend you $50."

10. <u>Nor.</u> Use "or" after negative expressions and not "nor" to avoid drifting into a double negative.

11. <u>One.</u> When used as a pronoun for a generic person, "one" should not be followed by "his" or "hers".

<u>Wrong</u>	<u>Right</u>
One must pay his obligations.	*One must pay one's obligations.*

12. <u>Presently.</u> Has two meanings: "in a short while" and "currently." One technique to avoid ambiguity: use "presently" to convey the first meaning and "currently" the latter.

13. <u>Principle & Principal.</u>

     a. *Principal,* an *adjective* meaning most important or the base amount of an investment (the "principal sum, plus interest"). *Also a noun* meaning "one with controlling authority."

     b. *Principle,* a *noun,* a fundamental law, doctrine or assumption upon which all things are based or which guides conduct.

     c. *Mnemonic:* Money and the head of your elementary school can be your friend, your pal (Princi*pal*); but fundamental princi*ples* are different.

14. <u>Secondly, Thirdly, Etc.</u> Consistency would lead one to begin with *firstly.* So use *first, second, third,* etc. If you choose to use secondly, thirdly, and the like, begin with *initially* to avoid the awkwardness of firstly.

15. <u>Split Infinitives</u>. Avoid interposing an adverb between "to" and the infinitive it governs unless you wish to place unusual stress on the adverb. Splitting infinitives drives some people absolutely crazy. Know your audience.

16. <u>That & Which</u>. "That" is the defining, or restrictive term; "which" is the non-defining, or nonrestrictive, and usually descriptive term. In most cases, if the phrase is properly set off by a comma, use "which." If no comma is needed, use "that."

> *The contract that is incomplete should be rejected. (Tells which one.)*

> *On the floor sat many boxes of documents, all of which would need to be reviewed.*

N. Quotation Marks.

Proper English grammar requires quotation marks to close after the terminal punctuation of a sentence.

"Oh, no."

The parties exclaimed "We have a deal!"

Many lawyers, however, place the quotes before the terminal punctuation in order to avoid the implication that the punctuation has itself been quoted. The same effect can be generated with the use of square brackets to indicate the inclusion of the punctuation.

The first word of the sentence is "help[.]"

The recommended method is proper English grammar—quotes after terminal punctuation—unless there is substantial concern about confusion, in which case the square bracket method should be used to indicate that the terminal punctuation is a modification of the quoted language.

If you are only quoting one word, you have some discretion. Periods and commas should be included inside the quotation marks, but question marks and exclamation points may be either inside or outside the marks at the drafter's discretion. Colons and semi-colons should be placed outside the quotation marks.

O. Spacing After Sentences.

Two spaces are used after a sentence's terminal punctuation (period, exclamation mark, question mark) and the capitalized first letter of the next sentence. This aids the reader when skimming or speed-reading the document by providing the eye with a double space to identify the beginning of the next sentence.

QUESTIONS & CLAUSES FOR CONSIDERATION

Twenty–Five Contract Drafting Considerations that Comprise a Philosophy.

1. The standard that we should strive to attain in drafting contracts is that a person of reasonable intelligence who knows nothing about the transaction can understand the deal after one reading of the contract.

2. An attorney is almost always a salesman. We are advocates for our clients whether we are practicing in the courtroom or not. When drafting a contract we are persuading the other party to sign now and to perform voluntarily later, and we are persuading a later court to enforce the contract if the other party does not comply.

3. Think like an attorney, but try not to sound like an attorney.

4. It is easier to resolve problems before they happen then after they happen. In drafting contracts we need to *anticipate* problems and provide solutions.

5. There is no such thing as a perfect document. There are bad documents, good documents, and better documents. Every document can be improved.

6. Usually our goal is both precision and clarity.

7. Concepts should be arranged in a logical order.

8. The answer to most questions about whether a provision is needed is, "It depends." It depends upon the facts and the client's needs for this particular transaction.

9. Easy reading is the result of hard drafting. Easy drafting is the result of hard thinking.

10. Every paragraph, sentence, and phrase should have a unique purpose.

11. We should constantly ask, "why, why, why?"

12. The person who drafts the contract has a significant advantage over the person who reviews a contract. Subtle refinements can be included by the drafter that are easily overlooked by the reviewer.

13. Never change your language unless you wish to change your meaning, and always change your language if you wish to change your meaning.

14. The use of defined terms enables us to simplify and clarify and can prevent inadvertent changes of language. Defined terms also help us to be gender-neutral.

15. Defined terms carry the extra baggage of the generic meaning of the words we choose to use. Careful selection of defined terms can help us to clarify and to be subtly persuasive.

16. When using a form or a prior document, we never leave in a provision because we do not understand its purpose, and we never take out a provision because we do not understand its purpose. First, we figure out its purpose. Then we determine whether it should be retained, deleted, or modified.

17. Word processing can enable us to dramatically improve the quality of our documents and the efficiency with which we produce them. Word processing can also enable us to make mistakes faster than we have ever been able to make them before and memorialize them forever.

18. The appearance of a document can increase or decrease its credibility. Neatness counts.

19. Usually we use:

    (a) "will" to state future fact,

    (b) "shall" to state an obligation,

    (c) "may" to state an option or a right, and

    (d) "must" to state a condition precedent.

20. Usually we use the present tense because we are stating continuing obligations.

21. Usually we use the active voice because it more clearly identifies the actor.

22. Usually we use gender-neutral language.

23. Do it once. Do it right. Save it.

24. Our work needs to be cost effective for our client.

25. Our client usually cannot make money unless we find a way to make the deal work. Be a deal maker, not a deal breaker, and you add value to the transaction for your client. Identify your client's business goals and then choose the correct structure for the transaction, which may be one that your client has not thought of or used before.

Note that many of the 25 considerations listed above are phrased as less than an absolute rule—i.e. most apply "usually." Look over the considerations that use this phrasing. When would you want to deviate from the rule? Why?

*

Chapter 4

DOCUMENT REVIEW
AND COMMENTS

———————

Before discussing contract drafting further, a few remarks are in order regarding the process that takes place *after* you have drafted a contract or other legal document: review by others, and the inevitable comments and criticism—"feedback"—that you will receive.

A. Comments and Mark–Ups Indicate Interest in Your Work.

When someone reviews your work and proceeds to mark it up or otherwise make comments, this is not a sign of failure. In fact, to the extent that the reviewer, be it client, supervising attorney, or opposing counsel, makes any comments at all, this expresses interest in the document and shows that you have their attention. When given a document to review, most lawyers reach for a pen, knowing that they will use it. Receiving comments and mark-ups of your work is par for the course, and you should get used to it as soon as possible to avoid unnecessary pain and anguish.

B. Different Considerations for Different Reviewers.

Who will be doing the review and providing the comments?

1. Your Colleagues and Supervisors.

Especially when starting out, the first group to review your documents will probably be your colleagues and supervisors in a firm. These comments will be designed to improve the documents and your client's position. As such, you should receive them as what they are: constructive commentary from a different perspective, produced with the benefit of different experiences and knowledge that are meant to improve the final work product. They are *not* a personal indictment of your failure to grasp what needs to be done!

First, make suggested changes that improve the document, then make the other ones that don't harm the document (this is much easier than explaining why you don't think they are necessary). Disregard, *with* explanation, the ones that harm the document. Even if you are in the unfortunate position of receiving comments that appear designed to undermine your confidence and sense of self-worth (which does happen from time to time), you should look for the constructive, beneficial points hidden within what may appear to be venom. Even comments that seem minor or purely stylistic are important—and should be internalized so that the next project involving that commentator incorporates the feedback from the last project in its first draft. Do not incorporate these changes into all your projects in the future, unless (a) you like them or (b) you are working with another client, colleague, or opposing counsel with similar style.

A very effective technique to minimize your reviewer's time and effort and to focus attention on the areas that most require review is to use "black lining." In a black lined document, revisions are indicated by using ~~strikeout~~ text to indicate deletions from a prior draft and underlining to indicate additions. The "track revisions" features of WordPerfect· or Word· will suffice, although add-on programs also exist. The beauty of black lining is that, when reviewing successive generations of drafts, the reviewer knows exactly what is new and needs to be reviewed, the other material presumably having been approved earlier. Black lining may even be appropriate at the first draft stage if you are basing the document on an exemplar, especially one prepared by your reviewing attorney. Appendix 4 contains a revision of a settlement agreement that uses black-lining to show changes from a prior draft.

If you use black lining it must be accurate and complete. Inaccurate black lining will establish your reputation as sloppy within your firm and with your client. With opposing counsel it is likely to create distrust and concern about your ethics.

It is also valuable to communicate to the reviewer what you need reviewed, when you need it back, and other contextual matters. Find out how they like to get this information, what information they like to get, and the best method for getting it to them.

To minimize comments about your work that may impact negatively upon your reputation or advancement within a firm or enterprise, take great care to make your document as good as you can be *before* turning it over for review. Attorneys and clients are busy people for whom time and effort are valuable resources. Skilled practitioners can spot a misspelled or misused word, a grammatical mistake, or even an extra space from a mile away, and these distractions impede their review of the substance of your prose—they feel compelled to scratch in a correction with their pen.

Learn the rules of your supervising attorney and follow them slavishly before turning in work for review. Although most supervising attorneys will clean up your grammatical and typographical mistakes, this is not their job. Forcing them to do so is not good for your career. Develop an eye for detail as early as possible.

Finally, especially for attorneys new to practice, it is easy to find yourself in a cycle of endless revisions that are rather pointless. After a certain point, polishing results in no further material increase in quality. If you bill your client for the time spent on these rounds of revisions, your work product will be overpriced. If you do not bill for the time, you will be working without compensation. If you find yourself making endless rounds of non-substantial changes, such as changing all instances of "Seller's" to "of the Seller" or vice versa, and are making no meaningful changes to meaning or to correct objective, mechanical errors—Stop.

2. Client Review.

The next category of reviewer is your client. The degree of depth of this review depends upon your client representative's level of interest and training. Inside counsel and accountants can be expected to give the document a relatively thorough reading and rarely require much in the way of explanatory cover letters. For those without such detail-intensive backgrounds, you may want to enclose a cover letter highlighting the most important points in the documents or this round of revisions to ensure that the client is "on notice" to these items and will pay attention to them during the review.

Some clients will not want to review the documents at all, or will be happy to review them at the same time that the other side reviews them (transmitted with a cover letter stating that the documents have not yet been reviewed by your client and are therefore subject to modification). It is a good idea to make sure that your client reviews the documents at least once prior to the final draft and that you take note of their comments and modify the documents accordingly. This ensures that you really do understand the directions your client has given to you.

Remember, clients rarely care if you fail to incorporate comments from "the other side," but they do mind when their comments—however minor, however inconsequential, however wrongheaded you believe them to be—are not incorporated or at least discussed with them and discarded after that discussion.

3. Review by Opposing Counsel.

You have transmitted the documents to the opposing counsel—is your review over? *No.* Take a break, so that your next review of the document will be conducted with fresh eyes. Then, without waiting for opposing counsel to get back to you, review the document one more time and note any corrections that appear. Things will be readily apparent to you at this stage that you could not see earlier. You will then be prepared to raise them in your first conversation with opposing counsel, thus avoiding protests based on notions of waiver, closure, or re-opening negotiations. Your changes will also provide you with a selection of trading points to use as consideration for changes requested by opposing counsel.

Encourage opposing counsel to provide you with a marked-up copy of the document showing specific line-edits that are desired, not vague comments like "we need an indemnity here" or "this won't work." It is usually a waste of time for this mark-up to be accompanied by lengthy commentary in the cover letter explaining and justifying each change, and those letters are costly. They should be generated only when it is important to make a detailed record of the negotiations beyond what marked-up drafts would show. This may be the case in extremely large multi-party transactions where one attorney is collecting and synthesizing the comments of many lawyers and re-broadcasting the modified document to the crowd; in situations when negotiations are going badly and may fall apart, perhaps precipitating lawsuits in the future; or when they are required by clients who wish to receive this sort of costly narration and entertainment.

Comments from opposing counsel fall into one of four categories and should be responded to as follows:

Category of Comment	Response
Those beneficial to all parties or that benefit the document and the deal.	Make the changes, perhaps thanking opposing counsel for their insight and contribution in the cover letter, fax cover sheet or cover e-mail.
Those that are matters of style or personal "nits" of opposing counsel and do no harm to the documents or your client's position.	Consider making the changes. It is less expensive than trying to negotiate out opposing counsel's pet peeves. But also consider how acquiescence across the board can affect the way you are viewed by opposing counsel and your colleagues; acquiescence can be perceived as a sign of weakness. Sometimes you have to put your foot down and say "no" to a change that would not really matter to maintain authority and credibility.
Those that harm either your client's position or the smooth operation of the document.	Reject the changes, with an explanation of the problem that they cause. If the effect that opposing counsel was aiming for is evident, and you believe the effect may be desirable or merely neutral, consider suggesting an alternative method of reaching the same end without doing violence to your client's interests or the document.
Those that are valid points for future negotiation.	Consider what, if anything, you would request in exchange for

Category of Comment	Response
	the change, or be tentative about making the change—perhaps inserting the requested change into the document as an alternative to the original provision, which is also retained—and make reference to the trade off, if any, or to keeping the issue open in your cover letter, fax, or e-mail. *Do not acquiesce without receiving something in return* unless you and your client have run out of points, issues, and comments. Once you give something away it is difficult or impossible to come back and try to charge for it!

For each comment you receive from opposing counsel (or anyone else for that matter), think: What is the point of this comment? What substantive effect are they trying for? Then determine if that effect is acceptable to your client (this may require checking with your client and gaining authority for the change). If acceptable, ask yourself, "is this the best way to gain this effect?" If it is not, respond with an alternative change that has the same effect, pointing out that it addresses the same issue, but is better because it is more elegant, will take less time to institute, will not affect other issues, is less costly, etc.

For example, a landlord's counsel may demand a large cash security deposit from a start-up tenant with little or no track record. This may be unacceptable or impossible for your client—but they could obtain a letter of credit from a reputable bank or provide a guaranty from a well-heeled shareholder. Either of the alternatives should satisfy the landlord's legitimate desire for some form of security or credit support. But, unlike the security deposit, they do not require your client to part with cash at the present time. If the effect is unacceptable, you will have to respond by rejecting the comment or change and, if necessary, explaining why it is unacceptable.

C. Control of the Document, Making Revisions, and Subsequent Drafts.

Assuming that your client has the resources and is willing to expend them, the best possible strategy is for you to control the drafting and revision process. This allows you to craft the document's nuances. If you perform the unglamorous word processing services, you will have the opportunity to be the master of the document's intricacies and will be in the best position to protect your client at every opportunity. Indeed, you will likely be the attorney who knows the document the best.

After you have made the changes you and your client are willing to make in response to the other comments received from opposing counsel, go over the document one more time looking for conforming changes. If the same language that was changed appears in other locations and it is appropriate to make the changes there as well, do so.

D.   Reviewing Documents—A Ten Point Checklist.

When reviewing documents drafted by others and when critically examining your own drafting, use the following questions to focus your review:

1.   *Parties, Dates, Dollar Amounts, and Interest Rates.*

   Does the document identify the correct parties in their proper capacities? Are the dates used correct? Are all currency amounts and interest rates correct and complete? Never assume that any factual statement is correct; trust, but verify.

2.   *Appropriate Structure.*

   Does the document and the overall structure of the transaction suit your client's needs? Do you understand the deal that is at issue? Is there an alternative structure that is more desirable for your client, perhaps for reasons other than those in the immediate transaction such as accounting and tax treatment? Does the document match your client's expectations and earlier description of the deal to you?

3.   *Clear, Mandatory Duties, and Optional Rights.*

   Does the document contain clear mandatory duty provisions regarding all performances by other parties due to your client? Are mandatory duties specified using the words "shall" or "must?" Are rights or options expressed in terms of "may?" Do these provisions clearly state "who" does "what" to or for "whom" or "what," "when?" Timing of performance is essential; do not neglect to specify the "when."

4.   *Representations and Warranties.*

   Does the document contain representations and/or warranties running in favor of your client regarding all facts, statements, and assurances upon which your client is relying? If these representations and warranties prove false, is there a mechanism—perhaps a covenant coupled with an indemnity—for recovering from a credit-worthy entity or for rescinding or otherwise modifying the transaction? Does the document require your client to make broad or unnecessary representations and warranties and can these be estimated, narrowed, or limited in temporal or geographic scope? Can a materiality threshold limiting the representation to things over a certain amount (*e.g.,* claims in excess of $25,000) be added to limit the breadth of the statement? Can a knowledge limitation be inserted so that a representation, especially as to the lack of something, is limited to the knowledge of a specific individual at a specific time? Are those representations and warranties that are made factually correct?

5. *Internal and External Consistency.*

Does the document "fit" the desired structure? Is it complete and consistent internally and with any other documents involved in the transaction? Defined terms and boilerplate should generally be consistent across all documents in a transaction to avoid confusion and potential ambiguity. Do all the documents contain a non-severability clause? Are they governed by the same integration, merger, choice of law, choice of forum, and alternative dispute resolution provisions?

6. *Substantive Understanding.*

Do you understand each provision of the document? Review each of them until you understand them completely and their interaction with the other sections of the document and related documents.

7. *Hypothesize Performance.*

Think through the life of the transaction and the document under various fact patterns. What will happen, moment by moment, if the parties comply with all the terms in a timely manner? Sometimes it is useful to think of this life cycle through in reverse to determine if the final product is supported in all respects by the agreement's provisions. Are performances required in the proper order?

8. *Hypothesize Non–Performance and Default.*

What if one or both parties fail to perform all or part of the agreement—are the consequences of failure to perform stated and closely linked to the performance required? Does the document address other issues and problems that are likely to arise in the course of performance? Resolve issues and problems now, at the drafting stage, rather than waiting for the parties to reach the problem and negotiating at that time. It is likely that the parties will never be more amenable to working out details than they are at the inception of the deal. Capitalize on the opportunity to prevent trouble before it occurs.

9. *Address Bankruptcy Risk.*

Analyze what will happen if one of the parties files a bankruptcy petition or becomes subject to a receivership. Will property or rights that are important to the other party become "property of the estate" under 11 U.S.C. § 541? Will performance be stayed or affected by the automatic stay of 11 U.S.C. § 362? Will the document be considered an "executory contract" subject to assumption or rejection under 11 U.S.C. § 365? If so, will this assumption or rejection be possible independently from assumption or rejection of the other documents in the deal? If so, is there a way to structure the transaction so that this property or these rights are held by a third party that is unlikely or unable to be the subject of a bankruptcy case? Can the document be made part of, incorporate, or be incorporated into other documents from which it should not be divisible or severable? Do the recitals in the contract make clear what performances and property rights are important to each of the parties and what injury and damage they may suffer if they are deprived of them? Can you provide for a lien, security interest, or third party credit support such as a guaranty or letter of credit to secure the opposing party's payment and performance obligations?

10. *Consider the Worst Case Scenario.*

Assume that the document is executed and the parties become openly hostile, seeking to undermine each other at every opportunity. Will the document provide sufficient guidance to govern the relationship? Will it provide sufficient guidance to a court interpreting the document or imposing remedies if the parties are locked in mortal combat with no thought to the opportunity or litigation costs involved? Although this may be a worst-case scenario, that is the appropriate test for a well-drafted transactional document.

Chapter 5

CONSIDERATION AND THE TERM OF THE AGREEMENT

A. Consideration.

With limited exceptions, in order to be enforceable, a contract must be supported by mutual consideration, i.e., there must be a benefit conferred or a detriment suffered by each party to the contract. Consideration takes a number of forms, including (i) cash, (ii) promissory notes, (iii) letters of credit, (iv) transfers of property, (v) services, (vi) transfers or surrender of rights, (vii) assumption of another's duty or liability or (ix) mutual promises. Generally lack of consideration is not an issue in real life, yet it bears remembering. In some jurisdictions there are presumptions of consideration that arise when a written contract recites that consideration has been "had and received" or similar formulations. *See, e.g.,* Cal. Civ. Code § 1614. Do not forget that not acting by forbearing or surrendering a right or option is consideration just as much as is affirmative action. *See In re* Dynamic Enters., Inc., 32 B.R. 509, 517 (Bankr.M.D.Tenn.1983) (a grant of the exclusive right to use a franchise trademark in a specific area was considered adequate consideration since the right "imposed substantial forbearance on the franchisor."); CAL. CIV. CODE § 1614.

Perhaps the time that consideration comes up the most is when contracts are modified, especially when the modifications amount to merely a decrease in the duties owed by a single party. A contract to modify an existing contract must generally be supported by mutual consideration. It is good practice to make sure this is the case by providing for consideration on both sides of the deal (the one-dollar-had-and-received formulation of yore), even if your jurisdiction has done away with the common law pre-existing duty rule (requiring more than a pre-existing duty to support a contract). *See, e.g.,* U.C.C. § 2–209(1) (pre-existing duty rule repealed by UCC for sales of goods).

Consideration is also an issue when one party's contractual obligations are supported by a third party's guaranty of payment or performance. In such a circumstance the guarantor may not appear to be receiving consideration for the guaranty as the only parties receiving benefits are those to the contract being guaranteed; the guarantee appears merely to be gratuitously sticking its neck out for another. Some transactional lawyers put their minds at ease over the guaranty/consideration issue by (a) ensuring that the guaranty states that it is being given by the guarantor to induce one or both of the parties to enter into the primary transaction *and* (b) having the guarantor sign the guaranty *before* the parties execute the primary transactional documents.

Most contracts include a "statement of consideration" section near the beginning of an agreement. Examples of statements of consideration include the following (which range from somewhat archaic and legalistic to plain English):

> *NOW, THEREFORE, premises considered and in consideration of the mutual covenants and agreements hereinafter set forth and in consideration of one dollar ($1.00) paid by Seller to Buyer, the receipt and adequacy whereof is hereby acknowledged, the Seller and Purchaser hereby covenant and agree as follows:*

—or—

> *NOW, THEREFORE, in consideration of the mutual promises set forth in this Agreement, the parties agree [as follows]:*

—or—

> *[Accordingly] The Parties agree:*

B. Allocation of Consideration.

This issue is most important in the purchase and sale context, where allocation of the purchase price will affect the buyer's tax basis in the items acquired and the seller's gains and income. Buyers generally favor allocating as much of the price as is reasonably possible first to non-capital assets such as accounts receivable, notes receivable, inventory and work in progress so as to minimize income later when those items are collected or sold and, second, to assets that can be quickly expensed or depreciated so as to quickly recover the cost. Sellers typically have the reverse preferences, although they may not object to allocations favoring non-capital assets if the capital assets involved have been subject to substantial appreciation over the buyer's holding period (*e.g.* land held over long periods).

Clauses allocating purchase price often refer to an attached schedule to cut down bulk in the body of the contract. The parties' duties are often phrased in terms of committing to report the transaction to tax and other authorities either "as stated" in the schedule or "in a manner not inconsistent" with the schedule.

QUESTIONS & CLAUSES FOR CONSIDERATION

Here is a sample provision allocating assets to the four classes defined by I.R.C. § 1060. The clause is from an acquisition agreement to purchase substantially all the assets of a business. Note the plain English approach and use of a tabular structure.

Section 7—Allocation of Consideration

(a) *Purpose of Allocation.*

The purpose of the allocations contained in this section is to comply with § 1060 of the Internal Revenue Code only and shall not be construed by the parties or any nonparty as having any other effect.

(b) *Allocation of Purchase Price.*

The purchase price for the assets shall be allocated among the four classes established by Internal Revenue Code § 1060 and related regulations as provided below:

(1) *Class I Assets.* The portion of the purchase price allocated to Class I assets (cash, demand deposits, and like accounts in banks and other depository institutions and similar items designated by the IRS) set forth on *Schedule* 7(b)(1), is based on a dollar-for-dollar value and is equal to $_____ dollars.

(2) *Class II Assets.* A portion of the remaining balance of the purchase price allocated to Class II assets (certificates of deposit, government securities, readily marketable stock and securities, and foreign currencies) set forth in *Schedule* 7(b)(2), is based on the relative fair market value of such assets and is equal to $_____ dollars.

(3) *Class III Assets.* The portion of the remaining balance of the purchase price is next allocated to the Class III assets (all assets not described in Classes I, II, or IV, consisting of tangible and intangible assets, including furniture and fixtures, land, buildings, equipment, accounts receivable, and covenants not to complete) as set forth on *Schedule* 7(b)(3) based on the relative fair market value of such assets in the amount of $_____ dollars.

(4) *Class IV Assets.* The remaining unallocated portion of the purchase price, if any, is allocated to the Class IV assets. Class IV assets consist of the intangible assets, assets in the nature of goodwill, and going-concern value.

C. Variable Consideration.

Provisions for variable consideration are appropriate when the consideration will depend upon future events. Such provisions can include formulas (*e.g.,* percentage of rent provisions, common in leases and licenses) as well as adjustments to base consideration depending upon the amount of assets such as receivables or inventory on hand when a sale transaction closes. It is crucial that the drafter think through all possible outcomes for the formula. On the opposite side of the deal, it is also important to understand the formula proposed by the drafter and any potential impact upon your client. It is often useful to include an example to illustrate the workings of a complex formula or adjustment provision.

QUESTIONS & CLAUSES FOR CONSIDERATION

Simple Formulas in Contracts.[1] A clause from a debt security reads, in part:

> Issuer shall make monthly payments to holders of bonds equal to the product of (i) the product of (x) the bond rate and (y) a fraction the numerator of which is the actual number of days in the related interest period and the denominator of which is 360 and (ii) the certificate principal balance as of the close of business on the last day of the preceding interest period.

Cumbersome but understandable if you take the time to decode it:

Monthly Payment = Bond Rate x $\underline{\text{#of Days in Period}}$ x Principal Balance
                                     360

Since you need to resort to this or similar mathematical notation to understand the clause, why bother to encode it in words in the first place? It is an invitation to mistakes in the encoding or decoding process. In these circumstances it is better to draft the clause using defined terms and formulas. Try it. Draft provisions requiring an Issuer to make the required monthly payments and providing for calculation of those payments using mathematical notations.

2.   Draft the consideration provision of a contract providing that an author assigns her copyright in a particular work to a publisher in exchange for a royalty of 20% of the gross revenues of publication of the work. Include defined term provisions as needed. Gross revenues should include all sales proceeds received by the publisher less all returns, credits, and refunds.

3.   In leases of retail real property, the landlord may charge rent based upon a fixed amount, a fixed base amount plus a percentage of sales, or solely percentage of sales. Tenants often prefer one of the two later formulations as they shift some of the risk of business downturns onto the landlord. Landlords may accommodate tenants in this regard, assuming that they will be rewarded for accepting this risk if sales are strong, which is, to some extent, a function of the location of the landlord's property, its development, and operation.

Assume that your client, a landlord, has come to you and requested that you draft a percentage rent provision. The client tells you that the

---

1. This exercise is based upon Howard Darmstadter's article "The Arithmetic Lawyer" in Business Law Today (ABA November/December 2000).

minimum annual rent desired is $25,000, and that the additional percentage rent is 5% of sales over $500,000. (Note how the minimum rent of $25,000 is 5% of $500,000—do you understand why this is? It is a guaranteed baseline rental: the risk of lower-than-$500,000 sales is placed on the tenant.) Minimum rent is to be payable monthly, with percentage rent payable quarterly, 60 days after the close of each calendar quarter. The tenant will give the landlord a financial statement showing sales for the prior quarter with each payment of percentage rent, and the landlord has the right to audit the tenant at the landlord's own expense to verify the accuracy of each financial statement unless the audit reveals that the tenant has understated sales by more than 2.5%, in which case the tenant must pay for the audit and also pay a fee of 1% of actual sales for the period to the landlord. Internet sales are not to be included in the calculation of gross sales for the purpose of percentage rent. (Why? Because internet sales have little or nothing to do with the benefits that the tenant derives from the landlord's property.) Sales and excise taxes, returned merchandise, credit card fees, employee sales, and sales of things other than normal merchandise are additional deductions from gross sales to be made prior to calculating percentage rent.

Draft the provision and any necessary definitions.

4. What follows is a complex provision from a real estate joint venture structured as a sale of property with so-called "seller-take-back" financing with an "equity kicker" in the form of a "waterfall" participating contingent interest in the profits from development. The terms in quotes are shorthand for very detailed provisions in the transactional documents. The "waterfall" contingent participating interest provisions appears here. This is a very confusing provision when encountered for the first time. Try reviewing it in a number of "passes," like an airplane pilot surveying unknown territory. Make your first pass at 35,000 feet and spot the big things. The next pass is made at 10,000 feet, to see some specific features. Then decrease altitude and fly over it at 500 feet, reducing your speed, and understand the nuances.

Brief background: In this transaction, the original owner of the property in question is selling the property to the developer and taking back a note secured by a deed of trust on the property. The developer is going to build a golf course, clubhouse, lots, and infrastructure (streets, curbs, gutters, electrical, gas, cable and sewage systems), around the golf course. The developer does not plan to build houses. It will sell the lots and memberships in the golf club, which it will operate until all lots have been sold, at which time the club and course will be turned over to the homeowners' association. Homeowners or merchant builders that purchase the lots will build the homes, within the parameters of the covenant, codes, and restrictions that the developer will record against all lots to ensure a certain uniformity of style and use for the development.

The note that the seller is taking back in exchange for the land—the "seller-take-back-financing"—provides for payments of two sorts: sums certain payable at times certain and a participating contingent interest (a variable payment) that allows the original owner/seller to benefit if the development is a success. In order to allow the developer to obtain financing for construction on the property, the original owner/seller/lender has agreed to subordinate its deed of trust securing the note to allow another lender (who provides the "Permitted Senior Debt" referred to in the provision) to make a construction loan that will be senior and have a first priority lien on the property to secure its loan. Under the note, the original owner/seller is the "Lender" because it is taking the note and deed of trust in exchange for the property. The developer is the "Maker."

You may want to draw a picture or otherwise diagram this transactional structure in order to provide context for your analysis of the provision below. Beginning drafters often do not recognize the value that pictures, graphs, and charts can have for understanding and organizing complex facts, rights, and relationships. It is critical to understand the business terms and structure of a deal like this before drafting or reviewing the agreements that are supposed to memorialize it.

[Beginning of Provision]

11.1   *Payments of Participating Contingent Interest.* As additional consideration for the sale of the Property by Lender to Maker, Lender shall be entitled to receive certain additional payments based upon the cash flow generated from management, sales and operations of the Property. The payments received by Lender pursuant to this Section 11 are referred to herein as the "Participating Contingent Interest." For purposes of calculating payments of Participating Contingent Interest to Lender hereunder, Cash Flow and Excess Cash Flow (as defined hereinbelow) shall be deemed held by a third party and distributed from time to time to Lender and Maker in accordance with the following priorities. Excess Cash Flow (defined herein to mean Cash Flow remaining after payment of any required payments of Unpaid Purchase Price under this Note or any optional payments made under section 6 hereof) shall be distributed from time to time as follows:

(a) First, to Maker until Maker has received distributions under this subsection (a) equal to Maker's Capital Investment plus an amount ("Preferred Return") sufficient to achieve an internal rate of return ("IRR") of 15% on Maker's Capital Investment (The Capital Investment plus Preferred Return are referred to collectively as the "Preference Capital"). Distributions of Cash Flow pursuant to this subsection (a) shall be deemed to be made first with respect to accrued and unpaid Preferred Return, with the balance applied and credited to Maker's Capital Investment.

(b) Next, Excess Cash Flow shall be distributed 75% to Maker and 25% to Lender until such time as Maker has been distributed an amount ("Additional Preferred Return") which, when added to amounts distributed to Maker pursuant to subsection (a) above, (x) is sufficient to achieve an IRR on Maker's total Capital Investment less Maker's Excess Capital Investment in the Property that is greater than or equal to twenty-five percent (25%), and (y) that is equal to 200% of Maker's total Capital Investment less Maker's Excess Capital Investment in the Property.

(c) Thereafter, Excess Cash Flow shall be distributed equally between Maker and Lender.

If distributions of Participating Contingent Interest are made pursuant to subsections (b) and (c) above, and Maker thereafter makes an additional Capital Investment ("Additional Capital Investment"), Preferred Return, Preference Capital and Additional Preferred Return with respect to such Additional Capital Investment shall be calculated from and after the date such Additional Capital Investment is made, and distributions of Excess Cash Flow shall be made in accordance with the priorities set forth in Section 11.1 with respect to the Preferred Return, Preference Capital and Additional Preferred Return payable with respect to such Additional Capital Investment. Notwithstanding the foregoing, in no event shall Lender be required to return any payments of Participating Contingent Interest theretofore paid to Lender on account of such Additional Capital Investment.

For purposes of this Promissory Note, the term "Internal Rate of Return" or "IRR" means the annual discount rate, determined by iterative process, which results in a net present value of approximately zero (0) when such discount rate is applied to Maker's Capital Investment from time to time and certain distributions in respect of Maker's Capital Investment from time to time. For purposes of determining Internal Rate of Return for purposes of this agreement, the formula below shall be utilized:

$$O \;=\; -CC + \frac{D_1 - C_1}{1 + r} \;+\; \frac{D_2 - C_2}{(1 + r)^2} \;+\ldots\; \frac{D - C}{(1 + r)^n}$$

"-C" = Maker's Initial Capital Investment.

"C_n" = Maker's additional Capital Investment invested in the period denoted in subscript.

"D_n" = All distributions to Maker in the period denoted in subscript.

"r" = Periodic discount rate expressed as a decimal equivalent to the annual "IRR" or internal rate of return.

For purposes of the above formula, Maker's Capital Investment made in any month shall be treated as having been made on the first day of such month and cash distributions in any month shall be treated as having been made on the last day of such month.[2]

In the event of a sale of all of the Property by Maker in accordance with the terms of this Note and the Deed of Trust, to the extent all of the consideration therefor shall have not been paid in cash, then the collection and distribution of Excess Cash Flow, as, when, and to the extent received, shall be administered by the Maker, or if Maker shall have been dissolved, by the former managing member of Maker, and distributed in accordance with the provisions of section 11.1 hereinabove.

Participating Contingent Interest, if any, shall be payable monthly on or before the fifteenth business day of each calendar month.

11.2 *Definitions.*

(a) *Capital Investment; Definition.* The term "Capital Investment" shall mean any and all capital (including Excess Capital Investment) contributed by the members of Maker in excess of Two Million Dollars ($2,000,000) as and to the extent expended by Maker on and after the Closing Date as defined in the Purchase Agreement with respect to the acquisition, construction, development, sales and marketing of the Property. Capital Investment shall also include any amounts borrowed by Maker and not secured by the Property as and to the extent such loan proceeds are expended towards the acquisition, construction, development, sales and marketing of the Property. Capital Investment shall also include letters of credit obtained by or on behalf of Maker and delivered in connection with Maker's acquisition and development of the Property ("Letters of Credit"); provided, however, that, with respect to any such letter of credit the collateral for which is limited to the Property and for which none of Maker's members has any liability, then unless amounts are drawn by the beneficiary of a Letter of Credit, the outstanding liability amount of such Letter of Credit shall not be deemed Capital Investment for purposes of calculating Preferred Return and Additional Preferred Return, and shall not be included in the principal amount of any Capital Investment.

(b) *Cash Flow; Definition.* "Cash Flow" for any calendar month is defined as Revenues during such month plus any cash reserves maintained by Maker which Maker reasonably, in the exercise of its good faith business judgment, determines to be unnecessary and therefore may be released, less the sum of:

(i) Costs during such calendar month;

(ii) Deposits into reserves (if any) made during such month; and

2. Why is this important?

(iii) Payments required and made during such month under the Permitted Senior Debt Documents.

(c) *Costs; Definition.* "Costs" shall mean, for a given calendar month, the aggregate of the following which are properly chargeable to the operation of the Property and as determined under the cash method of accounting unless otherwise provided herein.

(i) Real estate taxes and insurance premiums paid;

(ii) Service payments, maintenance contract payments, development fees, on-site employees' wages and fringe benefits; costs of repairs and maintenance; promotional and advertising payments; public relations and similar expenses; reasonable accountants' fees; fees and expenses of third party operators of the "Facilities," as defined below; and other reasonable operating expenses of the Property accrued during such calendar month;

(iii) With respect to sales of the Property and Memberships, all reasonable and customary costs and expenses incurred by Maker in connection with the sales of the Property and Memberships, including but not limited to, reasonable attorneys' fees of Maker, Lender, and Senior Lender, title insurance, reasonable travel and entertainment expenses, and brokerage fees at prevailing market rates;

(iv) Justified and reasonable refunds paid by Maker during the calendar month of any Revenues received in an arm's length transaction;

(v) Reasonable administrative and general overhead expenses of Maker and its managing member for expenditures incurred directly in connection with the operation and development of the property;

(vi) The actual costs of restoration of the Property incurred following a casualty to the extent of the permitted deductible under the applicable insurance policy or where there are no insurance proceeds therefor and Maker is not required to and does not carry insurance therefor;

(vii) Costs of construction and other hard costs to the extent not paid with advances under the Senior permitted Debt; and

(viii) Actual fees and other costs of issuance paid to the Senior Permitted Debt.

"Costs" shall not included fees, expenses, interest, preferred return, or other consideration paid by Maker (or any of its affiliates) with respect to debt or equity capital contributed by members of Maker. "Costs" shall include market rate fees paid to the issuers in respect of the issuance and/or renewal of Letters of Credit.

(d) *Excess Capital Investment; Definition.* The term "Excess Capital Investment" shall mean any amount by which Maker's Capital Investment exceeds $_____.

(e) *Revenues; Definition.* "Revenues" shall mean, for a given calendar month, all Revenues from the Property and the operation thereof, as determined under the cash method of accounting, received by Maker or its authorized managing agent for the Property during that calendar month. "Revenues" shall include, without limitation, (i) all consideration (including, when converted into cash, promissory notes or any other form of consideration) actually received by Maker from all sales of the Property, which consideration shall also include any forfeited deposits retained by Maker (in the case of a terminated escrow), option fees to purchase lots or monetary settlements with prospective purchasers, (ii) fees and revenues generated to Maker from the operation of those certain country club and golf course facilities ("Facilities") to be developed on the Property, including receipts with respect to charges for merchandise, services, rents, license fees and from all other sources derived by Maker (or its Affiliates) from the Facilities; (iii) fees for lessons, greens fees, tennis court fees, public and private banquets held at Facilities, membership dues and all other fees or charges of any kind paid with respect to the use of the Facilities; (iv) brokerage commissions, fees and any proceeds retained by Maker (or its Affiliates, but excluding the Sales Company referenced at Section 16.1 of the Purchase Agreement) in the transfer or sale of memberships or interests in the Facilities; (v) charges for all food served and sold at the Facilities, including alcoholic and non-alcoholic beverages; (vi) fees and revenues generated to Maker (or its Affiliates) in respect of the sale of membership interests in the Facilities and the sale of the Facilities, as may be permitted under the Deed of Trust; (vii) proceeds from financing, refinancing and further encumbrancing the Property as and to the extent permitted under the Deed of Trust including, without limitation, the Permitted Senior Debt proceeds; and (viii) any other funds or proceeds received from any other source derived from the Property, including casualty insurance proceeds and condemnation proceeds not applied to restoration of the Property.

[End of Provision]

A.   Think about this provision and how it works. Can you describe it so that your non-lawyer client, the original land owner, knows what the super-slick developer is proposing? The developer has merely described this as an "equity kicker" that will allow them both to share the profit. Your client wants to understand what is actually being proposed.

B.   Who bears the risk if things do not go as well on the project as expected?

C. What happens to Lender's participating contingent interest if, instead of getting a construction loan, Maker puts in its own funds (equity capital) to finance the development?

D. Redraft these provisions in plain English to improve their clarity and precision.

* * *

D. The Term of the Agreement.

1. *The Effective Date.* A contract is generally in force as of its execution, and in the case of execution on different dates, upon the later. This can, however, be varied by the parties through use of an "effective date"—either a date certain (*e.g.* June 22, 20xx), or a date variable (*e.g.* 30 days after execution of this contract by both parties).

2. *The Termination Date.* Contracts can continue indefinitely or terminate upon a fixed or variable date and can, of course, be extended or terminated by the parties. Extension or early termination can be the subject of an agreement external to the original contract or can be built into the initial contract. It may even be appropriate to define "termination" by reference to what effect "termination" has on the rights and obligations of the parties. Termination can be a multifaceted concept, embracing different modifications of the parties' rights, such as termination for or without "cause," termination by failure of condition precedent, or termination by condition subsequent. Each of these forms of termination can leave different provisions in force. As you are drafting, identify provisions that need to survive termination in order to achieve their purpose. For example, confidentiality, non-disclosure, return of trade secrets, and covenants not to compete are provisions that are needed after the termination just as much, if not more than, before termination.

3. *Termination and Renewal or Continuation and Cancellation.* A contract can be drafted so that it regularly terminates and must be renewed by both parties, or so that it continues until canceled by one or both parties. These two structures produce different relationships, motivations, and incentives for the parties. Cancellation-and-renewal, common in real property leases, forces the parties to regularly contemplate whether to renew the contract, providing a regular reminder and opportunity to renegotiate—an advantage for the party with the most leverage and power. It also limits bankruptcy risk, as a contract or lease that is extinguished automatically by its own terms is not extended when one of the parties files a bankruptcy petition. The bankruptcy estate takes the debtor's rights subject to the terms of those rights.[3]

On a practical note, however, many clients will be unable to administer an automatic contract cancellation and renewal program, especially

---

3. *See* 11 U.S.C. § 541. 11 U.S.C. § 108 may provide the bankruptcy estate with additional time to secure rights under a contract—but it does not extend the term of the contract itself.

if there are many such contracts or the initial terms are short. Remember: No matter how legally exquisite a structure may be, it has to be workable for the client! Otherwise, conduct that does not conform to the contract's terms may produce defenses to enforcement of the contract as written such as waiver, laches, modification by conduct, and the like.

QUESTIONS & CLAUSES FOR CONSIDERATION

1. Draft a provision establishing an effective date for a contract that is the date it is signed by all parties.

2. Draft a provision providing for termination of a contract one year from its effective date unless it is renewed by the parties at least a month before it would otherwise expire.

3. Draft a provision providing for monthly termination of a license to use copyrighted material unless both parties agree to extend the license for another month and the licensee pays another monthly license fee before the license terminates.

4. Draft an employment agreement providing that Ned Armstrong will employ you for a period of one year as his financial, business and legal counsel and advisor, for a salary of $50,000. You will be required to work a 40–hour week with additional time as needed (with no increase in compensation). You will be entitled to three weeks of vacation per year and five days of sick leave (these benefits accrue evenly over the year). The contract can be terminated by Mr. Armstrong for cause or no cause at all. If terminated for cause, you will not be entitled to compensation or benefits post-termination. If terminated without cause, you will receive all payments that would otherwise have been due as and when they would have come due. The contract should include confidentiality and non-disclosure provisions that survive termination.

Chapter 6

CONDITIONS

Conditions must be carefully drafted and integrated into the rest of the contract. First, you must take care to clearly draft the condition so its terms are clear. (Conditions generally trigger duties (shall clauses) or rights (may clauses)). The reader must be able to determine when the condition is satisfied and, if satisfied, or not, what consequences follow. Word choice is key.

In most contract negotiations, one party will seek to include many conditions, especially conditions to closing, and the other only a few. For example, in a purchase and sale agreement, the seller will try to limit the conditions to closing to as few *objective* conditions as possible, such as any needed third party approvals and the lack of any prohibitory injunction or other adverse ruling by governing bodies. By doing so, the seller is seeking to lock the buyer into the deal.

The buyer, on the other hand, will want to build in as many conditions, and to keep these conditions as *subjective* and dependent upon the buyer's own judgement, as possible. By doing so the buyer can more easily walk away if due diligence reveals that things are other than as expected, or enjoy the opportunity to later renegotiate terms in exchange for a waiver of the condition. For example, buyers may seek to include as a condition that its due diligence will conclude with satisfactory results (as judged by the buyer in its sole discretion). This sort of condition can also be framed as "lack of material adverse change" condition to closing.[1] Pay careful attention to what this means and who determines whether the condition has been met. Buyers, keep it as subjective as possible and attempt to maintain control over the determination that the condition has bee met. Vice-versa for sellers; also consider including a materiality threshold[2] to define a material adverse change.

---

1. *See generally In re* IBP, Inc. Shareholders Litig. v. Tyson Foods, Inc., 789 A.2d 14 (Del.Ch.2001) (refusing to allow party to invoke a material adverse change provision to cancel merger and discussing case law regarding such provisions).

2. A materiality threshold is a minimum measurement hurdle that must be met for the event to "count" for purposes of triggering other provisions of the contract. Examples include minimum levels for invento-

Another common condition is that of one party obtaining financing and final written approval by all internal and external entities with any jurisdiction over the transaction. Again, the buyer is motivated by two desires: (a) the ability to back out of the deal if it is no longer interested in proceeding for whatever reason, and (b) the ability to threaten to back out in order to gain more favorable terms.

Consider the benefits of linking your client's material duties to the condition that the other party use its "best efforts" to perform either all or an enumerated list of duties under the contract. This is especially worthwhile in the case of parties with unequal economic or bargaining power in which the weaker party's success is dependent upon the other party's performance. In those circumstances, a best efforts clause is to the weaker party's advantage. Examples include construction agreements, distribution agreements and intellectual property agreements.[3]

You must confront the fact that parties and courts often ignore or waive conditions. Contracts are often full of clauses providing that a party's failure to act or enforce a right or remedy shall not be deemed[4] to be a waiver of that right, and that any waiver of a current right shall not be a waiver of any other right or a future incidence of the same right. The litany continues: Time is of the essence; Non-severability; No amendment or waiver by conduct; All amendments and waivers must be in writing; Recitations that both parties have been represented by counsel, or at least had the opportunity to consult with counsel, have read the agreement and understand it.[5]

All these provisions are attempts by the parties to avoid having a court later refuse to enforce a condition by finding that it was waived by conduct, was unconscionable, would otherwise lead to a forfeiture, and the like. A determined court can generally find some way to excuse a failed condition should it choose to do so, and can usually do so in a ruling that is so fact-based that it is largely immune on appeal.[6] The

---

ry, receivables, and the like; limiting a "no undisclosed claims or lawsuits" condition, representation, or warranty to those "where the amount in controversy exceeds $100,000" or a requirement in a financing commitment that the potential borrower have submitted financing applications "to no less than 3 federally chartered financial institutions."

3. *See, e.g.,* Polyglycoat Corp. v. C.P.C. Distribs., Inc., 534 F.Supp. 200 (S.D.N.Y. 1982) (distributor violated best efforts clause when it chose to promote competing product rather than one manufactured by the plaintiff); Van Valkenburgh, Nooger & Neville, Inc. v. Hayden Publishing Co., 30 N.Y.2d 34, 330 N.Y.S.2d 329, 281 N.E.2d 142(1972) (publisher breached best efforts clause to promote author's book). Case law demonstrates that inclusion of a best efforts clause gives rise to an almost fiduciary level duty on the part of the burdened party. *See*

id.; Bloor v. Falstaff Brewing Co., 454 F.Supp. 258 (S.D.N.Y.1978) (retailer breached a best efforts clause when it allowed plaintiff's beer brand sales to plummet while retailer implemented a business strategy to maximize its own profits). Even without a best efforts provision, one may be implied into an agreement like an exclusive license. *See* Wood v. Lucy, Lady Duff–Gordon, 222 N.Y. 88, 118 N.E. 214 (1917) (best efforts to make designer's clothing implied in exclusive license per Cardozo, J.).

4. "Deeming" something to be the case is what lawyers and judges do when the something is not truly the case, but they want it to be.

5. This sort of boilerplate is discussed in Chapter 9 below.

6. Why are fact-based decisions more immune on appeal than purely legal determinations? Consider the applicable stan-

drafter can guard against this result best by (a) drafting the consequences of failure of a condition into the condition, not just leaving it to the default and remedy provisions of the agreement,[7] (b) employing good boilerplate to attempt to document the parties' intention that all the terms of the document be strictly construed, and (c) explicitly stating the reason that the condition was included and that it was a fundamental inducement for one or more of the parties to enter into the transaction.

When reviewing conditions, focus on what is likely to occur if the condition is not met. Does your client have an appropriate course of action—or cause of action—to pursue under the terms of the contract? If not, provide for one. Also, consider whether this test is met for the opposing party. If not, is it better for your client if this remains the case? Or is it better to attempt to fix the potential problem and fill the void? Answers to these last questions will vary enormously depending on the circumstances.

QUESTIONS & CLAUSES FOR CONSIDERATION

1. Biotech, Inc. ("BI"), has developed a process that reverses male pattern balding. A patent application has been filed and FDA approval is pending. BI has only two (2) shareholders, Jennifer Abbey and C.B. Beach. Each owns 5,000 shares. They want a contract that allows either of them to state a price per share at which he/she will either buy or sell. Once the price is announced, the other shareholder has to either buy or sell at the stated price. Apparently Ms. Abbey read about this "Russian roulette" procedure in a business magazine and thought it was brilliant. When the corporation was formed the shareholders entered into a plain vanilla buy/sell agreement triggered only by death or disability. Prepare the Russian roulette provision(s).

2. The following provisions are from a contract of sale between the Sellers (the "Parties of the First Part") and the Buyers (the "Parties of the Second Part").[8] Redraft this conditional forfeiture and remedy provision using plain English.

[beginning of provision]

A. In the case of the failure of said Parties of the Second Part to make either of the payments, or interest thereon or any part thereof or perform any of the covenants on their part hereby made and entered into, then at the election of the First Parties, the whole of said payments and interest provided for herein, shall become immediately due and payable and this Contract shall at the option of said First

---

dard of review, generally abuse of discretion (factual findings) or *de novo* (legal conclusions).

7. Default and Remedy provisions are discussed in Chapter 10 below.

8. The language is from the contract at issue in the malpractice case of Boles v. Simonton, 242 Mont. 394, 791 P.2d 755 (1990).

Parties be forfeited and terminated by giving to said Second Parties ninety days notice in writing of the intention of the First Parties to cancel and determine this Contract, setting forth in said notice the amount due on said Contract and the time and place when and where payment can be made by said Second Parties.

B. "IT IS MUTUALLY UNDERSTOOD AND AGREED by and between the Parties to this Contract that ninety (90) days is a reasonable and sufficient notice to be given to said Second Parties in case of failure to perform any of the covenants on their part hereby made and entered into, and shall be sufficient to cancel all obligations hereunto on the part of the said First Parties and fully re-invest them with all right, title and interest hereby agreed to be conveyed, and the Parties of the Second Part shall forfeit all payments made by them on this Contract and any right, title and interest in all buildings, fences or other improvements whatsoever, and such payments and improvements shall be retained by the said Parties of the First Part, in full satisfaction, and as a reasonable rental for the property above described and in liquidation of all damages by them sustained and they shall have the right to re-enter and take possession of the premises aforesaid. IT IS FURTHER AGREED that the Parties of the First Part in addition to all remedies set forth herein, shall have all other remedies available to them at law and in equity."

[end of provision]

Chapter 7

REPRESENTATIONS, WARRANTIES, COVENANTS, INDEMNITIES, GUARANTIES

Contracts frequently use "representations," "warranties," "covenants," "releases," "guaranties" and "indemnities." Each is a different type of provision, and it is important to select the proper type to generate the proper legal effect. Perhaps more than any other set of provisions, those described in this chapter highlight the litigation or default planning aspects of transactional practice and contract drafting. Each of these provisions gives rise to a particular set of causes of action in the event of breach or error.

Representations, warranties, covenants, and indemnities in particular are interrelated and reinforce each other. A represented fact will induce a party to enter into negotiation and documentation of a transaction. That representation will likely be converted into a warranty as to that fact that may survive closing. If the warranty is breached or is incorrect, a covenant is used to produce a duty on the part of the warranting party to make the facts as they were warranted. Finally, to the extent that the non-warranting party has been damaged by the breached or incorrect warranty, an indemnity creates a route for damage recovery against the warranting party or a third party.

Unlike the way you were probably taught to analyze a set of facts for tort, contract, or property claims (element by element with damages or other remedies last), when thinking about these sorts of clauses as a drafter, *you should approach the problem from the desired remedy first.* For example, if certain facts are misstated, what remedy do you wish to seek? Possibilities include rescission pre-closing, rescission post-closing, or consequential or liquidated damages from the other party or from a credit-worthy third party or fund. Then select the type of provisions that will produce a cause of action for your client that is ripe when needed, lies against the appropriate defendant, and provides the desired remedy.

A. General Rules for Representations, Warranties, and Covenants.

1. Representations.

Classically, a *representation* is a statement of presently existing facts that is intended to induce reliance and action by a party, such as entering into a contract.[1] An incorrect representation will support an action for rescission or damages sounding in contract (and tort if fraud is present).

Unless otherwise specified, the representation speaks as of the execution of the document in which it is contained. The cause of action is, therefore, generally ripe as of that time, which may be pre-closing. Pre-closing representations may terminate at closing by operation of law unless the contract specifies that they survive the closing. Check governing law in your jurisdiction on this point and, best of all, address the matter specifically in the contract

Representations are meant to give one party some reassurance or "comfort" that the other party's claims are true. In this sense they shift the risk that a stated fact is untrue to the representing party. Typical subjects for representations include the accuracy of financial statements, and the existence of adverse claims, breached or defaulted contracts, liens, encumbrances, and legal actions.

Representations are also used to shift the burden of investigation and disclosure in the due diligence process. For example, assume that your client wishes to purchase a business but wants to know if there are any claims or lawsuits against the business. You and your client could search relevant court records, perhaps nationwide. You could also dig through all of the business records looking for evidence of claims. These are burdensome and expensive activities. Alternatively, you could insert a representation into the purchase agreement in which the seller states that, except as disclosed on an attached schedule, no claims or lawsuits have been asserted against the company. This sort of blanket statement is known as a flat or unqualified representation. It shifts the burden of investigation and disclosure back to where it belongs, on the seller, which is the entity that should be the least-cost provider of the information.

Typically, the seller's counsel would respond with the suggestion that the representation be qualified, often by narrowing it to relate to claims or lawsuits over a certain size—a "materiality threshold"—or known to certain specific individuals—a "knowledge limitation." Depending on the circumstances this may be acceptable to your client. If so, make sure that either limitation is not overbroad. Materiality thresholds should be set at levels that sound appropriate alarms but filter out the noise generated by immaterial claims. Knowledge limitations should specify persons who are likely to know the *details* involved; rarely will it be sufficient to limit knowledge to that of the uppermost tier of manage-

---

1. BLACK'S LAW DICTIONARY 1301 (6th ed. 1990).

ment. In this way, the burden of necessary investigation and disclosure can appropriately and reasonably be shifted to the sellers.[2]

Representations are generally drafted in the form:

> *[Buyer, Seller, other defined term] represents [representation carefully stated as to scope and substance].*

Representations should almost always be drafted in the present or past but not the future tense to prevent them from being interpreted as covenants.

A representation is often combined with a warranty, in which case the form is:

> *[Buyer, Seller, other defined term] represents and warrants [representation and warranty carefully stated as to scope and substance].*

This combination ensures that a cause of action will lie post-closing if the representation has terminated as of closing but the warranty survives or as part of an overall "belt *and* suspenders" approach.

2.   Warranties.

Classically, a *warranty* is a statement made about certain facts whereby the warrantor promises to ensure that those facts are as stated.[3] A breached or incorrect warranty will support an action for damages sounding in contract, and the cause of action is ripe as of the closing of the transaction.

Warranties are generally drafted in the form:

> *[Buyer, Seller, other defined term] warrants that [warranted facts carefully stated as to scope and substance].*

Like representations, they should almost always be drafted in the present or past tense but not the future tense to prevent them from being interpreted as covenants.

3.   Covenants.

A *covenant* is a promise to act or not to act in the future.[4] It is essentially a single contractual duty within a document. Breach of a covenant will support an action for damages or specific performance sounding in contract (or tort under the theory of promissory fraud), and the cause of action is generally ripe at the time that the covenant was to be performed, although doctrines such as impossibility, prospective inability to perform, and voluntary disablement may accelerate the accrual of the cause of action.

---

2. The Question and Clauses for Consideration section of this chapter and the contracts in the appendices, particularly Appendix 2, provide additional examples of this technique

3. BLACK'S LAW DICTIONARY 1586 (6th ed. 1990).

4. BLACK'S LAW DICTIONARY 363 (6th ed. 1990).

Covenants are generally drafted in the form of a "shall clause"—an active voice statement that identifies the party making the promise and stating that promise directly. For example: Seller shall indemnify and defend Buyer from all adverse claims to title.

Test all of your covenants for the active voice, and ask, do they clearly state *who* is to do *what* to or for *whom, when,* and in *what manner, quality,* or *quantity.*

A final consideration when drafting covenants that is similar to the decisions faced when drafting representations and warranties: What degree of performance will be required. Some covenants are unqualified and provide that a party shall do something, period. Other times they are drafted in terms of "best efforts," "commercially reasonable efforts" or "reasonable efforts." When drafting or reviewing covenants, consider whether language qualifying the obligation is appropriate.

4. *The UCC Approach.*

In a sale of goods contract covered by the Uniform Commercial Code, however, any "affirmation of fact or promise made by the seller to the buyer which relates to the goods and becomes part of the basis of the bargain creates an express warranty that the goods shall confirm to the affirmation or promise."[5] This approach blurs the distinction between classic definitions and distinctions between "representations," "warranties," "covenants," and even "conditions."

5. *General Rules and Techniques: Typical*
Representations & Warranties.

Each of the general rules regarding representations, warranties, covenants, and conditions can be altered by language of the contract itself—so none can be drafted or interpreted in a vacuum.

Typical representations and warranties include (i) the transaction is not a breach of any other agreement and does not violate the law, (ii) a seller or lessor has good title to all assets being sold or leased, and those assets are free of liens and encumbrances, and (iii) all material facts have been disclosed. Each is often phrased as "except as disclosed on schedule *X* to this agreement, [representation or warranty]." As noted above, this structure makes the provision more than just a representation or warranty—it becomes a due diligence tool that shifts the burden of finding and discussing exceptions to the statement to the representing and warranting party. Representations and warranties of this type are often combined with a covenant to defend against claims that are adverse to any of the representations and warranties, and an indemnification (see next section) against losses caused by inaccurate representations or warranties.

That combination of provisions resembles "deal insurance" in that one party makes a representation and warranty and then agrees to

5. U.C.C. § 2–313.

indemnify and defend the other party from claims that render the representation or warranty incorrect. Remember, however, that insurance is only as good as the insurer when the claim is made! Do not take too much comfort in unsecured, unregulated insurance-like provisions—circumstances change and parties die, are dissolved, and become insolvent or judgment-proof. Due to the use of blanket and purchase money security interests to support business financing, the sale and securitization of rights to payments and payment streams, and the use of limited liability entities to separate assets and retained earnings from liability-creating operations, many, if not most, substantial businesses are judgement-proof beyond whatever insurance coverage they have. This does not mean clients should not contract with these businesses, just that counsel must focus on ensuring that their clients understand the risks involved and whether there is a creditworthy payor or other source of funds to look to in the case of an inaccurate or breached representation, warranty, or other provision.

As discussed above, in important method of reducing the scope of a representation or warranty, (and thus any covenant or indemnity linked to it), is a "knowledge" limitation. In light of the prior paragraph, it bears revisiting. For example, "the representations and warranties of section X below are limited to facts of which a, b, or c [people] have actual knowledge on the date of this agreement." This is a fair limitation, as long as the appropriate persons are specified: those who would naturally have the knowledge sought. Do not stop at the senior executive level—as knowledge there is generalized—but delve down into middle management and even to the operations level of a business, as appropriate.

6.   *Guaranties, Indemnities, and Releases.*

a.   Guaranties

A *guarantor* is one who promises that, if another party does not perform a duty, the guarantor will.[6]

The word "guarantee" when used in the colloquial sense of a warranty (on your microwave oven, for example) has one spelling, and "guaranty" when used in its formal legal meaning (a promise to perform a third party's obligation) has a different spelling. *There should be no double-e guaranties in your contracts!*

Remember that a guaranty is only as good as the guarantor.

b.   Indemnities

An *indemnity* is a collateral contractual obligation where one party, the indemnitor, engages to hold another, the indemnitee, harmless from losses to third parties.[7] A common indemnity is one that covers any losses from a breach or inaccuracy of any representation or warranty in

---

6. BLACK'S LAW DICTIONARY 705 (6th ed. 1990).

7. BLACK'S LAW DICTIONARY 769 (6th ed. 1990).

the agreement. The indemnitor need not be the other party to the contract. Like guaranties, indemnities are only as good as the indemnitor.

The basic issues that arise with indemnities are related to scope in a variety of dimensions. Scope of indemnification is defined or limited by (i) the time period during which claims can be asserted, (ii) the time period during which the event underlying the claim occurred, (iii) the minimum and maximum amount of any claim or of all claims in the aggregate, or over a particular period of time, (iv) the damages covered (actual pecuniary loss to third parties, consequential damages, punitive damages, liquidated damages), and (v) the mechanism for presenting claims and solving disputed claims.

c. Releases

A *release* of a right, claim or privilege is a cancellation of the right to assert a right, claim, or privilege.[8] A similar result may be achieved by "assignment" of the claim, which can have other different effects that are useful in creatively structuring a transaction, such as maintaining the subordinate priority of other claims or one party's judgment-proof status.

7. Cautionary Procedures.

At the outset, consider including a master provision that eliminates or "disclaims" as far as legally possible all express or implied representations, warranties, covenants, indemnities, and releases except as expressly provided in the contract. This is an attempt to "wipe the slate clean" of common law and statutory "implied" provisions such as the UCC's warranty of merchantability or fitness for intended use.[9] A disclaimer of warranties may be subject to different, peculiar drafting requirements that seem to indicate the potential judicial hostility to overreaching disclaimers and releases obtained by economically dominant parties.[10] Include a "merger" or "integration" clause to trigger the parol evidence rule to exclude evidence of any statements that could be construed as agreements, representations, warranties, covenants, etc., made during negotiations or earlier rounds of documentation.

The use of the incorrect type of provision can result in the provision working in unintended ways, limiting a party's rights, or giving rise to unintended defenses or consequences. For example, since warranties

---

8. BLACK'S LAW DICTIONARY 1289 (6th ed. 1990).

9. *But see* U.C.C. §§ 2–316(1) (disclaimers of express warranties in conflict with apparent warranty will be inoperative if that construction is unreasonable); 2–316(2), (3) (disclaimer of implied warranties with specific disclaimers, general disclaimers, buyer inspections, and course of performance).

10. *See, e.g.,* National & Int'l Brotherhood of Street Racers, Inc. v. Superior Court, 215 Cal.App.3d 934, 264 Cal.Rptr. 44, Street Racers 937 (1989) ("a release will be challenged as failing to mention the particular risk which causes a plaintiff's injury ... or as insufficiently comprehensive ... It will be attacked as totally ineffective if a key word is placed in the caption for emphasis but not repeated in the text ..., or if despite unambiguous language, the word "negligence" is not used....").

concern the present existence of facts, the characterization of a covenant as a representation or warranty may prevent the covenant from applying to a future breach of the obligation. Likewise, the characterization of a covenant as a representation or warranty may create fraud or misrepresentation tort liability—including potential punitive damages—for the promisor's breach, but that breach should only be a contract claim—limiting damages to compensatory ones in most jurisdictions—if a true covenant is used.[11]

Claims of breach or inaccuracy accrue and statutes of limitations run at different times depending upon the type of provision used. A claim for misrepresentation can arise at the time of signing a purchase and sale or other agreement. A breach of warranty claim generally arises at the time of the closing or sale. A breach of covenant claim accrues when the party does not honor the covenant, which may be in the distant, post-closing future.

Do not confuse a letter of credit with a guaranty. A letter of credit establishes a separate, direct, primary obligation between the issuer to the beneficiary. A guaranty creates an obligation "secondary" to that of the primary obligor. A guarantor has subrogation and reimbursement rights against the primary obligor, while an issuer of a letter of credit has only reimbursement rights and whatever security interest it negotiated.[12] The beneficiary of a letter of credit must comply strictly with the terms of the letter of credit, and the issuer has few defenses to payment, which may not be the case with a guaranty and a guarantor.

Failing to recognize a guaranty as a guaranty may lead to failing to include a waiver of the guarantor's suretyship defenses, exoneration rights, notice, presentment, exhaustion of claims against the primary obligor, or unique state law provisions, such as the anti-deficiency or "one form of action" statutes of many Western states.[13]

If an "indemnity" is used to cover a warranty claim, the "indemnitee" may not have a claim if the "indemnitor" can limit its liability to true indemnitor liability, which includes only reimbursement of the

11. *See, e.g.,* People v. Johnson, 213 Cal. App.3d 1369, 1375, 262 Cal.Rptr. 366 (1989) (a defendant who makes a "material representation about conduct in the future" is required to act in accordance with those representations "irrespective of what his intent or knowledge was at the time the representation was made.").

12. *See, e.g.,* Bank of Am., N.T. & S.A. v. Kaiser Steel Corp., 89 B.R. 150 (Bkrtcy. D.Colo.1988) (a bank, which paid a standby letter of credit, was not subrogated to rights of a creditor to proceed on its security interest in the debtor's assets).

13. Anti-deficiency statutes typically provide that a lender secured by a lien on real property may only look to that property to satisfy the debt upon default. *See, e.g.*

Cal. Civ. Proc. Code § 580b (anti-deficiency provision applicable to so-called seller-takeback financing for one-to-four unit dwelling occupied by borrower). "One form of Action" or "One Action Rule" laws limit a lender to first proceeding judicially against the collateral in a judicial foreclosure action and then, in that same action, obtaining a deficiency judgment against the borrower *or* electing to waive the result to seek a deficiency judgment by proceeding non-judicially against the collateral, such or by a deed of trust. *See, e.g.,* Cal. Civ. Proc. Code § 726. Pro-debtor laws of this sort were enacted in many Western states whose land and homes were financed by Eastern banks and financial institutions. Local counsel can be invaluable in identifying issues like this.

"indemnitee" for its liabilities to *third persons*—self-sustained and remedied damages are not included. This limitation can be drafted around in many jurisdictions by expressly including otherwise excluded damages.

An indemnity against "liability" becomes collectible immediately when the indemnitee become *liable* to a third person. An indemnity against anything else (such as "claims" or "damages") becomes collectible only after the indemnitee has *paid* the third person.

Finally, an indemnity may not be effective if the indemnitee's own negligence contributed to its obligation to a third party. Generally, an indemnitee can recover in these circumstances only if the indemnity expressly provides for recovery under those circumstances. Again, draft carefully!

QUESTIONS & CLAUSES FOR CONSIDERATION

1. State whether the following functional provisions are best drafted as representations, warranties, covenants, indemnities, guaranties, releases, or combinations of these types of provisions, and explain your reasoning:

    A. A provision concerning the amount of inventory and work in progress of a manufacturing business which a prospective Buyer wants to rely upon in deciding to move forward with the transaction.

    B. A provision concerning the amount of inventory and work in progress of a manufacturing business which a prospective Buyer wants to rely upon in deciding to waive an unmet condition and close the transaction.

    C. A statement that property to be sold is free of liens other than those disclosed by the Seller and that the Seller will defend the Buyer against any claims inconsistent with this statement and will pay off any undisclosed liens that are, in fact, valid.

    D. Susan's father is willing to repay a loan from a bank to Susan if she doesn't pay off the note in a timely fashion.

    E. Howard's mother will pay Howard's nurse for any liabilities to third parties caused by Howard while he is under the nurse's care.

    F. Same as in "E" above, but Howard's mother also promises to defend the nurse or pay the cost of the nurse's defense in any legal actions associated with those liabilities.

    G. A statement that a car's odometer reading is correct.

2. Draft each of the provisions above. Use generic defined terms for unknown specifics and feel free to invent qualities, dates, and other details as long as they are consistent with the facts stated.

3. Review the UCC sections cited in this section. Summarize the provisions and their meaning in five pages or less of plain English that would be understood by a non-lawyer.

4. Draft a general disclaimer of all warranties in a sale of goods transaction. Remember, it needs to be conspicuous. UCC §§ 2–316(2).

5. Draft a specific disclaimer of the warranty of merchantability under UCC § 2–314(1).

6. The following are sample representations/warranties drawn from actual contracts. Some of these provisions are cumbersome and do not, perhaps, reflect the optimum in clarity and plain language. In addition to illustrating the sorts of things that it is common for parties to represent and warrant, these provisions provide you with the opportunity to re-draft them more clearly, either through different use of language or formatting.

These would be introduced by an introductory lead-in clause in the form: [Buyer *or* Seller] [Represents *or* Warrants *or* Represents and Warrants, *as appropriate*] that:

A. *Representation/warranty on basis of preparation of financial statements.*

(a) Sellers have delivered to Buyer the balance sheet of the Company reviewed by the Company's Accounts, as of [*date 1*] and [*date 2*], and the related statements of income, shareholders' equity, and cash flows for the fiscal years then ended. Each of these financial statements (i) is complete and correct in all material respects; (ii) has been prepared in accordance with generally accepted accounting principles consistently applied by the Company; (iii) fairly presents the financial condition of the Company as of the date thereof and the results of operations, and changes in cash flows, respectively, of the Company for the fiscal years covered thereby; and (iv) reflects all liabilities, including taxes, of the Company as of the date thereof. The inventory valuations in each of such financial statements are based on the principal of inventories at weighted average cost or market in accordance with the established practice of the Company for a number of years, with all obsolete or unusable or not readily salable inventories having been either eliminated or properly written down (it being understood that such pricing is not to be construed as the fair market values of such Inventories). Except as set forth in Schedule ___ such financial statements set forth the Shareholders' Equity of the Company as of the respective date thereof, after full provision and reserves for all taxes and other liabilities for all periods up to the dates thereof. Except as set forth in Schedule ___, to the best knowledge of Sellers and the Company, there is no liability of the Company or any basis for the assertion against the Company of any liability not reflected or reserved against in such balance sheets.

(b) Sellers have delivered to Buyer the balance sheet of the Company as of [*interim date*], and the related statements of income, shareholders' equity, and cash flows for the [*interim period*] then ended. These interim financial statements (i) are complete and correct in all material respects; (ii) have been prepared in accordance with generally accepted accounting principles consistently applied by the Company; (iii) fairly present the financial condition of the Company as of the date thereof and the results of operations and cash flows of the Company for the interim [*defined period*] period; and (iv) reflects all liabilities, including taxes of the Company, as of the date thereof.

B. *Representation/warranty on absence of certain changes or events.*

Except as set forth in Schedule ___, since [*date*], there have been:

(a) To the best knowledge of Sellers and the Company, no change in the condition (financial or otherwise), properties, business, operations, or prospects of the Company which, either singly or in the aggregate, is materially adverse (as defined herein) to the Company;

(b) no sales of goods or services or other transactions of the Company other than those occurring in the ordinary and regular course of business;

(c) no change in the manner of conducting the business of the Company;

(d) no material adverse change in the working capital position of the Company, no unusual build up of its inventories, and no mark-up of its fixed assets or inventories;

(e) no financial or other commitments or obligations incurred by the Company, except such as may be incidental to carrying on the ordinary and regular course of business;

(f) no borrowing by the Company of any funds (other than advances under the Company's revolving credit agreement, the aggregate outstanding amount of which is set forth on Schedule ___) and no endorsing or guaranteeing payment by the Company of any loan or obligation, contractual or otherwise, of any other Person, and there are no such borrowings, endorsements, or guaranties by the Company presently outstanding.

(g) other than those occurring in the ordinary course of business, none of which exceeds $500, no loans or advances by the Company to any Person at any time;

(h) no capital additions or improvements to the properties of the Company in excess of $10,000 in the aggregate and no contracts therefore;

(i) except for finished products and component parts sold by the Company in the ordinary course of business, no sale, retirement, abandonment, or other disposition of any properties of the Company except the disposition of minor equipment in the ordinary course of business with an aggregate value of less than $10,000;

(j) no outstanding obligation by the Company, either for money borrowed or otherwise, other than as set forth in the financial statements delivered to Buyer pursuant to Section ____, except trade accounts payable and other current expenses and taxes incurred and accrued on its books and rising out of the ordinary day-to-day course of business, none of which obligations is in default or arrears of payment;

(k) no dividend on the capital stock of the Company or distribution to the stockholders of the Company and no money or other property set apart for the payment or for making any other distributions to or for the account of the stockholders of the Company;

(*l*) no acquisition or contract to acquire in any manner, directly or indirectly, any of the outstanding capital stock of the Company or of any other corporation;

(m) no payment of or any obligation to pay any amounts either in cash or other property to any Person for cancellation of any outstanding options or agreements to acquire shares of the Company's capital stock; and

(n) no change in the capital structure or articles of incorporation or by-laws of the Company.

C. *Representation/warranty for intellectual property.*

(a) Schedule ____ contains a complete and accurate list of all Intellectual Property material to the business of the Company as presently conducted. To the extent set forth in Schedule ____, the Intellectual Property has been duly filed in or issued by the United States and foreign Patent Offices or other appropriate governmental body. Except as set forth in Schedule ____, (i) the Company is the sole Person entitled to use the Intellectual Property, free and clear of all Claims; (ii) the Company does not use any of the Intellectual Property by consent of any other Person; and (iii) to the best knowledge of Sellers and the Company, there are no

Liens on any of the Intellectual Property. Except as set forth on Schedule ___, (A) the Company does not pay any licensing fee, royalty, or other payment to any other Person with respect to any of the Intellectual Property or the use thereof; (B) the Company's rights to use and transfer any and all of the Intellectual Property are unrestricted and not contractually restricted in duration; and (c) to the best knowledge of Sellers and the Company, the Intellectual Property neither infringes on the right of other Persons nor is being infringed on by other Persons.

(b) To the best knowledge of Sellers and the Company, the Intellectual Property, is sufficient for the business of the Company as presently conducted. Except as set forth on Schedule ___, the Company has not at any time been charged with any infringement of any adversely held patent, trademark, trade name, service mark, or copyright, and, to the best knowledge of Sellers and the Company, there are no unexpired patents (held by Persons other than the Company) with claims on products of the Company or on any apparatus, process, or other method applied by it in its business, or other patents or applications thereof which may have a material effect on the Company's business or prospects.

Chapter 8

EVENTS OF DEFAULT
AND REMEDIES

Notes, leases, and other contacts that govern continuing relationships feature specific sections that delineate events of default, procedures for declaring a default, and the remedies available to a non-defaulting party upon declaration of default. These provisions are the special concern of the lawyers because at the "front end of the deal"—the negotiation and documentation stages—the clients are primarily focused on performance, not on default.

In contracts courses, law students study common law rules regarding remedies, from limits on damages to the availability of specific performance and other equitable remedies. As a contract drafter, you need to plan you way *around* these legal rules to allow your client to recover as much as possible in the event of the other party's breach. Good transactional lawyers know the substantive law applicable to their transactions and then plan and structure transactions to take advantage of favorable law (*e.g.*, tax effects, validation of liquidated damages provisions, etc.) and to avoid, or "draft around," unfavorable law.

"Default" is a broader concept than "breach of contract." The default and remedy section of a contract should begin with a listing of what actual events are "events of default." Although the enumerated events of default generally include events that would be a breach of the contract under the common law without a specific default section—for example, non-payment of rent under a real property lease—they can also include many things that would otherwise not be considered a breach—such as changed financial status as measured by financial ratios and other "insecurity" provisions. Events of default or a declaration of default under one contract can also be a default or an event of default under another agreement, including an agreement involving a completely separate transaction and completely different parties. This is known as a "cross-default."

Events of default are, of course, selected for each transaction. Common events of default include:

- Failure to perform an obligation.

- Failure to pay monies when due.

- Failure to maintain a certain status (membership, financial condition, etc.).

- Breach or inaccuracy of a representation or warranty.

- Bankruptcy and similar insolvency-related condition and proceedings (although these are generally unenforceable if the contacting party is the subject of a bankruptcy case).

- Default under another agreement.

- General insecurity of the other party.

The contract can make the occurrence of an event of default an automatic default under the contract entitling the non-defaulting party to exercise its remedies, or it may require the non-defaulting party to give notice that the event of default has occurred and "declare" a default. The latter form gives the non-defaulting party more flexibility, but also requires more careful monitoring of the other party—especially if non-monetary defaults are involved. Remember, a notice of default or termination will generally not be effective if the defaulting party is in bankruptcy before the proper notice is given of an event of default.[1]

Many default provisions include the concept of a right to cure, or fix, the default and avoid application of the remedies provided in the contract. Different cure periods can apply to different events of default, and the contract should specify when the cure period begins to run. In drafting, one of two approaches is used to provide for cure rights. One either drafts a separate provision addressing the right to cure or builds the cure right into each event of default provision.

The provisions that establish a default are generally followed by provisions that specify (i) remedies, (ii) whether those remedies are automatic or elective on the part of the non-defaulting party, (iii) how the election of remedies, if any, is to be made and (iv) whether the remedies are mutually exclusive or cumulative. Consider the legality and enforceability of remedies as well. The most effective ones that you can imagine are often unenforceable or of limited enforceability.

The mutual foreseeability test of *Hadley v. Baxendale*[2] would limit liability unless the draftsperson used, among other provisions, a liquidated damage clause and a prevailing party attorneys' fee clause. Alternatively, the drafter could include recitals showing what damages were reasonably foreseeable by all parties. Similar issues arise in other areas, including provisions for acceleration of payment obligations, post-judgment attorneys' fees, interest, default interest, prepayment fees, or calculation of interest based upon an actual year or a 360 day "accounting" year. The drafter needs to assess all applicable issues, the limiting

---

1. *See, generally,* 11 U.S.C. § 362(a) (prohibiting taking action against a debtor or a debtor's property after a bankruptcy case is commenced and the order for relief is entered); *but see* 11 U.S.C. § 362(b) (listing exceptions and unstayed types of acts).

2. Hadley v. Baxendale, 9 Exch. 341 (Court of the Exchequer 1854).

or expanding effect of otherwise applicable law and possible "draft arounds" available to serve the client's interests.

A final note about default and remedies: When an event of default has occurred and it is time to declare the default, the notice of default (generally in the form of a letter) should be drafted in unequivocal language and should track the language and requirements of the contract exactly. There is no need to be overly kind or insulting in tone—a neutral description of the contract, the pertinent provisions, the event of default that has occurred, a declaration of the default, an election of remedies, if needed, and any demand for action will suffice. The notice of default should be transmitted exactly as specified in the contract. Failure to strictly adhere to the contractual requirements will afford the defaulting party a defense to enforcement and may allow additional time to cure and reinstate the agreement.

QUESTIONS & CLAUSES FOR CONSIDERATION

1. For an example of exactly how badly and ineffectively notices of default can be drafted, consider the following case.

BEAL BANK v. CRYSTAL PROPERTIES, LTD., L.P. (IN RE CRYSTAL PROPERTIES, LTD., L.P.)

United States Court of Appeals, Ninth Circuit, 2001.
268 F.3d 743.

WARDLAW, Circuit Judge:

Beal Bank ("Beal") appeals the district court's order affirming the bankruptcy court's grant of summary judgment in favor of the debtor, Crystal Properties ("Crystal"). Beal asserts that the bankruptcy and district courts incorrectly concluded that Crystal was not required to pay interest at the default rate on seven defaulted loans Beal acquired from the Federal Deposit Insurance Corporation ("FDIC"). The central issue is whether, and, if so, when, the default interest rate, as provided in the original loan agreement between Beal's predecessors and the Ngs (later Crystal) is triggered. Beal argues that the default interest rate was triggered the moment the Ngs failed to make interest payments to its predecessors (early 1995). Crystal contends that the default rate became applicable after the first quarter of 1997, when Beal recorded the notices of default. We agree with the bankruptcy and district courts, concluding under well-established authority, that the default interest rate did not apply to Crystal's loans until the first quarter of 1997, when the holder first took affirmative action to put the debtor on notice that it intended to exercise its option to accelerate, and thus invoked the default rate under the contract at issue. We have jurisdiction pursuant to *28 U.S.C. § 158*(d), and we affirm.

I. Background

This case arises out of nine loans issued by Guardian Bank ("Guardian") to Thien Koan Ng and Carol Ng, either directly or indirectly through one of the entities they controlled. Each of the loans was executed in California. The collateral for the loans consisted of real property and/or pledged promissory notes secured by real property in California. The contract rate set forth in each loan document was Bank of America's prime interest rate, plus one percent. Each loan also included a Premium Interest Rate Clause providing that the unpaid balance would accelerate on default and bear interest at a rate 5% higher than the contract rate. The premium interest rate clause or "default interest clause" in each note states:

> Should default be made in any payment provided for in this note, * * * at the option of the holder hereof and without notice or demand, the entire balance of principal and accrued interest then remaining unpaid shall become immediately due and payable, and thereafter bear interest, until paid in full, at the increased rate of five percent (5%) per annum over and above the rate contracted for herein. No delay or omission on the part of the holder hereof in exercising any right hereunder, * * * shall operate as a waiver of such right or any other right under this note * * **

Although the Ngs originally acquired at least nine loans from Guardian, only the seven loans set forth below are at issue in this appeal:

* * * * *

Of these seven notes, three (Loans E, F, and G) matured prior to the first quarter of 1997—the date upon which the parties agreed the default interest rate became applicable.

By early 1995, the Ngs had missed payments on their loans. Thien Ng entered into negotiations with Guardian to induce the Bank to accept a fifteen percent (15%) discount on the loan balances. On January 20, 1995, the FDIC placed Guardian into conservatorship. After the FDIC assumed control of Guardian's affairs, Thien Ng continued to attempt to negotiate a pay out.

On February 23, 1995, the FDIC secured a written demand that the Ngs bring their loans current and informed them that failure to do so would result in the FDIC imposing the default rate. The letter notified the Ngs that the FDIC had frozen three of their accounts at Guardian, but had not set off any outstanding loan balances against the funds held in the frozen accounts. Although the letter concluded that the loans "are in default, which invokes (sic) the default interest clause," it contained no statement regarding the amount of the default interest rate or whether the FDIC wished to accelerate the loans.

On March 6, 1995, the FDIC again demanded that the Ngs bring their loans current. This letter specifically stated that because the Ngs had transferred the real property security for three loans identified in the letter (only one of which is among the seven loans in this appeal) to a third party, the FDIC "had triggered the default interest provision of [the] Deeds of Trust." Notwithstanding that statement, the calculations of the principal and accrued interest owed to the FDIC set forth in the letter were based on the contract rate—and not the default rate.

On May 9, 1995, the FDIC communicated with the Ngs again (in a letter erroneously dated March 9, 1995). The correspondence included a list of the outstanding balances of remaining principal and unpaid interest calculated at the contract rate. This letter made no reference to the default interest clause.

Ten days later, on May 19th, the FDIC wrote to the Ngs outlining their negotiations about a possible 15% discount on the outstanding loans. The FDIC indicated that because Guardian had negotiated a 15% discount on the loans, it might be willing to consider a discount if the Ngs provided financial statements and agreed to keep interest payments current during the negotiations. The letter also represented that the FDIC would withhold taking action on the three loans discussed in the March 6th letter during discount negotiations.

The FDIC and the Ngs subsequently reached an agreement to allow the Ngs to pay off all outstanding loans at a 12.5% discount. On August 15, 1996, the FDIC sent the Ngs an accounting statement calculating the principal and accrued interest due on each loan at the contract rate. The letter also noted that the "agreement that we had entered into with you to allow a discounted payoff will expire on September 17, 1996." Despite reaching this agreement, the Ngs failed to make the negotiated payments to the FDIC and never tendered the loan balances.

Around December 1996, Guardian, through the FDIC, assigned its beneficial rights in the Ngs's loans to Beal. Because Beal could not reach any settlement agreement with the Ngs as to the overall payoff amount, Beal sent notices of acceleration and default to the Ngs. By the first quarter of 1997, Beal recorded notices of default for all seven loans, an act that the parties agree was legally sufficient to trigger the default interest provision in the notes.

On June 25, 1997, Crystal, a real estate venture corporation owned and controlled by the Ngs, commenced a bankruptcy proceeding by filing a Chapter 11 petition in the Central District of California. One day before Crystal filed its Chapter 11 petition, the Ngs transferred the real property collateral for the seven loans to Crystal. To determine the maximum amount of Beal's claims, Crystal filed a motion for estimation on August 19, 1997, which was granted. Beal filed proofs of claims for the seven loans on September 12, 1997.

In April 1998, the parties cross-moved for summary judgment to determine, inter alia, whether Beal was entitled to apply the default interest rate before the date it filed the notices of default. The bankruptcy court held that it was not:

The real question is, as has always been, can Beal Bank come in as a successor in interest and go back and retroactively apply default interest from a period long before it had any connection with this loan, notwithstanding anything else that went on, and the answer, I think, can't be yes.

The bankruptcy court further reasoned that it would be inequitable to allow Beal to recover the default interest rate in a period during which it was not actively enforced by Beal's predecessors in interest. It concluded that the FDIC and Guardian had waived their right to default interest for the periods in which they were holders of the notes.

The bankruptcy court ruled on the remaining issues presented in the cross-motions for summary judgment and entered final orders on May 28, 1998.

Beal timely appealed the single issue of applicability of the default interest rate to the district court, which heard argument on April 19, 1999. Affirming the bankruptcy court, the district court held that because Guardian and the FDIC did not take any affirmative action to exercise the option to accelerate, neither entity had triggered the default interest rate. The district court also concluded that the plain language of the notes precluded Beal from collecting default interest on the matured loans because the default interest clause was tied to the option to accelerate. Again, Beal timely appealed.

II. Right to Default Interest

A. Construction of the Contract

Beal argues that because the notes expressly state that default interest is due and payable upon default "without notice or demand," the default interest rate should begin to accrue the moment Crystal defaulted on the notes. Based on our reading of the notes at issue, we disagree.

"[A] written contract must be read as a whole and every part interpreted with reference to the whole." *Kennewick Irrigation Dist. v. United States*, 880 F.2d 1018, 1032 (9th Cir.1989) (quoting *Shakey's, Inc. v. Covalt*, 704 F.2d 426, 434 (9th Cir.1983)). Furthermore, "a court must give effect to every word or term employed by the parties and reject none as meaningless or surplusage...." *Cree v. Waterbury*, 78 F.3d 1400, 1405 (9th Cir.1996) (quoting *United States v. Hathaway*, 242 F.2d 897, 900 (9th Cir.1957)). Therefore, we must interpret the contract in a manner that gives full meaning and effect to all of the contract's provisions and avoid a construction of the contract that focuses only on a single provision of the note.

As noted above, all of the notes executed between Crystal and Beal's predecessors provide:

> Should default be made in any payment provided for in this
> note, * * * at the option of the holder hereof and without notice
> or demand, the entire balance of principal and accrued interest
> then remaining unpaid shall become immediately due and pay-
> able, and thereafter bear interest, until paid in full, at the
> increased rate of five percent (5%) per annum over and above
> the rate contracted for herein. No delay or omission on the part
> of the holder hereof in exercising any right hereunder, * * *
> shall operate as a waiver of such right or any other right under
> this note * * **.

Thus, "the entire balance of principal and accrued interest then
remaining" becomes immediately due and payable "at the option of
the holder." Therefore, the right to accelerate the unpaid debt is at
the lender's option. The notes further provide that if the option is
exercised, the notes will "thereafter bear interest * * * at the
increased rate of five percent (5%) per annum over and above the
rate contracted for herein." The use of the word "thereafter" can
only mean that the default interest rate does not become effective
unless the holder of the note exercises its option to accelerate.
Therefore, we read the contract language, as did the district court,
to require the holder to exercise its option to accelerate before the
default interest rate is triggered.

Nevertheless, Beal cites to *In re PCH Associates*, 122 B.R. 181
(Bankr.S.D.N.Y.1990), in support of its contention that the default
interest in the notes can be invoked without acceleration. Although
PCH Associates holds that the default interest rate in the PCH
Associates' contract was triggered even though the lender failed to
exercise its option to accelerate, the contractual language examined
by the court in PCH Associates differs significantly from the contractual language at issue here. The default interest provision in
PCH Associates stated: "Following the occurrence of an Event of
Default, interest shall accrue on the principal amount hereof at the
rate of twelve (12%) percent per annum and shall be payable upon
demand." *PCH Assocs.*, 122 B.R. at 187. The bankruptcy court
interpreted this and the other accompanying provisions as providing
the lender with two options: "[1] the option to accelerate the entire
debt, in which event interest would accrue on both the First and
Second Parts, or [2] simply accept the missed payments, albeit late,
at a higher [default] interest rate to compensate for the time value
of money." *Id.* at 197. Here, the provision we are interpreting
simply is not analogous to the contract provision at issue in PCH
Associates. The notes at issue in this case require that the default
interest provision be triggered after acceleration and only provide
the lender with one option. Therefore, PCH Associates is inapposite.

B. Option to Accelerate

1. Affirmative Action Required

Beal argues that even if it was required to exercise its option to
accelerate, it was not required to give Crystal notice of its intent to

apply the default interest rate. Crystal counters that despite the language in the contract, a creditor must take affirmative action to put the debtor on notice that it intends to exercise its option to accelerate. We believe that Crystal has the better of the argument.

While California law governs the issue * the question is closed to debate. Both state and federal courts have made clear the unquestionable principle that, even when the terms of a note do not require notice or demand as a prerequisite to accelerating a note, the holder must take affirmative action to notify the debtor that it intends to accelerate. See *Green v. Carlstrom*, 212 Cal.App.2d 240, 243, 27 Cal.Rptr. 850 (Cal. Dist. Ct. App. 1963) (holding that "the option to accelerate a promissory note does not operate automatically but some act is required to effect such acceleration.") (citation omitted); *Trigg v. Arnott*, 22 Cal.App.2d 455, 71 P.2d 330, 332 (Cal.Dist.Ct. App.1937) (holding that the holder of the note must act in a manner that effectively provides notice that the holder has exercised his option); What Is Essential to Exercise of Option to Accelerate Maturity of Bill or Note, 5 A.L.R.2d 968, 971 (1949) ("[A] party having an option to declare a note due and payable cannot simply by his own secret intention, never disclosed by act or word, claim that he declared the note due and payable. The addition of the words 'without demand or notice' does not alter the requirement of an affirmative act of the holder of the note for the valid exercise of the option."); see also *United States v. Rollinson*, 275 U.S.App.D.C. 345, 866 F.2d 1463, 1467 (D.C.Cir.1989) (following precedent holding that, "because acceleration was optional on the part of the holder, affirmative action * * * must be taken to make it known to the debtor that he has exercised his option to accelerate") (internal quotations and citation omitted) (alterations in original); *United States v. Feterl*, 849 F.2d 354, 357 (8th Cir.1988) (holding that, "as a general rule, * * * affirmative action by the creditor must be taken to make it known to the debtor that [the creditor] has exercised his option to accelerate.") (citation omitted); *United States v. Hosko*, 1989 WL 265041, *2 (M.D.Pa.1989) (citing Rollinson in holding that "where the acceleration of the installment payments in cases of default is optional, on the part of the holder, then the entire debt does not become due on the mere default of payment but affirmative action by the creditor must be taken to make it known to the debtor that he has exercised his option to accelerate"), aff'd, 884 F.2d 1386 (3d. Cir.1989) (unpublished disposition); *Curry v. United States*, 679 F.Supp. 966, 969–70 (N.D.Cal.1987) (concluding that "the general rule is that where the acceleration of the installment payments in cases of default is optional * * *, then the entire debt does not become due on the mere default of payment but affirmative action by the creditor must be taken to make it known to the debtor that he has exercised his option to accelerate.") (citation and internal quotations omitted) (alterations in original) (emphasis omitted); *United States v. Cardinal*, 452 F.Supp. 542, 547 (D.Vt.1978) ("The law is well settled that where the acceleration of the installment payments in cases of default is optional on the part of the holder, then the entire debt does not become due on the mere default of payment but affirmative action by the creditor must be taken to make it known to the debtor that he has exercised his option to accelerate, even though the note itself, as is the case here, waives notice of demand.") (emphasis added); *Moresi v. Far W. Servs., Inc.*, 291 F.Supp. 586, 588 (D.Haw.1968) (same); *In re Holiday Mart, Inc.*, 9 B.R. 99, 105 (Bankr.D.Haw.1981) ("It is well established that to exercise an option to accelerate the maturity of a note the holder must take some affirmative action that evidences its intention to accelerate. * * * This requirement applies even where the note provides for acceleration 'without notice.' ").[3]

We find the overwhelming weight of authority persuasive and note the lack of any law that would contradict the requirement of affirmative action to accelerate. We therefore conclude that the California Supreme Court would adopt the rule that the addition of the words "without demand or notice" does not alter the requirement that the holder of the note must carry out some affirmative act to exercise its option to accelerate.* * * Even though the note here provides that upon default the note can be accelerated "without notice or demand," Beal or its predecessors must take some affirmative action before acceleration and, in turn, before the default interest rate becomes effective.[4]

This conclusion is further supported by the language of the deeds of trusts for each loan, which provides that the: "Beneficiary may declare * * * all sums secured hereby immediately due and payable by delivery to Trustee of written declaration of default and demand for sale and of written notice of default and of election to cause said property to be sold, which notice Trustee shall cause to be duly filed for record." Because "[a] note and a deed of trust * * * must be read and construed together," *Kerivan v. Title Ins. & Trust Co.*, 147 Cal.App.3d 225, 230, 195 Cal.Rptr. 53 (1983), the language in the deed of trust supports the conclusion that Beal was required to take some affirmative action "declaring" that it had exercised its option to accelerate and thus triggered the default interest clause.

Therefore, the district court did not err in holding that Beal and its predecessors were required to give Crystal notice of its intent to exercise its option to accelerate the note.

---

3. See, e.g., *Butner v. United States*, 440 U.S. 48, 55, 99 S.Ct. 914, 59 L.Ed.2d 136 (1979) (holding state law governs property interests in bankruptcy proceedings "unless some federal interest requires a different result. . . .").

4. See *NLRB v. Calkins*, 187 F.3d 1080, 1089 (9th Cir.1999) (where state's highest court has not addressed an issue, federal court's task is to "predict how the highest state court would decide the issue using intermediate appellate court decisions, decisions from other jurisdictions, statutes, treatises, and restatements as guidance") (internal citations omitted).

2. Notice and Demand Not Provided

Beal argues, in the alternative, that the two letters sent by the FDIC, its immediate predecessor in interest, constituted affirmative action and notice sufficient to accelerate notes A, B, C, D, and G. It contends that, because the letters accelerated these notes and notified Crystal that it was invoking the default interest rates, the default interest rate should be applied to the outstanding loan amounts dating from the date of each letter, February 23, 1995, and March 6, 1995, not from the recordation dates in the first quarter of 1997. Because these letters did not accomplish what Beal now urges, however, this argument is unavailing.

"The exercise of the option to accelerate must be in a manner that is clear and unequivocal and effectively informs the maker that the option to accelerate has been exercised * * *" *In re Holiday Mart, Inc.*, 9 B.R. 99, 105 (Bankr. Haw. 1981); see also *First Bank Investors' Trust v. Tarkio Coll.*, 129 F.3d 471, 475 (8th Cir.1997) (" 'A right to accelerate * * * should be clear and unequivocal, and if there is a reasonable doubt as to the meaning of the terms employed preference should be given to the construction which will * * * prevent acceleration of maturity.' ") (alterations in original) (citation omitted); 11 Am. Jur. 2d Bills and Notes § 196 (1997) ("The creditor must perform some clear, unequivocal affirmative act evidencing an intention to take advantage of the acceleration provision * * *").

Neither the February 1995 letter, the March 1995 letter, nor any other correspondence from the FDIC "clearly and unequivocally" triggered Beal's option to accelerate and, concomitantly its right to apply the default interest rate.

a. The February 23, 1995 Letter

On February 23, 1995, the FDIC wrote:

> The FDIC has not setoff any account, nor has it taken any action of any kind under either real property secured or personal property secured loans. All the FDIC has done is to freeze accounts for which there are delinquent loans outstanding. Your loans however, are in default which invokes (sic) the default interest clause.

(emphasis in original). The letter is silent as to the FDIC's option to accelerate. If any inference is to be drawn from this letter, it is that the FDIC had not exercised its option to accelerate because it states that the FDIC had not used Crystal's accounts at Guardian to pay down the loan. Although the FDIC did warn Crystal that its loans were in default, it failed to discuss acceleration, a necessary predicate for invocation of the clause.

The Eighth Circuit has found less ambiguous language in a letter from the lender to be insufficient to trigger an option to accelerate and a default interest clause. See *Tarkio Coll.*, 129 F.3d at 474–76. In Tarkio College, the holder of the note, First Bank, on May 14, 1991, wrote the debtor:

> This is to advise you, ... that First Bank deems Tarkio College in default of its promissory note to First Bank with respect to the referenced loan transaction. Accordingly First Bank requests Tarkio College to now come forward within the next ten (10) days with full payment of the unpaid principal, $862,396.39, and unpaid and accrued interest of $38,793.70 as of this day, 05/14/91. Interest is accruing at a rate of $283.528 per day.

Id. at 474. Even though this letter clearly stated that the debtor was required to come forward with the full amount within ten days and that interest was accruing at a higher rate, the Eighth Circuit concluded that it "was ambiguous and, therefore, was not a 'clear and unequivocal' statement of the bank's intent to accelerate the loan." *Id.* at 475.

Because acceleration clauses are often considered "a penalty and inserted for the benefit of the creditor," *Stewart v. Claudius*, 19 Cal.App.2d 349, 353, 65 P.2d 933 (1937), and because "if there is a reasonable doubt as to the meaning of the terms employed preference should be given to the construction which will * * * prevent acceleration of maturity," *Tarkio Coll.*, 129 F.3d at 475 (citation omitted), the February 23, 1995, letter from the FDIC, like that in Tarkio College, did not trigger the option to accelerate or the default interest clause.

b. The March 6, 1995 Letter

As Judge Morrow's well-reasoned order concluded, the March 6, 1995, letter from the FDIC to Crystal is even less persuasive evidence of an unambiguous intent to accelerate.

The letter contains conflicting statements that also fail to clearly invoke the option to accelerate and the default interest clause. The March letter, which actually pertains to only one loan on appeal (Loan G, the Montclair Property) provides:

> Because you have transferred title to the following properties without permission of the FDIC as required by the Deeds of Trust, your actions have triggered the default interest provision of those Deeds of Trust * * * In addition to the above, there is a 5% default interest due on all remaining principal and unpaid interest. Unless we receive payment in full of all principal and accrued interest by May 31, 1995, on [3 of the loans] where you have sold the property, we will be filing a Notice of Default.

Although, in this letter, the FDIC states that Crystal's "actions have triggered the default interest provision" with respect to three identified loans, it calculates the debtors' outstanding principal and interest balances at the contractual interest rate. And although the FDIC later states that "a 5% default interest rate will apply * * * in addition" to the contract rate, the manner in which the letter is phrased merely advises the debtors that the FDIC could invoke the default interest clause in the future. See *Tarkio Coll.*, 129 F.3d at 475 (lender's letter did not clearly state an intention to accelerate or charge the default interest rate when it "applied the contractual interest rate of twelve percent in computing the amounts and * * * did not state clearly when, if ever, the [default] interest rate of sixteen percent would apply to the outstanding balance of the loan"). Beal argues that Tarkio College is "clearly distinguishable" on its facts because the promissory notes at issue in Tarkio College were "ambiguous as the letter specifically applied the contractual interest rate in computing the amounts noted in the letter." This argument fails because the FDIC's March 6th letter to the debtors, like the letter in Tarkio College, applied the contractual interest rate in computing the amounts calculated in the letter.

Moreover, the last sentence in the March 6, 1995, letter reads: "Unless we receive payment in full of all principal and accrued interest by May 31, 1995 * * * we will be filing a Notice of Default." This statement threatening future action demonstrates that the acceleration option had not been exercised and that the FDIC was not demanding immediate payment. Because the debtors were given almost three months to pay the outstanding balances on their loans, the letter did not "clearly and unequivocally" accelerate the loan or trigger the default interest clause.

Finally, in its papers before the district court, Beal admitted that the March 6th letter did not invoke the default rate. Specifically, Beal noted that: "in [the March 6th] letter, Ng was notified that a Premium Interest Rate would be imposed if the loans were not brought current." Although Beal did not make this same admission in its appellate briefs, it did not deny having made it before the district court. Because a judicial admission made at the district court is binding on this court, see *United States v. Bentson*, 947 F.2d 1353, 1356 (9th Cir.1991) (judicial admissions before district court that defendant failed to file tax returns for years at issue are binding on the appellate court), Beal is bound by its admission.

c. Subsequent Correspondence from the FDIC to the Debtors

Correspondence between the debtors and the FDIC following the March 6, 1995, letter also fails to indicate any affirmative action or invocation of the default interest provision. On May 9, 1995, the FDIC wrote to the debtors setting forth its calculations of the remaining balances on the loans at the contract rate, and failed to mention its option to accelerate or the default interest clause.

On May 19, 1995, Ruth Daugherty from the FDIC sent a letter to the debtors stating that the FDIC was still considering a 15%

discounted settlement. Specifically, the letter noted that Ms. Daugherty was "willing to forestall the filing of Notices of Default without waiving [her] rights to do so in the future, provided [that the debtors would] work toward a resolution at a reasonable discount." The letter made no reference to the default interest rate. In fact, the letter noted that if the 15% discount were granted, the FDIC would expect the debtor to pay off the loans "within a shorter period of time than the 90 days to which [the debtor] referred." The letter actually lends support to our interpretation of the March 6, 1995 letter. By referencing the March 6th letter as a previous agreement "to [have debtor] repay all of [its loans] within 90 days for a 15% discount of all outstanding principal and interest," it reiterates that the FDIC had agreed to allow the debtor to pay the amounts due without exercising the default interest clause.

Finally, in an August 15, 1996 letter, the FDIC sent a letter to the debtors calculating "the principal amount due, [the] accrued interest due, and the daily accrual." The letter specifically recognized that the interest rate had been calculated at the rate "per the signed note previously held with Guardian Bank" and not at the default interest rate. See *Tarkio Coll.*, 129 F.3d at 475–76 (calculating the interest of a note at the contract rate negates an inference of intent to charge at the default interest rate). The letter also acknowledged that the debtor and the FDIC reached a discount agreement negotiated at the contract rate.

This subsequent correspondence weighs in favor of a finding that Beal's predecessor, the FDIC, never exercised its option to accelerate or invoked the default interest clause in a clear or unequivocal manner. Beal cannot assert rights that the FDIC declined to exercise. See *In re Chappell*, 984 F.2d 775, 781–83 (7th Cir.1993) (Because predecessor did not assert its right to interest during the life of the plan despite several opportunities to do so, the successor in interest was barred from obtaining any interest on a second mortgage).

C. Matured Loans

Beal argues that no affirmative act was required to trigger the default interest clause in the three loans (Loans E, F, and G) that matured before the first quarter of 1997. It contends that the default interest rate was automatically due and payable as of the date of maturity because there was no unpaid balance left to accelerate on these loans. This argument ignores the plain language of the contract. The default provision in all seven loans provides:

> Should default be made in any payment provided for in this note, * * * at the option of the holder hereof and without notice or demand, the entire balance of principal and accrued interest then remaining unpaid shall become immediately due and pay-

able, and thereafter bear interest, until paid in full, at the increased rate * * *

The two critical clauses—"should default be made in any payment * * * " and "the entire balance * * * shall become immediately due and payable"—cannot be applied to a debt that has matured. Thus, as noted supra, this provision is an acceleration clause in which the lender's ability to charge default interest is tied to its option to accelerate. Because on maturity there is no debt left to accelerate, see *In re Entz–White Lumber & Supply, Inc.*, 850 F.2d 1338, 1342 (9th Cir.1988) (noting that on maturity, acceleration is unnecessary), the default interest provision in the debtor's note only applies to payment defaults that occur during the term of the note where the lender elects to accelerate. By its very terms, the default interest provision cannot be charged post-maturity.

Although Beal asserts that the district court erred in its analysis, it does not refute the district court's interpretation of the contract. Instead, Beal reiterates that it is "axiomatic" that once a note matures, the total balance is due and payable and therefore the default interest provision should apply. Beal misses the point of the district court's holding. The district court did not rule contrary to the notion that a "matured note" is "due and payable" on the day of maturity. Rather the district court held that, under the plain language of the contract, the default interest "provision contemplates that default interest will be payable only if the lender elects to accelerate and the full principal balance comes due prior to the 'maturity date.'" Therefore, the district court concluded that because the matured notes are "due and payable" and thus cannot be accelerated, the plain language of the contract precluded Beal from applying the default interest provision after the loans matured.

As Judge Morrow correctly noted in her order, Beal's predecessors easily could have drafted a provision that triggered the default interest provision either upon maturity or acceleration. See, e.g., *Tarkio Coll.*, 129 F.3d at 474 ("Any unpaid balance remaining under the note after the maturity date of July 1, 1995, or after acceleration of the loan by First Bank would accrue interest at a 'post-maturity rate' of sixteen percent per year.") (emphasis added); *In re Pikes Peak Water Co.*, 779 F.2d 1456, 1457–58 (10th Cir.1985) ("The principal or unpaid balance thereof ... shall draw interest at the rate of thirteen per cent (13%) per annum after the maturity date of any respective payment or upon declaration of default.") (emphasis added); *In re Realty Associates Securities Corporation*, 163 F.2d 387, 390 (2d Cir.1947) ("After an 'event of default' (non-payment at maturity being specified as one such event) [an interest rate of five per cent (5%) per annum] ... shall be applied to payment of the principal and interest then owing.") (emphasis added); *RTC Mortg. Trust v. J.I. Sopher & Co., Inc.*, 1998 WL 132815, *5 (S.D.N.Y.1998) ("In the event of the occurrence of a default beyond the applicable cure period, if any, or the non-payment of this Note on the Maturity

Date, then interest shall accrue at the Maximum Rate until this Note is paid in full.") (emphasis added); *FDIC v. Widefield Homes, Inc.*, 916 F.Supp. 1074, 1079 (D.Colo.1996) (discussing note that provided: "upon default, including failure to pay upon final maturity, Lender, at its option, may also * * * increase [the interest to the default interest rate]") (emphasis added); *F.D.I.C. v. Boyarsky*, 1995 WL 373483, *1 (S.D.N.Y.1995) ("The Note had a maturity date of July 1, 1992 and provided for a default interest rate at the adjustable rate plus 3%, to apply after the maturity date or upon acceleration after an event of default.") (emphasis added); *In re Route One W. Windsor Ltd. P'ship*, 225 B.R. 76, 78 (Bankr.D.N.J.1998) ("The Barclays note provides that upon and following either the (i) maturity date or (ii) default by the debtor, the note shall bear interest at * * * the 'default rate.' ") (emphasis added); *In re Ace–Texas, Inc.*, 217 B.R. 719, 721 (Bankr.D.Del.1998) ("Pursuant to the terms of the Notes, ... interest on unpaid principal and interest accrues at a default rate * * * [from and after maturity]."); *River Bank Am. v. Tally–Ho Assocs., L.P.*, 1991 WL 35719, *6 (Del.Super.Ct.1991) ("The Mortgage Note which is involved here provides that the 'Default Rate' shall be paid 'In the event of (a) the maturity of the entire indebtedness evidenced hereby, or (b) any default hereunder.' ") (emphasis added).

Beal further argues that the Uniform Commercial Code ("UCC") supports its claim that the default interest clause should apply on a matured note. The UCC provision, § 3–304, as adopted by the California Commercial Code, provides: "If the principal is payable in installments and a due date has not been accelerated, the instrument becomes overdue upon default under the instrument for non-payment of an installment, and the instrument remains overdue until the default is cured." This language, however, does not lend support to Beal's argument. Although it is true that an instrument becomes overdue upon default, the UCC provision does not state that despite contrary contractual language, a default interest provision automatically applies once a loan matures.

Beal also argues that the district court erred in holding that the default interest clause could not apply to the matured loans, contending that the bankruptcy court found otherwise. It points to isolated language contained in the transcript of the hearing before the bankruptcy court:

> Four of the loans were all due and payable, I think it appears to me that notice with regard to the default rate of interest rate is not required because there is nothing to accelerate.

It is not entirely clear whether the bankruptcy court actually made a finding that the default interest rates were triggered on the matured loans (Loans E, F, and G). The bankruptcy court stated in its oral holding: "I think what I said at the beginning is that on the mature loans, it's not clear to me that notice is necessary, but it was not an issue that I had to essentially reach on the matured loans."

However, even if the bankruptcy court did hold that an affirmative action was not necessary for the matured loans, and thus the default interest rate may be applicable, this has no bearing on our de novo review of the district court's order. We have held that an appellate court may affirm a district court's order to affirm "on any ground finding support in the record, even if the district court relied on the wrong grounds or wrong reasoning." *Laboa v. Calderon*, 224 F.3d 972, 981 n. 7 (9th Cir.2000) (citing *Marino v. Vasquez*, 812 F.2d 499, 508 (9th Cir.1987)). "Because the district court functions as an appellate court in reviewing a bankruptcy decision and applies the same standards of review as a federal court of appeals, the district court may also affirm a bankruptcy's order ... on any ground supported by the record." *Bogart v. Peter–Douglas, G.R.*, 2000 WL 1132189, *3 (D.Or.2000). See also *In re Daniels–Head & Associates, 819 F.2d 914, 918 (9th Cir.1987)* (When reviewing a bankruptcy court's decision, "the district court acts as an appellate court."); *In re Webb*, 954 F.2d 1102, 1103–04 (5th Cir.1992) ("When reviewing a bankruptcy court's decision ..., a district court functions as [an] appellate court and applies the standard of review generally applied in federal court appeals") (footnote omitted); *In re St. Mary Hospital*, 120 B.R. 25, 28 (Bankr.E.D.Pa.1990) ("The district court may affirm the decision of the bankruptcy court on any basis that finds support in the record."), aff'd, 931 F.2d 51 (3d Cir.1991) (unpublished disposition).

Finally, Beal argues that the bankruptcy court erred in finding that the principles of waiver and estoppel precluded Beal from applying the default interest rate to the matured loans. Because, like the district court, we conclude that the plain language of the contract precluded the default interest rate from applying to the matured loans, we need not reach the issues of waiver and estoppel.

AFFIRMED.

After reading *Beal Bank*, analyze what the drafters of the original and subsequent defective default letters did wrong. Draft a letter that, if substituted for the original *Beal Bank* letter, would have been an effective notice of default triggering all remedies provided for in the documents.

2. Here is an example of a default and remedies provision from a note secured by a deed of trust that encumbers a real estate development project. What is the intent behind each of the events of default? Similarly, what is the meaning and intent of the remedies?

[beginning of provision]

9. *Events of Default; Acceleration.*

9.1 *Events of Default.* The occurrence of any of the following events shall constitute an "Event of Default" hereunder:

(a) Any default by Maker in the repayment of any indebtedness owing to Lender, including, without limitation, Unpaid Purchase Price, Participating Contingent Interest, and any deposit, fee or other amount required to be paid under this Note or the Deed of Trust, for any purpose or reason, which indebtedness is not paid within five (5) days after the date when due under the terms of this Note or the Deed of Trust, whether at stated maturity, by acceleration or otherwise;

(b) Any breach by Maker of any of the non-monetary covenants and conditions contained in this Note or the Deed of Trust, other than those specific breaches described in this Section 9, which breach is not cured to Lender's satisfaction on or before the expiration of any applicable cure period set forth herein or in the Deed of Trust, or if none is so specified, within thirty (30) days following Maker's receipt of written notice regarding such breach; provided, however, that if such failure was not intentionally caused by Maker, cannot be remedied by the payment of a sum or money, and is capable of being remedied, but not within thirty (30) days, then Maker shall have an additional period of time within which to remedy such failure, not in any event to exceed sixty (60) days;

(c) Any representation, warranty, or disclosure made to Lender by Makers proves to be materially false or misleading;

(d) The recording of any claim or lien against the Property or any part thereof other than the lien of the Permitted Senior Debt (as defined in the Deed of Trust) and Permitted Encumbrances (as defined in the Purchase Agreement); provided, however, that no default shall exist hereunder as long as Maker has fully complied with the provisions set forth in the Deed of Trust regarding contesting of liens;

(e) Any event, act or omission occurs which constitutes a default under the Permitted Senior Debt Documents (as defined in the Deed of Trust);

(f) Other than as permitted by the provisions of this Note or the Deed of Trust, Maker sells, transfers, hypothecates, encumbers, or assigns its interest in the Property, or any portion thereof, whether voluntarily or involuntarily, or by operation of law;

(g) Without Lender's prior written approval, which approval shall not be unreasonably withheld, there shall have occurred any transfer or sale of any controlling interest of Maker or of a controlling interest in any managing member of Maker. As used herein, "controlling interest" shall mean ownership of more than fifty percent (50%) of the voting and economic interest in an entity;

(h)(i) The filing of a petition by Maker for relief under the federal Bankruptcy Code, or under any other present or future state or federal law regarding bankruptcy, reorganization or other debtor-relief law; (ii) the filing of any pleading or an answer by Maker in any voluntary proceeding under the Bankruptcy Code or other debtor-relief law which admits the jurisdiction of the court or the petition's material allegations regarding Maker's insolvency; (iii) a general assignment by Maker for the benefit of creditors; (iv) Maker applying for, or the appointment of, a receiver, trustee, custodian or liquidator of Maker or any of its property; (v) the failure of Maker to effect a full dismissal of any involuntary petition under the bankruptcy code or under any other debtor-relief law that is filed against Maker or in any way restrains Lender regarding the enforcement of its rights and remedies under the Note and Deed of Trust, prior to the earlier of the entry of any court order granting relief sought in such voluntary petition, or thirty (30) days after the date of filing of such involuntary petition; or (vi) the occurrence of any of the events specified in the preceding clauses (i) to (v) as to any person other than Maker who is obligated to Lender under the Note and Deed of Trust; or

(i) Maker's default under Section 12.1 of the Purchase Agreement

9.2 *Remedies.* Upon the occurrence of an Event of Default, Lender may, in addition to any other remedies which Lender may have hereunder or under the Deed of Trust or by law,

(a) Declare the Note immediately due and payable;

(b) Directly or through a court-appointed receiver, enter upon the Property and complete construction, development, and sale of the Property in accordance with the Approved Development Plan, with such changes therein as Lender may from time to time and in its reasonable judgment deem appropriate, all at the risk and expense of Maker. Lender shall have the right at any time to discontinue any work commenced by it in respect to the Property or to change any course of action undertaken by it and not be bound by any limitations or requirements of time whether set forth herein or otherwise. Lender shall have the right and power (but shall not be obligated) to assume any construction contract or subcontract made by or on behalf of Maker in any way relating to the Property and to take over and use all or any part of the labor, materials, supplies, and equipment contracted for by or on behalf of Maker whether or not previously incorporated into the Property, all in the reasonable discretion of Lender. In connection with any work of construction undertaken by Lender pursuant to the provisions of this Section 9.2(b), Lender may (i) engage builders, contractors, architects, engineers, and others for the purpose of furnishing labor, materials, and equipment in connection with the work of construction, (ii) pay, settle, or compromise all bills or claims which may become liens against the Property or which have been or may be incurred in any manner in connection with completing construction of the Property or for the discharge of liens, encumbrances, or defects in title of the Property, (iii) take such other action, including the employment of watchmen to protect the Property, or refrain from taking action under this Agreement as Lender may in its discretion determine from time to time. Maker shall be liable to Lender for all sums paid or incurred for completing construction of the Property, whether the same shall be paid or incurred pursuant to the provisions of this Section 9.2(b) or otherwise, and all payments made or liabilities incurred by Lender hereunder of any kind whatsoever shall be paid by Maker to Lender upon demand, with interest at the Default Rate, and all of the foregoing shall be deemed and shall constitute advances under this Note and be secured by the Deed of Trust.

All remedies of Lender provided for herein and in the Deed of Trust are cumulative and shall be in addition to all other rights and remedies provided by law. The exercise of any right or remedy by Lender hereunder shall not in any way constitute a cure or waiver of default hereunder or under the Deed of Trust or invalidate any act done pursuant to any notice of default, or prejudice Lender in the exercise of any of its rights hereunder or under the Deed of Trust unless, in the exercise of said rights, Lender realizes all amounts owed to it under the Note and Deed of Trust.

[end of provision]

3. Draft a letter/notice of default under the default/remedies section in question 2, above. The events of default that have occurred are failure to make one month's payment and the recordation of a mechanics' lien against the property for no less than $60,000 of unpaid work done on the air conditioning, (a.k.a. "HVAC") systems. Remember to clearly notice the default and select the remedies that you would like to exercise. You may invent any factual details that you need as long as they are not contrary to the facts given.

4. Draft a simple default/remedies set of provisions for a lease of real property. The events of default will be (a) non-payment of rent for 10 days after it is due (no notice to tenant required), (b) failure to maintain normal business hours after receiving 10 days notice of the failure to do so, and (c) operation as any kind of business besides a

card and gift store (give some thought to how to define this operation). Upon default, the landlord (x) is entitled to 10% interest on all unpaid rent, compounded monthly, (y) is entitled to immediate possession of the premises and all its contents and (z) may sell the contents to satisfy unpaid rent and other charges, subject to the rights of any party with a security interest (secured creditor) or ownership interest (consignment items) in the contents. Upon default the landlord may re-let the space immediately. Do not take into account state law limitations on remedies or unlawful detainer procedures.

5. Your client is a commercial landlord. Draft a default and remedies provision that will make your client whole (or as "whole" as possible) in the event the tenant does not pay rent for 6 months, is evicted after a contested court proceeding, and refuses to pay the resulting judgment after it is issued by a local court.

6. Default and remedies provisions are fine as far as they go. What other devices might be used to support performance under a contract? Who would be the parties to such support devices?

7. Specific performance is generally regarded as an "extraordinary" remedy, largely in the discretion of the court. What, if anything could the drafter of a contract do to increase the chances that a court would issue a specific performance decree.[5] Draft a clause or clauses implementing your suggestion. You may make up whatever facts about the parties, the subject matter of the contract, etc.

8. Injunctions are useful in protecting parties' rights—especially preliminary injunctions or temporary restraining orders. These and other equitable remedies are largely within the court's discretion when they are available at all. How could you increase the chances of an injunction issuing? Does it help if you know the traditional 4 part test for an injunction?[6] Draft a provision implementing your solution.

9. Draft a provision limiting damages under a commercial sale of goods contract governed by UCC § 2–715.

10. Research the law in your jurisdiction and determine what limits it imposes on ordinary contract damages in an action at law or equity. Are drafters free to alter those results by contract? If so, are there limits on these alterations?

---

5. *See* U.C.C. § 2–716.

6. *See, e.g., New Jersey Hosp. Assoc. v. Waldman*, 73 F.3d 509, 512 (3d Cir.1995) (the four factors are (i) substantial likelihood of prevailing on the merits, (ii) irreparable injury if the injunction does not issue, (iii) balance of the harms, (iv) public policy). There is some variation of this standard among the circuits and states, especially on the issue of whether all four factors must be met or if a strong showing of one will overcome an absence or negative finding on another. The drafter should thus be familiar with the standard in the applicable jurisdiction that will entertain contract disputes, often specified in a choice of forum or choice of law clause.

Chapter 9

THE IMPORT AND SCOPE OF BOILERPLATE

"Boilerplate" is the term used for those "standard" provisions inserted at the end of almost every transactional document. The term makes them sound routine and unimportant; nothing could be farther from the truth. These provisions commonly come into effect when there is a problem or disagreement between the parties—so they must be carefully considered and drafted to ensure that they work correctly when they are needed most. They represent another opportunity for pre-litigation planning—something that every business lawyer must keep in mind when drafting.

The term boilerplate is derived from the word for flat-rolled steel between one-quarter and one-half inch thick used to make steam engine boilers and the hulls of ships. In the early days of newspaper syndication the term was also used to describe the plates of non-movable type that publishers delivered to local newspapers and which contained the syndicated text and advertising that the local paper would adopt in full, adding its own stories and advertising to supplement the syndicator's standard material.

Applied to contracts, "boilerplate" refers to an assortment of "standard" provisions that cover issues are common to most contracts such as choice of law, choice of forum, severability, integration or merger, execution in counterparts, notice, and the like are typical "boilerplate." Like real boilerplate making up a boiler, in the hull of a ship, or for a local paper, these provisions are routine, but very important. Without good boilerplate, the boiler explodes, the ship sinks, and the paper consists only of local interest stories and farm reports. One authority refers to these provisions as "housekeeping" provisions.[1] Like the term "miscellaneous," this term tends to denigrate their importance. The term "boilerplate," when understood, reflects their fundamental importance as well as their routine nature.

---

1. Barbara Child, Drafting Legal Documents, Principles and Practices 141 (1992).

Never take boilerplate for granted or simply incorporate "standard" provisions without thought and analysis. When reviewing contracts drafted by others, do not just skim the boilerplate: Much mischief can be hidden there! Students and lawyers that do not have a transactional practice sometimes claim that this advice is hypertechnical and exaggerated. But transactional lawyers, many of whom have served as adjunct professors, partners, or opposing counsel with the author confirm the import and potential mischief of boilerplate. Just as beginning litigators are advised never to agree to the "standard" stipulations in a deposition without knowing what those stipulations are, transactional attorneys are cautioned against taking the other side's boilerplate for granted.

QUESTIONS & CLAUSES FOR CONSIDERATION

1. Revise the following boilerplate provisions into grammatically correct plain English. Use the active voice and present tense. It may be necessary to divide these provisions into multiple sections for clarity of purpose. To demonstrate that you understand the point (or points) of each of the resulting provisions, include headings for each of these provisions capturing their essence.

   A. This Agreement may be executed in several counterparts and all so executed will constitute one agreement which will be binding on all the parties hereto, notwithstanding that all of the parties are not signatories to the original or the same counterpart.

   B. This agreement shall bind and ensure to the benefit of Purchaser and Author and their respective heirs, legal representatives, successors, and assigns, and all or any part of Purchaser's rights hereunder may be licensed or assigned by Purchaser. The term "Purchaser" as used herein means and includes Purchaser herein named, and its successors and assigns. If more than one Author is mentioned herein or executes this Agreement, this Agreement shall be binding jointly and severally upon each such person, and the word "Author" as used herein shall then have a plural meaning. With respect to any and all material and rights sold or assigned to Purchaser pursuant to this Exhibit, Author agrees to execute and deliver to Purchaser such other instruments in a form satisfactory to Purchaser as it may be necessary to or desired by Purchaser for the transfer to it of the material and/or rights so sold or assigned; it being expressly agreed that all material and/or rights so sold or assigned to Purchaser shall vest in and inure to the benefit of Purchaser forthwith, whether or not such assignments and/or instruments are executed by Author or delivered to Purchaser. Purchaser may assign this Agreement and/or rights hereunder to any person or entity. Irrespective of the place of execution or performance this Agreement shall be governed by, and construed and enforced in accordance with, the laws of California applicable to agreements to be executed and wholly performed in California. The parties hereto expressly consent and submit to the jurisdiction of any court of competent jurisdiction within the State of California and agree to accept service of process outside the State of California in any matter to be submitted to any such court pursuant hereto. If any term hereof is adjudged void or enforceable, the same shall not affect any other term hereof, nor the enforceability thereof. This Agreement expresses the entire understanding of the parties hereto and replaces and all former agreements, understanding or representations relating in any way to the subject matter hereof, and Author expressly waives any other or further representations, warranties, or agreements not herein set forth, and this Agreement cannot be changed or terminated orally.

C. No failure on the part of any party to exercise or delay in exercising any right hereunder shall be deemed a waiver thereof, nor shall any single or partial exercise preclude any further or other exercise of such or any other right, and waiver of any breach of any term or condition of this Agreement shall not be deemed to constitute the waiver of any other breach of the same or any other term or condition.

D. A default on the part of any one person comprising the Maker or any guarantor of this Note shall be deemed a default on the part of the Maker hereunder.

E. Maker hereby waives presentment, demand of payment, notice of dishonor, protest, notice of nonpayment and any and all other notices and demands whatsoever except as expressly provided in this Note and Deed of Trust. No covenant, condition, right or remedy in this Note or the Deed of Trust may be waived or modified orally, by course of conduct or previous acceptance or otherwise unless such waiver or modification is specifically agreed to in writing executed by Lender. Without limiting the foregoing, no previous waiver and no failure or delay by Lender in acting with respect to terms of this Note or the Deed of Trust shall constitute a waiver of any breach, default or failure of a condition under this Note, Deed of Trust or any obligations contained therein or secured thereby. The undersigned further waives exhaustion of legal remedies and the right to plead any and all statutes of limitation as a defense to any demand on this Note, or to any agreement to pay the same, or to any demands secured by the Deed of Trust, or any other security for this Note. Maker hereby expressly waives any right of setoff or to otherwise withhold payment or assert as a defense against payment with respect to any and all sums payable under this Note and Deed of Trust as a result of any liability, breach or alleged breach of Lender under the terms of or in connection with the execution and delivery of the Purchase Agreement.

F. All sums referred to herein shall be calculated by reference to and payable in the lawful currency of the United States. This Note, Deed of Trust, and any other documents executed in connection with this Note have been reviewed and negotiated by Maker and Lender at arms length with the benefit of or opportunity to seek the assistance of legal counsel and shall not be construed against either party, regardless of who drafted such documents. The titles and captions in this Note are inserted for convenience only and in no way define, limit, extend, or modify the scope or intent of this Note. Any reference to Lender in this Note shall include any successor to or assignee of Lender. Time is of the essence of this Note and of each and every provision hereof.

G. If any section or provision of this Note is declared invalid or unenforceable by any court of competent jurisdiction, said determination shall not affect the validity or enforceability of the remaining terms hereof. No such determination in one jurisdiction shall affect any provision of this Note to the extent it is otherwise enforceable under the laws of any other applicable jurisdiction.

H. All notices, demands, requests, or other communications to be sent by one party to the other hereunder or required by law shall be in writing and shall be deemed to have been validly given or served by delivery of the same in person to the intended address, or by depositing the same with Federal Express or another reputable private courier service for next business day delivery, or prepaid telephone, telex, or telecopy, or by depositing the same in the United States mail, postage prepaid, registered or certified mail, return receipt requested, in any event addressed to the intended addressee at the addresses set forth below or at such other address as may be designated by such party as herein provided. All notices, demands and requests shall be effective upon such personal delivery, or one (1) business day after being deposited in the United States mail as required above. Rejection or other refusal to accept or the inability to deliver because of changed address of which no notice was given as herein required shall be deemed to be receipt of the notice, demand or request sent. By giving to the other party hereto at least fifteen (15) days prior written notice thereof in accordance with the provisions hereof, the parties hereto shall have the right from time to time to change their respective addresses and each shall have the right to specify as its address any other address within the United States of America.

If to Lender:	*[Lender Name]* *[Lender Address]* *[Lender City, State, Zip]* Attn: *[Lender contact person]* Fax: *[Fax]*
With copies to:	*[Lenders Counsel]* *[Lender Counsels Address]* *[Lender counsel City, State, Zip]* Attn: *[Lead Attorney]* Fax: *[Fax]*
If to Maker:	*[Maker Name]* *[Maker Address]* *[Maker City, State, Zip]* Attn: *[Maker contact person]* Fax: *[Fax]*
With copies to:	*[Makers Counsel]* *[Maker Counsels Address]* *[Maker counsel City, State, Zip]* Attn: *[Lead Attorney]* Fax: *[Fax]*

I.   The venue of any action brought to interpret or enforce the provisions of this Note shall be in Cook County, Illinois.

J.   Maker represents that it has the full power and authority to execute and deliver this Note, and this Note constitutes the valid and binding obligation of Maker, enforceable in accordance with its terms.

K.   The Relationship between Maker and Lender is that of borrower and lender, and no partnership, joint venture, or other similar relationship shall be inferred from this Note. Maker shall have no right or authority to make representations, act, or incur debts or liabilities on behalf of Lender. Maker is not executing this Note as an agent or nominee for an undisclosed principal, and no third-party beneficiaries are or shall be created by the execution of this Note.

2.   "Severability" boilerplate provisions are common. They provide that if a clause or provision in the contract is found to be illegal or unenforceable, that provision will be severed (ignored) and the balance of the contract will be enforced according to its remaining terms. Consider when you would want a contract to be severable— that is, if one clause is declared invalid or unenforceable, it can be severed from the rest of the contract, which can be enforced accord-

ing to its remaining terms. When would you want to provide for severability? When non-severability?

3. Are there options to a severability clause apart from the binary choices of "severable" or "not severable"? Draft a severability clause that allows for severance of illegal or unenforceable provisions and enforcement of the remaining contract as long as the essential deal— the sale of machinery in exchange for payments of $1,000 per month for 10 months, which are guaranteed by the buyer's corporate parent, with title to pass upon the seller's receipt of the last payment— remains intact. In this contract, severance of minor or tangential provisions is acceptable, but if the essential terms, such as the payments or the guaranty are somehow declared invalid, the remaining contract will not be enforced and the parties will be returned, as far as possible, to their pre-contract positions.

4. Draft a provision that will save a charge or fee from complete invalidation if it is declared unenforceable or void as excessive, usurious, or a forfeiture.

5. Draft a choice of law clause that applies the law of your local jurisdiction.

6. Draft a choice of forum clause that requires suit to be brought in your local jurisdiction if the plaintiff is seeking an injunction or other equitable relief, or anywhere in your state if it is just a suit for legal damages. Be sure to address what happens in the second instance if the defendant counterclaims seeking equitable relief.

7. Consider the problem of inconsistent paragraphs or sections of a contract. In case of inconsistency, how should one decide which applies? Draft a provision providing for the rule of decision and interpretation that you favor.

Chapter 10

ARBITRATION AND OTHER ALTERNATIVE DISPUTE RESOLUTION PROVISIONS

The cost and expense of litigation is something that all businesses hope to avoid. One possible solution is arbitration, a form of alternative dispute resolution. Although arbitration has its fans and adherents, it can be dangerous or inappropriate and should only be included in a contract after careful consideration.

Virtually all contracts can provide that disputes between the parties must be settled through arbitration. Courts routinely enforce such provisions, and will grant motions to dismiss by parties that seek to litigate rather than arbitrate upon objection of the defendant. Since the early 1980's when the ADR movement gained momentum, arbitration has been considered to be beneficial, featuring more privacy, less cost, and more speed than traditional litigation, and eliminating the wildcard decision-maker that is a civil jury.[1]

In fact, the mere elimination of the jury is often enough to allow for early settlement of a dispute. Without a jury, the parties are faced with the cold, hard facts of their cases and the legal arguments involved, and have less incentive to "roll the dice" with a lay jury that may be swayed by theatrics, passion, rhetoric, and prejudice. This has led to contract provisions that stop short of arbitration, but eliminate the jury wild card—waivers of the right to a jury trial. These waivers are particularly appealing to banks, insurance companies and large institutions, which benefit from the procedures and opportunities for review afforded by the court system, but feel unfairly vulnerable to juries bent on redistributing wealth and resources.

It is important to recognize that arbitration can have its negative aspects. Its flexibility, if not addressed by the drafter, can lead to

---

1. *See* Keating v. Superior Court, 31 Cal.3d 584, 183 Cal.Rptr. 360, 645 P.2d 1192 (1982) (recognizing arbitration in the "commercial context is quite common, and reasonably to be anticipated." As such, franchisees are not in a position to claim that an arbitration clause did not "fall within [their] reasonable expectations.").

113

undesired results. In many states, the decision of an arbitrator acting under a binding arbitration clause is final and cannot be reviewed by a court unless the decision violates fundamental public policy or the arbiter is shown to be deranged or incompetent. These are high standards to meet. Even a clear mistake of law on the arbitrator's part is generally not grounds for review and reversal. The lesson to take from this state of affairs is that, while arbitration may be useful or appropriate in many circumstances, careful thought should go before it is adopted, and any arbitration provision should be carefully drafted to control the resulting process.

So, what are the concerns to take into account when drafting an arbitration clause? First, an arbitration provision drafted to favor one side may be challenged as unconscionable[2] and thus the provision should be drafted to pass a test of fundamental fairness.[3]

Second, since the right and duty to arbitrate is created by the agreement, it is the agreement that governs the procedures.[4] The drafter may incorporate the rules of a specific arbitrating body, such as the American Arbitration Association (the "AAA"), or may incorporate federal or state rules or procedures, or may make up a procedure out of whole cloth. The last is rare. The danger of the first approach is that it is very easy to simply adopt the rules and procedures of the AAA or other organization without even knowing what they are, and which side they might benefit in your particular situation. Arbitration groups often have different sets of rules for different types of disputes, which could result in application of a procedure other than the one intended. Before incorporating rules and procedures into a contract, the prudent attorney will know what procedure is being incorporated and the relative costs and benefits of that particular procedure, and perhaps include the stipulation that the rules will be the rules in effect on the date of the contract, not some future set of rules that could be adopted after the contract is singed but before the incident resulting in arbitration arises.

Issues that need to be addressed in any arbitration provision, either by explicit drafting or by knowing the procedures of an outside arbitration service include: How does a party start the arbitration process? How

---

2. Stirlen v. Supercuts, Inc., 51 Cal. App.4th 1519, 1520, 60 Cal.Rptr.2d 138 (1997) (A compulsory arbitration clause in a contract of adhesion ("a standardized contract, which, imposed and drafted by the party of superior bargaining strength, relegates to the subscribing party only the opportunity to adhere to the contract or reject it") is deemed unconscionable.).

3. Engalla v. Permanente Medical Group, 15 Cal.4th 951 985, 64 Cal.Rptr.2d 843, 938 P.2d 903 (1997) (unfairness found in an arbitration requirement because the insurance company established the arbitration system with a bias toward giving itself the advantage (taking advantage of its repeat-player status)); Hull Dye & Print Works, Inc. v. Riegel Textile Corp., 37 A.D.2d 946, 325 N.Y.S.2d 782, Engalla 985 (1971) (refusing to enforce an arbitration provision that purported to give only one party the option of arbitration or litigation).

4. Parker v. Babcock, 37 Cal.App.4th 1682, 1687, 44 Cal.Rptr.2d 602 (1995) ("Private arbitration [as opposed to judicial arbitration] occurs only pursuant to agreement, and it is the agreement which determines the details of the process.... Typically, those who enter into arbitration agreements expect that their dispute will be resolved without necessity for any contact with the courts.").

is an arbiter selected? How will the parties present their cases? Will there be discovery or disclosure of facts? Do rules of evidence apply? What substantive law will apply? Is there an opportunity to challenge the arbiter's ruling and if so, how? Is the ruling binding or merely advisory?

Finally, if you or your client are unwilling to give up the procedural and substantive rights afforded by resort to the court system, but wish to provide for some chance of resolution short of a lawsuit, a mediation provision may be adopted. Drafting mediation provisions involves considerations similar to arbitration provisions. How does a party instigate the mediation process? Who is to serve as the mediator? What will the process be for educating the mediator about the parties, the contract and the dispute? Are only certain types of disputes suitable for mediation? How and when can the parties determine that the mediation is fruitless and seek redress in the court system? What portions, if any, of the mediation are confidential, non-discoverable, and inadmissible in later court proceedings? For those seeking to create disincentives for litigation, a waiver of jury trial coupled with a pre-suit mediation provision may accomplish this goal without subjecting the parties to the potential dangers of binding, non-reviewable arbitration.

QUESTIONS AND CLAUSES FOR CONSIDERATION

1. Draft an arbitration clause that provides for (a) notice and demand for arbitration procedure, (b) selection of a forum and arbiter, and (c) procedural rules. The provision should identify whether the arbitration is binding or merely advisory and whether it is subject to court review.

2. Draft a mediation provision providing for a demand for mediation, selection of a mediator, rules, and whether or not mediation is the sole or mandatory first remedy of the parties.

3. Draft a waiver of the right to jury trial for an action arising under a contract.

*

Chapter 11

SIGNATURE BLOCKS

A. Introductory Language for Signatures.

Before the signature blocks at the end of the body of the agreement where the parties sign, there is usually some introductory language. Like other standard provisions in agreements, there is a tendency for this language to have become ossified and exhibited dated legalese. It is better to delete phrases such as "In Witness Whereof" and "as of the date that first appears above" and use a modern, plain English provision. It should simply establish that, by signing the document, the parties are agreeing to its terms.

The Parties agree to the terms of this Agreement above.

To show that they have agreed to the terms of this agreement, the Parties have executed this Agreement below on [the date stated on page 1 or the date(s) indicated below].

In order to avoid inconsistent dating of documents, the introductory language to a signature block often refers to a date appearing on the first page or paragraph of the document. This is fine, as long as that date is filled in! Too many times, in the heat of closing, the parties, simply flip to the last page of the agreement (which they have reviewed many times before in negotiations, so why read it again?) and fail to note that the date on page 1 has been left blank. In another form that is common in practice, the agreement is dated "as of" a date contained on the first page (filled in early in the drafting process) and the signature blocks are undated or contain the dates of execution by the parties.

B. Traditional Signature Blocks.

Signature blocks accomplish two sets of purposes if properly drafted. First, as the place where the parties will sign the agreement, when executed, they indicate mutual assent to the contract. Secondly, they establish the formal identity and capacity of the entities that are parties to the agreement and the individuals expressing that assent.

Signature blocks for an individual (a person), look like this:

<u>Form</u>	<u>Example</u>
[defined term for the party]	Seller

[party name, typed], [capacity if other than self] [if the party's address does not appear elsewhere, include it here to assist in identification, Social Security numbers are also used but take into account privacy and identity theft concerns]	John W. Doe 1234 W. Willow Way Wonderland, Wyoming

Signature blocks for an incorporeal entity (LLC, Corp., Partnership, etc.) look like this:

<u>Form</u>	<u>Example</u>
[defined term for the party] [name of party entity]	Buyer International Drain Systems, LLC, a Delaware limited liability company

[name of signing person], [title]	By[1] Mary Ann Vortex, President

For either of these forms, following the name of party or capacity, include any information relevant to or qualifying that capacity, such as "subject to approval of the [bankruptcy or probate] court [give details of court and case or other identifying information]", or "as trustee for Joan Jenrett, a minor child," etc.

---

1. There is some variance in practice as to whether or not to use a colon after the word "By" "Its", "Title", and the like. One convention is to use the colon when the document is prepared as a form or when the signing party is unknown at the time of drafting and will be filled in at the time of execution. If the identity of the signing person is known when the documents are prepared, no colon is necessary. Conventions like this vary jurisdiction to jurisdiction, firm to firm, and attorney to attorney.

A complex signature block may result if one is dealing with multilevel incorporeal entities.[2] For example:

Portofino Properties, LLC

_____

By   Floorboard Associates, LLP,
       Its Managing Member

_____

By   Wainscott Investments, LLC
       Its General Partner

_____

By   General Interiors, Inc.
       Its Managing Member

_____

By   Assiduous Perry,
       President

In this style, Mr. Perry would sign on all lines as the authorized representative of the entities indicated. Alternatively, the intervening signature lines are omitted, and he only signs once, as President of General Interiors, and the authority of that signature flows through the corporate structure to Portofino Properties, as shown below:

Portofino Properties, LLC

By   Floorboard Associates, LLP,
       Its Managing Member
       By   Wainscott Investments, LLC
              Its General Partner
              By   General Interiors, Inc.
                     Its Managing Member

_____

By   Assiduous Perry,
       President

Styles like this vary from region to region and firm to firm. The key is (a) to identify the proper chain of authority through the incorporeal entities to the actual person signing the document, and then (b) ensure that the signature block you create accurately reflects this chain of authority.

Take care with party names and make sure you get them _exactly_ right. Especially easy to miss are issues of punctuation, such as commas and periods. For example "Allen Bates & Lebowitz LLP" could be a

2. Multi-level corporate structure is used to, among other things, isolate income and liability producing assets from other assets, including profits previously drawn off from these assets, to diversify ownership and risk in particular economic activities among various investors, and to realize tax advantages.

limited liability partnership that is the successor to "Allen, Bates & Lebowitz" and is legally distinct from the former entity, a general partnership including professional corporations. Many jurisdictions do not prohibit the formation of entities with very similar names, which might differ only by a comma or spelling out the word "and" rather than using an ampersand (&). Train your eye to notice details of this nature. It is embarrassing when the client catches the mistake at the closing. It is even worse when the error is not uncovered until subsequent litigation has ensued.

Related to signature blocks of the parties are witness signature blocks and notary jurats. Witness and notary requirements vary from state to state and transaction to transaction. It is important to research and comply with the applicable requirements.[3] Local counsel or the law digests in the Martindale Hubble legal directory can be useful sources of information as to these forms and other local requirements.

Little more need be said about signature blocks beyond noting that even the most seemingly mundane portions of a transactional document are driven by detail and require review with a keen eye to avoid mistakes.

C. E-Sign and Related Matters.

1. The E–Sign Act

The Electronic Signatures in Global and National Commerce Act, 15 U.S.C. §§ 7001 to 7006, 7021 and 7031, validates the practice of recognizing either a clicked "I accept" button on an Internet site or a faxed or e-mailed signature for contract law purposes. The E–Signature Act provides that:

> Notwithstanding any statute, regulation, or other rule of law ..., with respect to any transaction in or affecting interstate or foreign commerce: (1) a signature, contract, or other record relating to such transaction may not be denied legal effect, validity, or enforceability solely because it is in electronic form; and (2) a contract relating to such transaction may not be denied legal effect, validity, or enforceability solely because an electronic signature or electronic record was used in its formation.

15 U.S.C. § 7001(a) (West 2000). An electronic signature is defined by the Act as "an electronic sound, symbol, or process, attached to or logically associated with a contract or other record and executed or adopted by a person with the intent to sign the record."[4]

Complying with E–Sign will negate a statute of frauds defense based on Federal law and state law statute of frauds defenses if the state in

---

3. *See, e.g.,* Simon v. Chase Manhattan Bank (*In re* Zaptocky), 250 F.3d 1020 (6th Cir.2001) (invalidating mortgage as 2nd witness required by Ohio law not proven to have attended closing).

4. 15 U.S.C. § 7006(5).

question has not enacted The Uniform Electronic Transactions Act ("UETA," discussed in the next section of their text).

The E–Sign Act preempts any state law that invalidates signatures, contracts, and records solely because they are in electronic form, unless as noted above, the state has enacted the UETA, in which case the UETA preempts the E–Sign Act.[5] All other substantive requirements of state contract law remain in place.

The act includes a number of restrictions on contracts related to consumer transactions. A consumer is "[a]n individual who obtains, through a transaction, products or services which are used primarily for personal, family, or household purposes."[6] As to consumers, the act mandates that a business may only use electronic records if: the consumer (1) has affirmatively consented to their use; (2) has not withdrawn their consent; and (3) is given a clear and conspicuous statement informing them of the right to have the record provided in a non-electronic form, informing them of their right to withdraw consent and notifying them of the technology and software requirements needed to access the electronic documents.[7] Moreover, the consumer must consent to the electronic records in a form that reasonably demonstrates that the consumer can access the information in electronic form. These consumer restrictions do not apply to business-to-business transactions.[8]

The E–Sign Act contains a number of exceptions to its enforcement that may limit its effect. The act does not apply to contracts or records governed by the Uniform Commercial Code (other than sales, leases, waivers, and the statute of frauds).[9] Thus, the act does not apply to negotiable instruments (Article 3), bank deposits (Article 4), fund transfers (Article 4a), letters of credit (Article 5), documents of title (Article 7), investment securities (Article 8) or secured transactions (Article 9). The act does apply to sales (Article 2) and leases (Article 2a). Thus, one may be able to enter into a valid electronic contract for the sale of goods or the lease of commercial property, but the financing documents for transaction will have to be in hard copy and bear actual signatures. The act also does not apply to: (1) wills, codicils, or testamentary trusts, (2) state statutes or regulations (actual hard copy thereof), (3) court documents and notices, (4) notices of cancellation or termination of utility services, (5) default, foreclosure, or eviction notices on a primary residence, (6) notices canceling or terminating health or life insurance, (7) product recalls, or (8) any document required to accompany the transportation or handling of hazardous or toxic materials.[10]

In areas where the E–Sign Act does not apply, state and local law must be consulted to determine the effectiveness of e-mail signatures, "I accept" buttons, and fixed signatures.

5.   15 U.S.C. § 7001.

6.   15 U.S.C. § 7006(1).

7.   15 U.S.C. § 7001(c).

8.   15 U.S.C. § 7006(1).

9.   15 U.S.C. § 7003(a)(3).

10.   15 U.S.C. § 7003(a) & (b).

2. The Uniform Electronic Transactions Act

Many states have enacted or are considering enactment of the Uniform Electronic Transaction Act (the "UETA"), which supplants and is broader than the E–Sign. The UETA has been widely criticized by consumer groups and technical computer groups that are not associated with pro-business groups. The main feature of the UETA is section § 5(b) which provides that a party's consent to engage in transactions by electronic means is determined in "the context and surrounding circumstances" of the transaction and the conduct of the parties. This is a looser and less well-defined standard than those of the E–Signature Act, and has been the focus of critics concerned with consumer interests.

If issues involving electronic transactions and signature arise in a transaction, counsel will be well advised to consult not only the E–Sign Act but applicable local laws, including any enacted version of the Uniform Electronic Transactions Act, for current requirements and regulations. Non-conforming versions of the UETA have been enacted in some jurisdictions, so carefully checking the actual text of the applicable state statute is key.

Chapter 12

COVENANTS AND AGREEMENTS
NOT TO COMPETE

A special type of covenant is a covenant not to compete. It is often found in contracts for the sale of a business or employment contracts, but may also be the subject of a stand-alone agreement.

It is basic hornbook law throughout the United States than non-compete agreements will be enforced if they are reasonable in duration, geographic area, and scope of employment or activity prohibited. These fact-specific tests are extremely circumstance dependent.

To maximize the chances of strict enforcement, counsel for the beneficiary of the agreement should take care to craft such a provision as narrowly as possible while still accomplishing the goal of protecting the client. Conversely, counsel for the party to be restrained may be well served by accepting an over-broad provision on the theory that it is more likely to be found completely unenforceable than a narrowly phrased negotiated provision. This strategy, however, runs the risk that instead of invalidating the provision in total, a court will reform it in what it considers "reasonable" terms in light of available evidence of the parties intent.

Finally, if negotiating the provision, realize that there are trade-offs between the various dimensions of the provision's scope. For example, a shorter duration may make a wide geographic and industry clause reasonable; a world-wide non-compete in a narrow product or industry could be reasonable in an internet business context. Also, don't forget the ultimate trade off: Price. Parties should be prepared to pay for the privilege of enjoying the benefits of a covenant not to compete and employees and sellers of businesses should be aware that part of the price being paid for their labor or business is for a lack of competition. Consider whether it makes sense for the non-compete to terminate if the other party defaults on other obligations.

QUESTIONS & CLAUSES FOR CONSIDERATION

A. With a partner, negotiate and draft a non-compete provision for an employment contract. One client is a nationally prominent real estate brokerage with an office in your home town that will expend significant time and money training new sales associates and assisting them in gaining their real estate license over the first year of their employment. The other client is a prospective employee who does not have any real estate sales experience or training, but has extensive general sales training and experience based on five years of selling recreational vehicles, motorcycles, boats, and personal water craft to the public. Use your own judgment to negotiate a clause that you could recommend to your client under the circumstances.

B. With a partner, negotiate and draft a stand-alone non-compete agreement that will be executed by a seller of a business in favor of the buyer of the business at the closing of the sale. All of the assets of the business are being sold, including goodwill, which is substantial. Assume that the business is comprised of four well-regarded eye glass and hearing aid stores with locations in Orlando, St. Augustine, Ft. Lauderdale, and Miami, Florida. Assume further that the parties intend that the seller will work for the buyer for one year post-closing, after which she intends to retire and split her time between her homes in Naples, Florida, and Chicago, Illinois.

C. Exchange your assignments (1 or 2, above) with another student. Edit the exercise you receive, performing both a line edit and providing specific explanations of the changes you make along with the reasons for making the changes. Also explain whether or not you believe that the non-compete is reasonable and enforceable as originally drafted and as modified by your edits, and why.

D. Your client, Television Company, LLC ("TC"), has made a job offer to Sid Lawson, a newscaster at a large television station in a neighboring market. TC plans to use their standard employment agreement but would like to include a covenant not to compete in Mr. Lawson's contract. None of the current "personalities" at the station have a non-competition agreement. TC plans to invest nearly $800,000.00 in advertising and promoting Mr. Lawson and wants the covenant to be as broad as possible, but in the words of the station manager, "it better stick." The station and Mr. Lawson already have "an agreement in principle" but nothing has been signed. Salary, benefits, scheduling and a start-date are firm. Non-competition has been mentioned but the details have not been discussed. Prepare a non-competition provision to be included in Mr. Lawson's Employment Agreement. The parties should be referred to as "Lawson" and "TC".

E.   Generally, a severability provision in a contract provides that if a clause or provision of a contract is found to be illegal or unenforceable, that provision will be severed (ignored) and the balance of the contract will still be enforced according to its remaining terms. If a non-compete agreement is found to be unreasonable and unenforceable as written, a court could thus simply strike it under such a severability provision. Draft a severability provision that would direct a court to reform an offending or unenforceable covenant not to compete into an enforceable one if possible rather than striking it altogether.

*

Chapter 13

AMENDING AND RESTATING AGREEMENTS

Often, contracts and other transactional documents require amendment after they have been executed. There are three basic methods of amending a contract.

The first is crude but effective: The parties manually change the provisions by hand, striking out or inserting text on the original document and then initialing each change. It may be a good idea to add new signature blocks at the end of the document, or on a separate sheet, where the parties reexecute the agreement "as amended."

The second method is to prepare a second document, entitled "Amendment Number __ to [name original document]," and then to specify the amendments that are being made, perhaps including recitals that give context to the amendment for later use in understanding what went on and why the document was amended. In essence, this sort of amendment acts as an instruction sheet for later use in "virtually" cutting and pasting the two documents together into the new, resulting agreement.

The third method is called "amending and restating" the document. Using this method, the original contract terms, as amended, are written out or typed fresh as a new contract. The contract can be prepared to reflect the original contract date, the amendment date, or both. This is the best method for situation where there are many amendments to be made at once. Sometimes, an original agreement has been amended piecemeal many times using the second method described above, and it may make sense to amend and restate the amendments. This would result in the original agreement accompanied by a consolidated amended and restated set of amendments.

In choosing the method used, consider how often the document will be referred to by the parties or counsel for guidance. If the answer is seldom, then either of the first two methods may be used effectively. If it will be reexamined often, amending and restating or restating amendments is appropriate. The major risk in embarking on a complete restatement of a document is that it may reopen issues for negotiation that had been previously settled.

When the amendment is complete, ensure that it is distributed to all those that have or had the original document and ask them to include the amendment with their copy of the original documents. When amending documents that have been filed or recorded with governmental offices, it is probably necessary for the amendments, an amended and restated document, or, at a minimum, an abstract of them, to be filed with the same office to be "perfected" or "good against the world." This is generally the case with recorded deeds, encumbrances, lease abstracts, UCC–1 financing statements, and the like. In refiling, thought must be given to the effect of intervening filings by the parties or third parties, and the effect of those filings and the new filings on lien priority and similar issues. Title policy endorsements are available to provide "no loss of priority" protection in some cases.

QUESTIONS & CLAUSES FOR CONSIDERATION

Contracts are not confined to business transactions; some are basic to our society—and even these must be amended from time to time. Consider the amendments to the U.S. Constitution. The first are contained in the Bill of Rights, which employs the second method of amendment discussed earlier, restating amendments. Each subsequent amendment, is accomplished using the basic separate amendment approach. In contrast is the wholly amended and restated document that was the Constitution of the Confederate States of America. Alternatively, instead of viewing the Confederate Constitution as an amended and restated version of the United States Constitution, it can also be viewed as a wholly new document prepared using the U.S. Constitution as an exemplar or precedent document.

Excerpts of the two constitutions[1] are laid out below, side by side, with the amendments in the Confederate Constitution laid out italics. Omissions not covered by italics are indicated by "[?]." Note how the amendment and restatement process raised and, at least textually, resolved some of the most critical constitutional debates of the first 100 years of the Republic. Some of these issues, continue to occupy public debate today. Note also the careful conforming changes that have been made throughout the Confederate document.

---

1. The quoted portions of the U.S. Constitution feature the original punctuation and spelling, which was not yet standardized English.

CONSTITUTION OF THE UNITED STATES OF AMERICA.

CONSTITUTION OF THE *CONFEDERATE* STATES OF AMERICA.

We the People of the United States, in order to form a more perfect Union, establish Justice, insure domestic Tranquility, provide for common defense, promote the general Welfare and secure the Blessings of Liberty to ourselves and our Posterity, do ordain and establish this CONSTITUTION for the United States of America.

We, the People of the *Confederate States, each State acting in its sovereign and independent character, in order to form a permanent Federal Government,* establish *justice,* insure domestic tranquility, [^] and secure the blessings of *liberty* to ourselves and our *posterity—invoking the favor and guidance of Almighty God—*do ordain and establish this *Constitution* for the *Confederate* States of America.

ARTICLE I.

ARTICLE I.

SECTION 1. All legislative Powers herein granted shall be vested in a Congress of the United States, which shall consist of a Senate and House of Representatives.

SECTION 1. All legislative *powers* herein [^] *delegated* shall be vested in a Congress of the *Confederate* States, which shall consist of a Senate and House of Representatives.

SECTION 2. The House of Representatives shall be composed of Members chosen every second Year by the People of the several States, and the Qualifications requisite for Electors of the most numerous Branch of the State Legislature.

SECTION 2. The House of Representatives shall be composed of *members* chosen every second *year* by the *people* of the several States; and the [^] *electors in each State shall be citizens of the Confederate States, and* have the qualifications requisite for electors of the most numerous branch of the State Legislature; *but no person of foreign birth, not a citizen of the Confederate States, shall be allowed to vote for any officer, civil or political, State or Federal.*

* * * * *

The House of Representatives shall choose their Speaker and other officers; and shall have the sole Power of Impeachment.

The House of Representatives shall choose their Speaker and other officers; and shall have the sole *power* of *impeachment, except that any judicial or other Federal officer, resident and acting solely within the limits of any State, may be impeached by a vote of two thirds of both branches of the Legislature thereof.*

* * * * *

SECTION 7. All Bills for raising Revenue shall originate in the House of Representatives; but the Senate may propose or concur with Amendments as on other Bills.

SECTION 7. All *bills* for raising *the* revenue shall originate in the *house* of Representatives; but the Senate may propose or concur with *amendments*, as on other *bills*.

* * * * *

If any Bill shall not be returned by the President within ten Days (Sundays excepted) after it shall have been presented to him, the Same shall be a law, in like Manner as if he had signed it, unless the Congress by their Adjournment prevent its Return, in which Case it shall not be a Law.

If any bill shall not be returned by the President within ten days (Sundays excepted) after it shall have been presented to him, the same shall be a law, in like *m*anner as if he had signed it, unless the Congress, by their *a*djournment, prevent its *r*eturn; in which *c*ase it shall not be a *law*. *The President may approve any appropriation and disapprove any other appropriation in the same bill. In such case he shall, in signing the bill, designate the appropriations disapproved; and shall return a copy of such appropriations, with his objections, to the House in which the bill shall have originated; and the same proceedings shall then be bad as in case of other bills disapproved by the President.*

* * * * *

SECTION 8. The Congress shall have Power—

SECTION 8. The Congress have Power—

To lay and collect Taxes, Duties, Imposts and Excises, to pay the Debts and provide for the common Defense and general Welfare of the United States; but all Duties, imposts and Excises shall be uniform throughout the United States;

To lay and collect *t*axes, *d*uties, imposts, and excises, *for revenue necessary* to pay the *d*ebts, provide for the common defense [^], *and carry on the Government of the Confederate States; but no bounties shall be granted from the Treasury; nor shall any duties or taxes on importations from foreign nations be laid to promote or foster any branch of industry; and all duties, imposts, and excises shall be uniform throughout the Confederate States;*

To borrow Money on the credit of the United States;

To borrow *money* on the credit of the *Confederate* States;

To regulate Commerce with foreign Nations, and among the several States, and with the Indian Tribes;

To regulate *commerce with foreign nations, and among the several States, and the Indian tribes; but neither this, nor any other clause contained in the Constitution, shall ever be construed to delegate the power to Congress improvement intended to facilitate commerce; except for the purpose of furnishing lights, beacons, and buoys, and other aid to navigation upon the coasts, and the improvement of harbors and the removing of obstructions in river navigation, in all which cases, such duties shall be laid on the navigation facilitated thereby, as may be necessary to pay the costs and expenses thereof;*

To establish an uniform rule of Naturalization, and uniform Laws on the subject of Bankruptcies throughout the United States;

To establish [^] uniform [^] *laws of naturalization, and uniform laws on the subject of bankruptcies, throughout the Confederate States; but no law of congress shall discharge any debt contracted before the passage* of the same:

* * * * *

To establish Post Offices and post Roads;

To establish *post-offices and post routes; but the expenses of the Post-Office Department, after the first day of March, in the year of our Lord, eighteen hundred and sixty-three, shall be paid out of its own revenue;*

* * * * *

SECTION 9. The Migration or Importation of such Persons as any of the States now existing shall think proper to admit, shall not be prohibited by the Congress prior to the Year one thousand eight hundred and eight, but a Tax or Duty may be imposed on such Importation, not exceeding ten dollars for each person.

SECTION 9. The [^] *importation of [^] Negroes of the African race, from any foreign country other than the slaveholding States or Territories of the United States of America, is hereby forbidden; and Congress is required to pass such laws as shall effectually prevent the same.*

Congress shall also have power to prohibit the introduction of slaves from any State not a member of, or Territory not belonging to, this Confederacy.

* * * * *

No Bill of Attainder or ex post facto Law shall be passed.

No *bill* of *attainder* [^], ex post facto *law, or law denying or impairing the right of property in Negro slaves* shall be passed.

No Tax or Duty shall be laid on Articles exported from any State.

No *tax* or *duty* shall be laid on articles exported from any State *except by a vote of two thirds of both Houses.*

* * * * *

Every law, or resolution having the force of law, shall relate to but one subject, and that shall be expressed in the title.

* * * * *

No State shall, without the Consent of Congress, lay any duty of Tonnage, keep Troops, or Ships of War in time of Peace, enter into any Agreement or Compact with another State, or with a foreign Power, or engage in War, unless actually invaded, or in such imminent Danger as will not admit of Delay.

No State shall, without the consent of Congress, lay any *duty* [^] on tonnage, *except on sea-going vessels for the improvement of its rivers and harbors navigated by the said vessels; but such duties shall not conflict with any treaties of the Confederate States with foreign nations. And any surplus revenue thus derived shall, after making such improvement, be paid into the common Treasury; nor shall any State* keep *troops* or *ships* of *war* in time of peace, enter into any *agreement* or compact with another State, or with a foreign *power,* or engage in *war* [^] unless actually invaded, or in such imminent danger as will not admit of delay. *But when any river divides or flows through two or more States, they may enter into compacts with each other to improve the navigation thereof.*

* * * * *

ARTICLE II.

SECTION 1. The executive Power shall be vested in a President of the United States of America. He shall hold his Office during the Term of four Years, and, together with the Vice President, chosen for the same Term, be elected as follows:

ARTICLE II.

Section 1. The *Executive power* shall be vested in a President of the *Confederate* States of America. He *and the Vice–President shall hold their offices for the term of six years; but the President shall not be reeligible. The President and the Vice–President shall be elected as follows:*

* * * * *

ARTICLE V.

The Congress, whenever two-thirds of both Houses shall deem it necessary, shall propose Amendments to this constitution, or, on the Application of the Legislatures of two-thirds of the several States, shall call a Convention for proposing Amendments, which, in either Case, shall be valid to all Intents and Purposes, as Part of this Constitution, when ratified by the Legislatures of three-fourths of the several States, or by Conventions in three-fourths thereof, as the one or the other Mode of Ratification may be proposed by the Congress: Provided that no Amendment which may be made prior to the Year one thousand eight hundred and eight shall in any Manner affect the first and fourth Clauses in the Ninth Section of the first Article; and that no State, without its Consent, shall be deprived of its equal Suffrage in the Senate.

ARTICLE V.

SECTION 1. [^] *Upon the demand of any three States, legally assembled in their several conventions, the Congress shall summon a Convention of all the States, to take into consideration such amendments to the Constitution as the said States shall concur in suggesting at the time when the said demand is made; and should any of the proposed amendments to the Constitution be agreed on by the said Convention—voting by States—and the same be ratified by the Legislatures of two thirds of the several States, or by conventions in two-thirds thereof—as the one or the other mode of ratification may be proposed by the general convention—they shall thenceforward form a part of this Constitution. But* no State shall, without its consent, be deprived of its equal *representation* in the Senate.

ARTICLE VI.

All Debts contracted and Engagements entered into, before the Adoption of this Constitution, shall be as valid against the United States under this constitution, as under the Confederation.

ARTICLE VI.

The Government established by this Constitution is the successor of the Provisional Government of the Confederate States of America, and all the laws passed by the latter shall continue in force until the same shall be repealed or modified; and all the officers appointed by the same shall remain in office until their successors are appointed and qualified, or the offices abolished.

All *d*ebts contracted and *e*ngagements entered into before the *a*doption of this Constitution shall be as valid against the *Confederate States* under this *Constitution* as under the *Provisional Government.*

* * * * *

ARTICLE VII.

The ratification of the Conventions of nine States, shall be sufficient for the Establishment of this Constitution between the States so ratifying the Same.

ARTICLE VII.

The ratification of the Conventions of *five* States shall be sufficient for the *e*stablishment of this Constitution between the States so ratifying the *s*ame.

When five States shall have ratified this constitution, in the manner before specified, the Congress under the Provisional Constitutional shall prescribe the time for holding the election of President, and Vice–President, and for the meeting of the electoral college, and for counting the votes, and inaugurating the President. They shall also prescribe the time for holding the first election of members of Congress under this Constitution, and the time for assembling the same. Until the assembling of such Congress, the Congress under the Provisional constitution shall continue to exercise the legislative powers granted them; not extending beyond the time limited by the Constitution of the Provisional Government.

Chapter 14

LETTERS OF INTENT

A letter of intent, a memorandum of understanding or term sheet is a preliminary transactional document, generally prepared by a lawyer or lawyers, which captures some or all of the key deal points that the parties have agreed upon. It is usually *not* the final document that will govern the transaction, and the final transactional documents will generally supercede the letter of intent, usually expressly through integration or merger clauses. Here, we focus on a letter of intent. Drafting considerations for memoranda of understanding and term sheets are similar.

A. Why Use a Letter of Intent.

1. *To commit the other side prior to preparation of definitive documents.* This is important in a deal of any real significance, as substantial time, effort, and attorneys' fees will be generated in arriving at final documentation and performing due diligence. It is often prudent to memorialize the parties' present agreement on key points as well as those areas that have not yet been agreed upon, before proceeding to incur additional transaction costs.

2. *To establish an exclusive right to negotiate.* Buyers (and others similarly situated) may achieve this goal with an express provision to this effect in the letter of intent. As a practical matter, however, even if the letter of intent is silent it will achieve this result to some degree. After all, what buyer would want to expend precious time, effort, and money negotiating and performing due diligence when they are second in line? Sellers should be reluctant to enter into a letter of intent for this reason alone, unless they receive separate consideration (generally a payment of money or perhaps a loan on favorable terms) from the buyer. Otherwise the seller will find that it has given the other party a "free option" and will have difficulty interesting third parties in negotiations. When a seller is subject to an option and can no longer use the potential of another buyer (the

market) to drive the price and other terms in the seller's favor, she is at a significant disadvantage.

3. *To allow for information sharing under a confidentiality and non-disclosure arrangement.* Such provisions should be contained in the letter of intent, and it is best to provide, explicitly, specific remedies in case of breach.

4. *To outline the basic agreement.* This can allow the parties to seek necessary financing prior to the negotiation and documentation of definitive final documents (which can be costly). It also allows the parties to seek approvals from boards of directors, loan committees, junior lien holders and the like prior to incurring substantial transaction costs.

B. The Risks of Using a Letter of Intent.

1. *Premature Contractual Obligation.* The parties may be obligated before all terms are worked out, and this may mean that a party is forced to conclude a transaction that is very much different than the one it contemplated at the time of entering into the letter of intent.

2. *Rigidity.* The existence of the letter of intent may cause or increase rigidity in the parties position, and this may have negative impacts upon the negotiation process.

C. Enforceability and Drafting Points for Letters of Intent.

Courts can and will enforce letters of intent if they are convinced that (a) the parties intended to be bound to the agreement and (b) the agreement is sufficiently definite to be enforced.[1] As a result, when deciding to use a letter of intent, the parties should determine if it is to be binding or not. *They should then explicitly and unambiguously express this intent.* If enforceability is contemplated, including express remedies in the letters of intent will assist a later court in concluding the parties mean the letter of intent to be binding and enforceable and in determining the appropriate measure of damages or the equitable remedy.

Failure to address the binding or non-binding nature of the letter of intent can dramatically increase the uncertainties faced by the parties and their exposure to litigation risk. For example, the corporate oil giant Texaco was forced to take refuge in bankruptcy when a Texas jury found that a letter of intent between Penzoil and Getty Oil that was ambiguous as to its binding nature *was* binding and, therefore, Texaco had interfered with Penzoil's contractual advantage. The verdict against Texaco was $10.53 billion, a sum it could not bond around to obtain a stay of execution pending consideration of its appeal. Thus it sought protection in Chapter 11.[2] Whether a letter of intent is binding or not is important indeed.

1. *See, e.g.,* Arcadian Phosphates, Inc. v. Arcadian Corp., 884 F.2d 69 (2d Cir.1989).

2. Kevin J. Delaney, Strategic Bankruptcy, 126–159 (University of California

QUESTIONS & CLAUSES FOR CONSIDERATION

Here is a sample Letter of Intent which has been annotated with footnote questions to direct your attention to various issues, problems, and solutions. This sample does not always feature good plain English construction.

LETTER OF INTENT

(Asset Purchase/Sale)

[LETTERHEAD OF PURCHASER]

[date]

CONFIDENTIAL
[Addressee]
[Address]

>Re: Acquisition of Assets from *[Company name]*,
>   a [type of entity & jurisdiction of formation][3]

Dear *[Addressee]*:

    This letter confirms our understanding of the mutual present intentions of *[Full, Formal Name of Purchaser]* (the "Purchaser") and *[Full, Formal Name of Seller]*, (the "Seller") with respect to the principal terms and conditions under which the Purchaser will acquire substantially all of the Seller's assets (the "Assets"). This transaction is referred to as the "Acquisition" and the Seller and Purchaser are referred to, collectively, as the "Parties."[4]

    This letter is written with the understanding that the Seller is, among other things, *[disclose any material information that, if left undisclosed, could constitute such a material discovery that one or both parties could back out of their deal claiming surprise, misrepresentation, material omission, frustration of purpose, or impossibility, e.g., bankruptcy or conservancy of a party, the need for board, regulator or other approval, and the like.]*

    [If non-binding: The Parties acknowledge that this letter does not contain all matters upon which an agreement must be reached in order for the Acquisition to be consummated. Further, among other conditions specified herein or otherwise agreed to by the parties, the obligations of the Parties hereto to consummate the Acquisition are subject to the negotiation and execution of the Purchase Agreement and Loan Documents referred to below. Accordingly, this letter is intended solely as a

---

Press 1992 & 1998).

   3. Could you define "Seller" here in the "re" line? Are there any other definitions that could be conveniently placed here? Yes and yes. One style of drafting would set up the "re" line to define Buyer, Seller and the Assets to be acquired.

   4. Are these two definitions necessary or desirable?

basis for further discussion and is not intended to be and does not constitute a legally binding agreement; provided, however, that the provisions set forth in paragraphs 6, 7, 9, 10, 11, and 12 below and this paragraph shall be binding upon the Parties and, only with respect to paragraphs 9, 10, 11, and 12, shall survive termination.][5]

1. *Purchase of Assets.* At the closing (the "Closing"),[6] subject to the satisfaction of all conditions precedent contained in the Purchase Agreement, the Purchaser will purchase from the Seller, and the Seller will sell to the Purchaser, all of the Seller's Assets except those listed on Exhibit A hereto,[7] if any. The Purchaser may assign some or all of its rights hereunder prior to the Closing to one or more of its subsidiaries.[8]

2. *Purchase Price.* The purchase price for the Assets will be $_____, payable to the Seller, in cash, when [*specify time, condition, or event triggering closing*].

3. *Definitive Agreement.* The Purchaser and the Seller shall use reasonable diligence to commence good faith negotiations in order to execute and deliver a definitive agreement relating to the Acquisition (the "Purchase Agreement") acceptable to the parties hereto on or prior to [*date certain*].[9] [*Specify what happens if this does not occur including whether or not there are legal, binding obligations.*] All terms and conditions concerning the acquisition shall be stated in the Purchase Agreement, including representations, warranties, covenants, and indemnities that are usual and customary in a transaction of this nature and as may be mutually agreed upon between the parties.[10] Subject to the satisfaction of all conditions precedent contained in the Purchase Agreement, the Closing will take place no later than [*date certain*] or as soon thereafter as possible.[11]

5. What is this all about? Is "termination" an unambiguous term? Is it the same as a material breach of a contract? Or can termination mean different things to different people at different times? Can there be different types of "termination" with different consequences in the same contract? If so, explain and provide examples. Draft a multiple termination provision (use your imagination for the facts).

6. Is this definition needed? Why or why not?

7. Does this provision create an ambiguity or circularity? Check the definition of "Assets" in the first paragraph. If there is a problem here, how could you fix it?

8. Applying general contract law, would this letter of intent, if it is a contract, be assignable by the buyer? If so, does this sentence narrow that right to assign? Why or why not?

9. Examine this sentence closely. On first blush it may appear to be a pretty firm commitment to move forward with the transaction. The author intended the reader to assume that meaning. On closer reading, however, it becomes clear that the only firm obligation is to "use reasonable diligence to *commence*" further negotiations. Even implying a duty of good faith and fair dealing into this contract will not make this obligation a very firm one for either party. Read covenants very closely to ensure that the obligations are exactly what they are intended to be.

10. What does this mean? If this is a binding letter of intent, could this provision be enforced? How? Is it merely an agreement to agree?

11. What does this paragraph address? List the issues or problems to be solved and their possible solutions that are involved here. What happens if things break down on the way to the final documents? Does it matter if they break down through no fault of the parties? How about because of intentional foot dragging by one of the parties who no longer wants to consummate the transaction? Could this provision be improved to address the problems, if any, that you identified? How?

4. *Representations and Warranties.* The Agreement will contain representations and warranties customary to transactions of this type, including without limitation, representations and warranties by the Seller as to (a) the accuracy and completeness of the Company's financial statements; (b) disclosure of all the Seller's contracts, commitments, and liabilities, direct or contingent; (c) the physical condition, suitability, ownership and status of liens, claims, and other adverse interest with respect to the Seller's assets; (d) the Seller's ownership of the Assets; (e) the absence of a material adverse change in the condition (financial or otherwise), business, properties, assets of the Seller; and (f) the organization, valid existence, good standing, and capitalization of the Seller.

5. *Conditions to Consummation of the Acquisition.* The respective obligations of the parties with respect to the Acquisition shall be subject to satisfaction of conditions customary to transactions of this type, including without limitation, (a) execution of the Purchase Agreement by all parties; (b) the obtaining of all requisite regulatory, administrative, or governmental authorizations and consents; (c) approval of the Acquisition by the Board of Directors of the Purchaser; (d) absence of a material adverse change in the condition (financial or otherwise) of the Assets; (e) satisfactory completion by the Purchaser of due diligence investigation of the Company as provided in paragraph 2(b)(ii) above; and (f) confirmation that the representations and warranties of the Seller are true and accurate in all respects.

6. *Access to Company.*[12] The Seller shall give the Purchaser and its representatives full access to any personnel and all properties, documents, contracts, books, records, and operations of the Seller relating to is business. The Seller shall furnish the Purchaser with copies of documents and with such other information as the Purchaser may request.

7. *Other Offers.* The Seller (or the Seller's directors, officers, employees, agents, or representatives) may solicit, encourage or entertain proposals from or enter into negotiations with or furnish any nonpublic information to any other person or entity regarding the possible sale of the Seller's business, assets or stock so long as such activities do not unreasonably interfere[13] with the ability of the Purchaser to enter into and perform under the Purchase Agreement. The Seller shall notify the Purchaser of any proposals by third parties with respect to the acquisition of all or any portion of the Seller's business, assets, or stock and furnish the Purchaser the material terms thereof.[14]

8. *Conduct of Business.* The Seller shall conduct its business in the ordinary course, consistent with the present conduct of its business and

---

12. This provision is slanted in favor of one party. Which one? Provide specific line edits that could make the provision more balanced.

13. What does this standard mean? What is the intent behind it? Does it favor the buyer or the seller or both? Could it be

improved? Is there any benefit to be gained by not improving it? For the Buyer? For the Seller?

14. What is missing from this sentence? How could the missing information be best worked into this sentence, paragraph, or elsewhere in the letter of intent?

previous practices. Prior to the closing, and for a reasonable time subsequent thereto, the Seller will render management and consulting services to the Purchaser so as to allow the Seller to utilize the Assets to continue business in the normal course. The Seller will render such management and consulting services to the Purchaser on terms and conditions to be agreed upon by the Seller and the Purchaser prior to [*date certain*].[15]

9. *Expenses.* Each of the parties shall pay all of its expenses incident to this letter, the Purchase Agreement and consummation of the transactions contemplated hereby and thereby. The Seller and the Purchaser each represent and warrant that there are no brokerage or finder's fees which are or will be payable in connection with the Acquisition.[16]

10. *Confidentiality.* Each of the parties hereto agrees that it will not use, or permit the use of, any of the information relating to the Seller or the Purchaser respectively furnished to each other in connection with this letter, the Purchase Agreement or the Acquisition ("Confidential Information"), except publicly available or freely usable material as otherwise obtained from another source, in a manner or for a purpose detrimental to the Seller, the Seller or the Purchaser or otherwise than in connection with this letter, the Agreement, and the transactions contemplated hereby and thereby.[17]

11. *Disclosure.* Neither party will issue any public announcement concerning the transaction without the approval of the other party, except as may be required by law.[18]

12. *Termination.* Termination of negotiations by the Purchaser on the one hand and the Seller on the other prior to the execution and delivery of the Purchase Agreement shall be without liability and no party hereto shall be entitled to any form of relief whatsoever, including, without limitation, injunctive relief or damages. Upon the earlier of (a) the mutual written agreement of the parties hereto or (b) the failure by the parties here to execute and deliver the Purchase Agreement on or prior to [*date certain*], this letter shall terminate and the parties shall be

15. Another "agreement to agree?" What if no agreement is reached? How could this provision be improved without yet reaching the ultimate terms of the management and consulting services?

16. What if there are? For instance, what if, unknown to buyer, seller had hired a business broker to sell the business who later comes forward at or after closing to claim a commission? Who would pay whom what, and under what legal theories, in those circumstances?

17. Could a plain English restatement of this provision help? Try drafting one. Substantively, is this enough protection to achieve its purpose, or is it weaker than it may appear, providing only a false sense of security to the lawyers and their clients?

What else could be added to this provision? What does it mean to describe a provision like this as "having no teeth?" Draft a confidentiality provision with "teeth."

18. Could a procedure for requesting and gaining approval be useful here? What are the options for such a procedure? Distinguish carefully who has the burden of communicating a request and approval or disapproval (i.e., what should the "default" be in the case of no response to the request)? Draft a provision with such a provision in the role of the Buyer's counsel. How could a provision drafted by the Seller's counsel differ to better serve the Seller's interest?

released from all liabilities and obligations with respect to the subject matter hereof, except as provided in the second paragraph of page 1 of this letter.

13. *Counterparts.* This letter may be executed in one or more counterparts, each of which shall be deemed an original, and all of which together shall constitute one and the same instrument.[19]

If the foregoing correctly sets forth our mutual understanding, please so indicate by signing two copies of this letter in the spaces provided below and returning one copy to us no later than 5:00 p.m. on _____, 2001.

Very truly yours,

_____

[Signature of Purchaser]

Accepted and agreed as of the date first written above.

[Seller]

Signed: _____

By: _____
    Typed Name

Its: _____
    Title

1.   Respond to the questions in the footnotes to the letter of intent.

2.   Redraft the second paragraph of the letter to reflect the fact that the Seller is already a party to a similar letter of intent, and this letter of intent is a "backup" letter of intent that the parties will use to structure an acquisition if the "first" transaction fails to be consummated.

3.   Redraft the third paragraph of the letter to make it clear that the letter of letter is meant to be binding, and take care to include whatever provisions you think would be necessary to ensure that a court would enforce the letter of intent.

4.   Pre–Closing Bridge Loan. Modify the letter of intent to provide for the Buyer to make a bridge loan prior to closing to the Seller in the amount of $50,000 to provide working capital prior to closing. The loan should be secured by a "blanket" security interest in all of the Seller's assets, subordinate to existing financing. The unpaid proceeds of the loan and all accrued, unpaid interest should be treated as a prepayment of the purchase price, assuming that the acquisition closes.

19. What does this mean? What is its relevance in terms of contract law? What about evidentiary considerations?

5. Draft a letter of intent for an acquisition of the same business as that in the example letter of intent. Use plain English. In this transaction the acquisition will be structured as a stock acquisition, i.e., the Buyer will buy all of the outstanding shares of stock from the sole stockholder of the target company. Make sure you identify the proper parties to the agreement.

Chapter 15

OPINIONS OF COUNSEL

Opinions of counsel or "opinion letters" used in transactional practice form a very important part of modern law firm practice. The opinion letters discussed here are typical of sophisticated transactional practice, and are gradually becoming part of ever more basic transactions. Opinion letters are legitimately and commonly used to:

- Provide comfort that an intended course of action is legal or that certain definite legal consequences will follow;

- Provide comfort to the clients and opposing counsel by indicating that opining counsel has performed the due diligence investigation necessary to issue the opinion letter;

- Confirm the existence of specific legal relationships; or

- Provide for undertaking a detailed review of a legal issue that bears on a transaction and reaching a legal conclusion upon which other parties can rely.

Opinion letters are the subject of much discussion, debate, and disagreement as well as local practice differences. A complete understanding of legal opinion practice is far beyond the scope of this book, but there are a few key points that every lawyer involved in commercial transactions should know:

A. A legal opinion applies a body of law to a set of facts. *Lawyers do not opine as to the underlying facts.* They will reasonably assume certain facts, in reliance upon statements in documents, including other opinions of counsel, officers' certificates and the like. Making unreasonable assumptions, or assumptions that are at variance with known facts will not insulate the lawyer from liability in an action over an incorrect opinion.

B. A legal opinion is *not* a guaranty, a warranty, a representation, an indemnity, or an insurance policy. It is an *opinion*. If it is incorrect, the remedy is a malpractice claim, which requires a showing of damage caused by a breach of the applicable standard of care to one to whom a duty was owed.[1] Without putting too fine a point on it, if the issuing attorney or firm has met the appropriate standard of care in issuing it, he, she, or it may not be liable even if it is incorrect. This limits an opinion letter's efficacy as a protection for the client and others who rely on it.

C. Typically, opinions express legal conclusions as to (i) the existence and proper formation of an entity, (ii) an entity's good standing, (iii) the attachment, perfection and priority of liens, (iv) the legality and enforceability of all or part of a transactional document, (v) the validity of prior transactions, (vi) whether a transaction contravenes or breaches an applicable law, rule, regulation or contract, and (vii) similar matters.

D. There are two general forms of formal opinion letters: the "clean" opinion and the "reasoned" opinion. A clean opinion states an absolute opinion as its conclusion, while a reasoned opinion states what the lawyer or law firm concludes "should" be the conclusion of a court or other adjudicative body faced with the same facts and law. Obviously, clean opinions are more desirable to clients and others relying upon them, such as sources of financing and rating agencies.

E. Assumptions. Opinion letters contain assumptions, but attorneys can not rely upon a stated assumption if the attorney knows it to be untrue. In other words, the attorney must act reasonably when "assuming away" issues. Customary assumptions include: (a) due organization, and good standing of opposing parties, (b) genuineness of signatures, (c) enforceability of transactional documents against opposing parties, and (d) authenticity and completeness of documents.

F. Qualifications. Opinion letters also contain qualifications on the opinion given. Typical qualifications limit the opinion (a) to the laws of the state in which the opining attorney is licensed, (b) to exclude the effects of bankruptcy and other similar laws, and (c) future changes in law, whether by statute, rule, regulation, or covert decision particularly, future court decisions.

G. A Simple Rule of Honor in Opinion Letter Practice: Never request an opinion that you would not be willing to give if you stood in opposing counsel's shoes.

Transactional documents often include conditions involving an opinion. For example, a buyer may condition closing of a sale on receiving an appropriate opinion from seller's counsel opining that the seller is duly organized and in good standing under the laws of its home jurisdiction, etc. Whether or not the condition describes the desired opinion generally or attaches a form as an exhibit, counsel should at least preliminarily

---

1. Note the order of this description of the elements of a negligence cause of action. Do you see a benefit to analyzing a potential negligence claim in this order in practice rather than in the standard law school/bar examination order of duty, standard of care, cause in fact, proximate cause, and damages?

discuss and negotiate the terms of the opinion early on. Otherwise, the parties may expend considerable time and expense documenting a transaction and conducting due diligence only to find that closing is held up or prevented because one firm refuses to issue an opinion or one in the form required by the other party. Clients are not very understanding in such circumstances.

A list of authorities and sources of additional information on legal opinions is found in the bibliography.

QUESTIONS & CLAUSES FOR CONSIDERATION

1. The following is a sample opinion used in business acquisition transactions. Plain English techniques have not been consistently employed here.

[*Date*]

[*Addressee*]

RE: [Transaction]

Dear _____:

This Firm has acted as special[2] counsel to _____ (the "Seller") in connection with the _____ (the "Transaction") more particularly described below.

A. *Transaction Identification.* [*describe and define transaction and elements*]

B. *Statement of Assignment.* At the request of the Seller, we are providing you with this Opinion concerning the Transaction. We understand that this Opinion will be relied upon by the Buyer and _____ in determining whether _____. We also understand that this Opinion will be relied upon and copies of this Opinion may be furnished to _____.

C. *Documents Reviewed and Factual Matters.* In reaching the conclusions expressed in this Opinion, we have examined originals or copies satisfactory to us of the following documents in connection with the Project ("Transaction Documents"):

1. [*list Documents*]

The documents listed as documents __ through __ are sometimes hereinafter collectively referred to as the "Transaction Documents."

For purposes of rendering this Opinion, we have examined the Transaction Documents and such other records, books, documents, and matters as we have deemed necessary or appropriate for purposes of this Opinion. As to questions of fact material to this Opinion, we have relied, with your consent, solely upon the representations of _____ set forth in the Transaction Documents. Except as stated above, we have not under-

---

2. Most firms will seek to be characterized as "special" counsel, to avoid the implication that they are "general" counsel, which may imply a broader scope of knowledge about the client or set of transactions.

taken any independent investigation to determine the existence or absence of facts, and no inference as to our knowledge of the existence or absence of such facts should be drawn from the fact of our representation of Declarant.

D. *Assumptions*. For purposes of rendering this Opinion, we have made and relied, without independent inquiry, upon the following assumption:

    1.   The genuineness of all signatures and the authenticity of all Transaction Documents submitted to us as originals, and the conformity with the original documents of all documents submitted to us as copies.

    2.   There are no documents or other information which we have not been furnished which would materially alter, modify, or amend the Transaction Documents.

    3.   [*list other assumptions*]

E. *Attorney's Qualifications*. We are experienced in the practice of _____ law in the State of _____ and familiar with the laws, ordinances, regulations, and other legal requirements applicable to the Transaction within that jurisdiction. In preparing this Opinion we have reviewed, without limitation, [*list specific statutes and forms as implicated*].

F. *Opinions of Counsel*. Based upon our examination of the Transaction Documents and subject to the assumptions and qualifications set forth above, we are of the opinion that:

    1.   The Seller is a [*specify form of entity*], duly organized, validly existing and in good standing under the laws of the State of _____.

    2.   The Transaction Documents comply with applicable _____ law with respect to _____.

    3.   [*other opinions as needed*]

Except for the opinions specifically set forth in this Section F, no opinion is expressed with respect to any other aspect of the Transaction Documents. We express no opinion with respect to compliance with the securities laws of the State of _____ or any other jurisdiction.

G. *Limitations*. Our opinions herein are based upon the existing laws of the State of _____, and we express no opinion as to the laws or regulations of other states or jurisdictions, or with respect to the effect of noncompliance under any such laws or regulations. This opinion is furnished to you solely for your benefit and, except as provided in Section B, may not be relied upon nor copies delivered to any other person or entity without our prior written consent. The opinions expressed herein are based upon the laws of the State of _____ existing as of this date, and we expressly decline any other undertaking to advise you of any legal developments or factual matters arising subsequent to the date of this opinion which would cause us to amend any portion of it in part or in whole.

Very truly yours,

[firm signature][3]

2.   The following is a form of opinion letter that might be issued by counsel for a borrower to a lender. Again, plain English is not always optimally employed in this example, taken from practice.

[DATE]

———

———

———

     Re: ———

Dear Sir/Madam/Counsel:

We have acted as [special] counsel for [Name of Company] (the "Company") in connection with the transactions contemplated by the [Name of Principal Agreement] (the "Agreement") between the Company and [Name of Lender] (the "Lender"). This Opinion is furnished to the Lender pursuant to Section ——— of the Agreement.

We have examined originals or copies of the following documents, all dated as of ———, 200_, unless otherwise indicated (the "Documents"):

     A.   the Agreement;

     B.   ——— (the "Note");

     C.   ——— (the "Mortgage");

     D.   ——— (the "Security Agreement");

     E.   ——— (the "Financing Statements");

     (F)–(   ) [List other documents].[4]

In addition, we have examined such records, documents, certificates of public officials and of the Company, made such inquiries of officials of the Company, and considered such questions of law as we have deemed necessary for the purpose of rendering the opinions set forth herein.[5]

---

3. It is customary for opinions to be signed in the firm's name, and the identity of the individual lawyers involved in conducting and documenting the due diligence necessary to render the opinion is not formally revealed to the party to whom the opinion is issued by their personal signature. Records of who participated in the opinion preparation and issuance are generally kept within the firm, however, often by an "opinion committee" which establishes guidelines and approves opinions and the due diligence necessary to issue them.

4. Consider the need to distinguish or define certain "Documents" or groups of documents if opinions as to enforceability, etc., are not appropriate to certain of them (*e.g.* "Financing Statements") or if particular opinions relate only to certain ones (*e.g.* "Security Documents"). The use of subcategories is helpful in limiting opinions to specific types of documents, if appropriate.

5. Consider describing or attaching certificates on which one has relied in rendering particular opinions, using language like the following:

We have assumed (i) the genuineness of all signatures and the authenticity of all items submitted to us as originals and the conformity with originals of all items submitted to us as copies, (ii) that each party (other than the Company) to one or more of the Documents has the power and authority to execute and deliver, and to perform and observe the provisions of, the Documents to which it is a party, and has duly authorized, executed and delivered such Documents, and that such Documents constitute valid and binding obligations of such party.

With respect to the opinion expressed in paragraph (c) below, we have assumed that, at all times material to our opinion, (i) the Company has an interest of record in the real property described in the Mortgage (the "Real Property") at the time of the recording of the Mortgage, and (ii) the Company has "rights" in the personal property and fixtures described in the [Security] Documents (collectively, the "Personal Property") within the meaning of Section 9–203(1)(c) of the New York Uniform Commercial Code ("NYUCC").

With respect to the opinion expressed in paragraph (d) below, we have assumed that the Lender is acquiring the Note with no present intention of distributing the same other than in compliance with the requirements, if any, of all applicable state and federal securities laws.

We express no opinion as to (i) whether the Mortgage was duly recorded or the Financing Statements were duly filed, (ii) the enforceability of a security interest in any property excluded from the NYUCC by Section 9–104 thereof, (iii) the perfection or priority of the liens created by the [Security] Documents, or the effect of the absence of such perfection or priority, (iv) the state of title to the Real Property or the Personal Property, (v) the accuracy or legal sufficiency of the description of the Real Property or the Personal Property contained in the Mortgage, the Security Documents or the Financing Statements, or (vi) the effect of any regulation, law, covenant, or agreement relating to zoning, building codes, construction, use, occupancy, subdivision, or environmental control requirements as applied to the Personal Property or the Real Property.

The opinions hereinafter expressed are subject to the following further qualifications:

1. The effect of bankruptcy, insolvency, reorganization, arrangement, moratorium, or other similar laws relating to or affecting the rights of creditors generally, including, without limitation, laws relating to fraudulent transfers or conveyances, preferences, and equitable subordination.

In particular, our opinion in paragraph (a) below as to the [good standing] [qualification and good standing] [qualification or registration] of the Company is based solely upon certificates of public officials in the State[s] named in that paragraph, which certificates are dated _____. Our opinion in paragraph (e) below is based solely upon the certificate referred to in that paragraph and our review of the agreements described therein. We have made no independent investigation as to whether any of the certificates referred to in this paragraph are accurate or complete.

2. Limitations imposed by general principles of equity upon the availability of equitable remedies or the enforcement of provisions of the Documents and the effect of judicial decisions which have held that certain provisions are unenforceable where their enforcement would violate the implied covenant of good faith and fair dealing, or would be commercially unreasonable, or where a default under the Documents is not material.

3. The effect of statutes or judicial decisions rendering ineffective or limiting certain remedial provisions contained in the Documents. However, in our opinion, such statutes and judicial decisions do not operate to prevent the Lender from accelerating the maturity of the Company's obligations under the Documents in accordance with the terms thereof upon a material breach by the Company of a material covenant contained in one or more of the Documents or the occurrence of any other material Event of Default [(as defined in the Agreement)], or from exercising its remedy of foreclosure following such acceleration, provided the rules and restrictions set forth in such statutes and judicial decisions with respect to foreclosure are observed by the Lender.[6]

Based upon and subject to the foregoing, we are of the opinion that:

(a) The Company is a corporation duly organized, validly existing and in good standing under the laws of the State of _____ and is duly qualified and in good standing in the State[s] of _____.[7]

(b) The Company has the corporate [partnership] power and authority to execute and deliver, and to perform and observe the provisions of, the Documents. The Documents have each been duly authorized, executed and delivered by the Company.

(c) The Documents [(other than _____ and the Financing Statements)] constitute valid and binding obligations of the Company enforceable against the Company in accordance with their respective terms.

(d) No registration with, consent or approval of, notice to, or other action by, any federal or New York governmental entity is required on the part of the Company for the execution, delivery or performance by the Company of the Documents, or if required, such registration has been made, such consent or approval has been obtained, such notice has been given or such other appropriate action has been taken.

(e) The execution, delivery, and performance of the Documents by the Company are not in violation of its [Charter or Bylaws] [partnership documents]. The execution, delivery, and performance of the Documents

---

6. An example of such statutes is N.Y.U.C.C. §§ 9–501 *et seq.* which limit the enforceability of certain waivers and govern the disposition of personal property collateral upon the occurrence of a default. In some circumstances, it may be acceptable to substitute specific qualifications for the general qualification contained in paragraph (3) above. If the loan is unsecured, delete this paragraph.

7. Or modify as appropriate for other forms of entity, *e.g.*,

(a) The Company is a [general] [limited] partnership duly formed under the laws of the State of _____, with a stated term beyond the term of the Documents (in those cases where the Documents have a fixed term) (and is qualified or registered to do business in the State[s] of _____).

by the Company will not violate or result in the breach of any of the terms of or constitute a default under or (except as contemplated in the Documents) result in the creation of any lien, charge or encumbrance on any property or assets of the Company, pursuant to the terms of any indenture, mortgage, deed of trust or other agreement or order described in the certificate of _____, a copy of which is attached hereto as Exhibit___.[8]

We express no opinion as to matters governed by any laws other than the substantive laws of the State of New York (without reference to its choice of laws rules) and federal laws of the United States which are in effect on the date hereof.

This opinion is solely for Lender's benefit and may not be relied upon by, nor may copies be delivered to, any other person without our prior written consent.

Very Truly Yours,

[firm name]

8. If any agreement described in the above certificate may be governed by the laws of a jurisdiction other than one in which counsel is admitted, counsel should assume that such agreement is governed by the law of a jurisdiction to which she is admitted for purposes of the opinion referred to in paragraph (e). In addition, counsel should exclude from the scope of the opinion any potential violation of financial covenants contained in such agreements; the opinion recipient should rely on a representation of the chief financial officer or other appropriate officer of the Company as to those matters.

Additional Acknowledgments

George W. Kuney is an Associate Professor of Law and the Director of the Clayton Center for Entrepreneurial Law at The University of Tennessee College of Law. Prior to joining the faculty, he was in private practice with California-based firms where he concentrated on business law and reorganization under chapter 11 of the bankruptcy code nationwide.

The thoughts and material in this book were developed during the author's practice with Morrison & Foerster LLP, San Francisco, California; Howard, Rice, Nemerovski, Robertson & Falk, LLP, San Francisco, California; and Allen Matkins Leck Gamble & Mallory LLP, San Diego, California, and while teaching Legal Writing and Research, Contract Drafting, Bankruptcy & Creditors' Rights, Workouts & Reorganizations, and Representing Enterprises at the University of California's Hastings College of the Law, San Francisco, California; California Western School of Law, San Diego California; and The University of Tennessee College of Law, Knoxville, Tennessee. As such, they contain many points absorbed from others at these institutions. Additionally, the bibliography that follows lists books and other sources of authority that the author has worked with or think highly of, and which have unquestionably influenced the content of this book to one extent or another. Where specific attribution to a source was possible, it has been made in the text.

The author thanks Robert Barnes, Janice Claytor, James Giffen, Mark Jendrick, Robert Lloyd, Donna Looper, David Tipton, Nancy Rapoport, Stephanie S. Pierce, Carol Parker, and Peter Sherman for their input, review, and consultation regarding this text.

*

Bibliography

Brody, Susan L., Rutherford, Jane, Vietzen, Laurel A., Dernbach, John C. *Legal Drafting*. Boston, MA: Little, Brown and Co. Copyright 1994.

Burnham, Scott J. *Drafting Contracts*. Charlottesville, VA: The Michie Co., 2nd ed. Copyright 1987, 1993.

Child, Barbra. *Drafting Legal Documents, Principles and Practices*. St. Paul, MN: West Publishing Co., 2nd ed. Copyright 1992.

Darmstadter, Howard. *Hereof, Thereof, and Everywhereof: A Contrarian Guide to Legal Drafting*. Chicago, IL: American Bar Association. Copyright 2002.

Dickerson, Reed. *The Fundamentals of Legal Drafting*. Boston, MA: Little, Brown and Co. Copyright 1965.

Garner, Bryan A. *Advanced Legal Drafting*. Dallas, TX: Bryan A. Garner and LawProse, Inc. Copyright 1993.

Garner, Bryan A. *Advanced Legal Writing and Editing*. Dallas, TX: LawProse, Inc. Copyright 1993.

Garner, Bryan A. *The Red Book, A Manual on Legal Style*. St. Paul, MN: West Group. Copyright 2002.

Garner, Bryan A. *The Scribes Journal of Legal Writing*. New York, NY: Matthew Bender, vol. 7, 1998–2000. Copyright 2000.

Garner, Bryan A. *The Scribes Journal of Legal Writing*. St. Paul, MN: West Publishing Co., vol. 5, 1994–1995. Copyright 1996.

Haggard, Thomas, R. *Legal Drafting in a Nut Shell*. St. Paul, MN: West Publishing Co. Copyright 1996.

Haggard, Thomas, R. *Legal Drafting: Practical Exercises and Problem Materials*. St. Paul, MN: West Group. Copyright 1999.

Hayakawa, S.I. *Choose the Right Word, A Modern Guide to Synonyms*. New York, NY: Harper and Row, Publishers. Copyright 1968.

Oates, Laurel C., Enquist, Anne, Kunsch, Kelly. *The Legal Writing Handbook*. Boston, MA: Little, Brown and Co. Copyright 1993.

Ray, Mary B., Cox, Barbra J. *Beyond the Basics, A Text for Advanced Legal Writing*. St. Paul, MN: West Publishing Co. Copyright 1991.

Ray, Mary B., Ramsfield, Jill J. *Legal Writing: Getting It Right and Getting It Written*. St. Paul, MN: West Group, 3rd ed. Copyright 2000.

Schultz, Nancy L., Sirico, Jr., Louis J. *Legal Writing and Other Lawyering Skills*. New York, NY: Matthew Bender, 3rd ed. Copyright 1998.

Shertzer, Margaret. *The Elements of Grammar.* New York, NY: Macmillan Publishing Co., Inc. Copyright 1986.

Strunk, Jr, William, White, E.B. *The Elements of Style.* Macmillan Publishing Co., Inc., 3rd ed. Copyright 1979.

Drafting Business Contracts: Principles, Techniques and Forms. Berkeley, CA: The Regents of the University of California. Copyright 1994, 1996.

Sources of information regarding Opinion Letters:

Third Party Legal Opinion Report, Including the Legal Opinion Accord, of the Section of Business Law, American Bar Association, 47 Bus. Law. 167 (ABA 1991).

Report of the Business Law Section of the State Bar of California on the Third–Party Legal Opinion Report of the ABA Section of Business Law (State Bar of California May 1992).

1989 Report of the Committee on Corporations of the Business Law Section of the State Bar of California Regarding Legal Opinions in Business Transactions (Aug. 1989), 45 Bus. Law. 2169 (ABA 1990).

Report Regarding Legal Opinions in Personal Property Secured Transactions (Dec. 1988), 44 Bus. Law. 791 (ABA 1989).

Legal Opinions in California Real Estate Transaction, Real Property Law Section of the State Bar of California and Real Property Section of the Los Angeles County Bar Association, 42 Bus. Law. 1139 (ABA 1987).

March 1990 Addendum to Legal Opinions in California Real Estate Transactions, Real Property Law Section of the California State Bar Association (1990).

Report on Adaptation of the Legal Opinion Accord, Joint Drafting Committee of the Section of Real Property, Probate and Trust Law of the American Bar Association and the American College of Real Estate Lawyers, 29 Real Prop. Prob. and Tr. J. 569 (ABA 1994).

Blazer, D., Fitzgibbon, S., and Weise, S., *Glazer, Fitzgibbon and Weise on Legal Opinions* (1992).

Groh, M., *A Checklist for Preparing Opinion Letters in Standard Corporate Transactions,* 4 CEB Cal. Bus. L. Prac. 137 (Fall 1989).

APPENDICES

The appendices that follow consist of exemplars of different transactional documents. Portions of these exemplars are annotated with questions and comments in the footnotes. These annotations are designed to assist your analysis and understanding of each document.

These documents have been adapted from documents used in real transactions. They are not optimally drafted in terms of plain English and other principles described in this book. They represent, in general, documents that are merely above average in terms of good drafting. One exercise and opportunity for further practicing the drafting and reviewing skills described in the text is to redraft these exemplars to achieve Plain English documents.

*

Appendix 1

PROMISSORY NOTE

SECURED PROMISSORY NOTE

_____, _____ [1]

_____ _____, 20__ [2]

$_____ [3]

FOR VALUE RECEIVED, the undersigned ("Maker") promises to pay to the order of _____ ("Payee"), at _____, or at such other address as the holder of this Note shall direct, the principal sum of _____ Dollars ($_____), payable $_____ principal per month, plus interest (herein defined), commencing on _____ and continuing on the same date of each succeeding month, until the earlier of the following dates (the "Maturity Date"): _____, or the date the Loan and Security Agreement between Maker and Payee of even date (the "Security Agreement") terminates. On the Maturity Date the entire remaining unpaid principal balance of this Note, plus any and all accrued and unpaid interest, shall be due and payable.

Interest. This Note shall bear interest on the unpaid principal balance hereof from time to time outstanding ("Interest") at a rate equal to the "Reference Rate" (as hereinafter defined) plus __% per annum ("Interest Rate"). The Interest shall be calculated on the basis of a 360–day year for the actual number of days elapsed. "Reference Rate" shall mean the actual "Reference Rate" or the substitute therefor of _____ [4] whether or not that rate is the lowest interest rate charged by said bank. If the Reference Rate is unavailable, "Reference Rate" shall mean the rate published in the _Wall Street Journal_ on the first business day of the month, as the base rate of corporate loans at large U.S. money center banks. The Interest Rate applicable to this Note shall be adjusted monthly, as of the first day of each month, and the Interest Rate charged during each month shall be based on the Reference Rate in effect on the first day of the month. Accrued Interest shall be payable monthly, in addition to the principal payments provided above, commencing on _____, and continuing on the last day of each succeeding month. Any

---

1. These blanks are for the geographic description of where the note is to be entered into, such as San Francisco, California, or Knoxville, Tennessee.

2. This is the date of the note.

3. This is the original principal amount of the note.

4. This blank is for the name of a bank, generally a large money-center bank whose interest rate is used in the relevant area as a benchmark.

accrued Interest not paid when due shall bear Interest at the same Interest Rate as the principal.[5]

Time & Form of Payments. Principal and Interest on this Note shall be payable in lawful money of the United States of America. If a payment becomes due and payable on a Saturday, Sunday or legal holiday, the due date shall be extended to the next succeeding business day, and Interest shall be payable thereon during such extension.[6]

Events of Default. In the event any payment of principal or Interest on this Note is not paid in full when due, or if any other default or event of default occurs hereunder, under the Security Agreement, or under any other present or future instrument, document, agreement between Maker and Payee (collectively, "Events of Default"), Payee may, at its option, at any time thereafter, declare the entire unpaid principal balance of this Note plus all accrued Interest to be immediately due and payable, without notice or demand.[7] Without limiting the foregoing and Payee's other rights and remedies, the Maker agrees to pay immediately to Payee as liquidated damages an amount equal to 5% of the installment (or portion thereof) not paid to compensate Payee for the internal administrative expenses in administering the default. The acceptance of any installment of principal or Interest by Payee after the time when it becomes due, as herein specified, shall not be held to establish a custom, or to waive any rights of Payee to enforce payment when due of any further installments or any other rights, nor shall any failure or delay to exercise any rights be held to waive the same. Without limiting Payee's other rights and remedies, following the occurrence of an Event of Default, the Interest Rate shall increase by an additional 5% per annum until such Event of Default has been cured.

Application of Payments. All payments are to be applied first to costs and fees referred to hereunder, second to the payment of accrued Interest and the remaining balance to the payment of principal. Any principal prepayment shall be applied against principal payments in the inverse order of maturity. Payee shall have the continuing and exclusive right to apply or reverse and reapply any payments.

Maker agrees to pay all costs and expenses (including, without limitation, attorney fees) incurred by Payee in connection with or related to this Note or its enforcement, whether or not suit be brought. Maker waives presentment, demand for payment, notice of dishonor, notice of nonpayment protest, notice of protest, and any other notices and demands in connection with the delivery, acceptance, performance, default,

---

5. Note the detail of the provisials regarding interest. Note also how all the interest provisions are grouped together.

6. Again, note the subject matter grouping. This paragraph could be titled "payments."

7. The case of Beal Bank v. Crystal Properties, Ltd., L.P. (*In re* Crystal Properties, Ltd., L.P.), 268 F.3d 743 (9th Cir. 2001), at page 83 of this book deals with a hapless lender's attempts to declare a default under a clause very similar to this and demonstrates the perils of precatory language.

or enforcement of this Note.[8] Maker waives the benefits of any statute of limitations with respect to any action to enforce, or otherwise related to, this Note.

This Note is secured by the Security Agreement and all other present and future security agreements between Maker and Payee (collectively, "Security Documents"). Nothing herein shall be deemed to limit any of the terms or provisions of the Security Documents and all of Payee's rights and remedies under the Security Documents are cumulative.

Severability. In the event any one or more of the provisions of this Note shall for any reason be held to be invalid, illegal, or unenforceable, the remaining provisions of this Note shall remain in full force and effect.

No waiver or modification of any of the terms or provisions of this Note shall be valid or binding unless set forth in a writing signed by a duly authorized officer of Payee, and then only to the extent therein specifically set forth. If more than one person executes this Note, their obligations shall be joint and several.

THIS NOTE HAS BEEN DELIVERED FOR ACCEPTANCE BY PAYEE IN _____, AND SHALL BE GOVERNED BY AND CONSTRUED IN ACCORDANCE WITH THE INTERNAL LAWS (AS OPPOSED TO THE CONFLICTS OF LAW PROVISIONS) OF THE STATE OF _____, AS THE SAME MAY FROM TIME TO TIME BE IN EFFECT. MAKER HEREBY (i) IRREVOCABLY SUBMITS TO THE JURISDICTION OF ANY STATE OR FEDERAL COURT LOCATED IN _____ OVER ANY ACTION OR PROCEEDING ARISING FROM OR RELATED TO THIS NOTE; (ii) WAIVES PERSONAL SERVICE OR ANY AND ALL PROCESS UPON MAKER, AND CONSENTS THAT ALL SUCH SERVICE OF PROCESS BE MADE BY MESSENGER, CERTIFIED MAIL, OR REGISTERED MAIL DIRECTED TO MAKER AT THE *ADDRESS SET FORTH BELOW* AND SERVICE SO MADE SHALL BE DEEMED TO BE COMPLETED UPON THE EARLIER OF ACTUAL RECEIPT OR THREE (3) DAYS AFTER THE SAME SHALL HAVE BEEN POSTED TO MAKER'S ADDRESS; (iii) IRREVOCABLY WAIVES, TO THE FULLEST EXTENT MAKER MAY EFFECTIVELY DO SO, THE DEFENSE OF AN INCONVENIENT FORUM TO THE MAINTENANCE OF ANY SUCH ACTION OR PROCEEDING; (iv) AGREES THAT A FINAL JUDGMENT IN ANY SUCH ACTION OR PROCEEDING SHALL BE CONCLUSIVE AND MAY BE ENFORCED IN ANY OTHER JURISDICTION BY SUIT ON THE JUDGMENT OR IN ANY OTHER MANNER PROVIDED BY LAW; AND (v) AGREES NOT TO INSTITUTE ANY LEGAL ACTION OR PROCEEDING AGAINST PAYEE OR ANY OF PAYEE'S DIRECTORS, OFFICERS,

---

8. For a discussion of this sort of sentence and its development from case law as easy as 1703 and continuing through the 1952 version of the Uniform Commercial Code, *see* Howard Darmstadter, *Hereof, Thereof, and Everywhereof: A Contrarian Guide to Legal Drafting* at 159–160 (ABA 2002). Darmstadter points out that, under the 1990 UCC, "Maker waives presentment" should be sufficient to accomplish the intended result. *Id.*

EMPLOYEES, AGENTS, OR PROPERTY, CONCERNING ANY MAT-
TER ARISING OUT OF OR RELATING TO THIS NOTE IN ANY
COURT OTHER THAN ONE LOCATED IN _____. NOTHING IN
THIS PARAGRAPH SHALL AFFECT OR IMPAIR PAYEE'S RIGHT
TO SERVE LEGAL PROCESS IN ANY MANNER PERMITTED BY
LAW OR PAYEE'S RIGHT TO BRING ANY ACTION OR PROCEED-
ING AGAINST MAKER OR MAKER'S PROPERTY IN THE COURTS
OF ANY OTHER JURISDICTION.[9]

**WAIVER OF JURY TRIAL. PAYEE, BY ITS ACCEPTANCE
OF THIS NOTE, AND MAKER EACH HEREBY WAIVE THE
RIGHT TO TRIAL BY JURY IN ANY ACTION OR PROCEEDING
BASED UPON, ARISING OUT OF, OR IN ANY WAY RELATING
TO: (i) THIS NOTE; OR (ii) ANY OTHER PRESENT OR FUTURE
INSTRUMENT OR AGREEMENT BETWEEN PAYEE AND MAK-
ER; OR (iii) ANY CONDUCT, ACTS, OR OMISSIONS OF PAYEE
OR MAKER OR ANY OF THEIR DIRECTORS, OFFICERS, EM-
PLOYEES, AGENTS, ATTORNEYS OR ANY OTHER PERSONS
AFFILIATED WITH PAYEE OR MAKER; IN EACH OF THE
FOREGOING CASES, WHETHER SOUNDING IN CONTRACT
OR TORT OR OTHERWISE.[10]**

_____,
a _____ corporation

By _____
President

By _____
Secretary

Address of Maker:

_____

_____

_____

Address of Payee:

_____

_____

_____

9. What do you think of the use of ALL CAPS here? Does it make this provision easier to read? More conspicuous?

10. How about the addition of **bold** type face to the ALL CAPS—does this make the waiver of jury trial any plainer or more conspicuous?

Appendix 2

ASSET PURCHASE AND SALE AGREEMENT

ASSET PURCHASE AGREEMENT AND ESCROW INSTRUCTIONS[1]

This ASSET PURCHASE AGREEMENT AND ESCROW INSTRUCTIONS (the "Agreement") is entered into and effective as of [date], at [city], [state],[2] by and between _____ (the "Seller"), and _____ ("Buyer"), on the basis of the following facts and constitutes (i) a contract of purchase and sale between the Parties, and (ii) escrow instructions to _____ ("Escrow Agent"), the consent of which appears at the end of this agreement. Buyer and Seller are collectively referred to in this document as the "Parties."

RECITALS:[3]

A. Seller has determined that it is in the best interests of its shareholders to enter into this Agreement, whereby Seller will sell to Buyer, for the Purchase Price and on the terms and conditions set forth below, all of the Debtors' assets (other than the Excluded Assets, as defined in Section 1.2 below).

B. [Recitals as appropriate][4]

AGREEMENT

For good and valuable consideration, the receipt and sufficiency of which is hereby acknowledged,[5] the Parties agree that the above Recitals are true and correct to the best of their knowledge[6] and further agree as follows:

---

1. The escrow features of this form of agreement can be used or omitted. An escrow is recommended for large transactions or transactions involving non-corporeal entities with equity ownership beyond a single individual or family—if something goes wrong and the deal does not close—or, worse yet, closes with an incomplete exchange of consideration, counsel and the officer conducting the transaction can point to the escrow for protection or the escrow agent for monetary recovery.

2. Why include all these specifics regarding where the contract was entered into?

3. Or "Statement of Background."

4. What sorts of things are appropriate to include in the recitals? What is the purpose of recitals? Are they part of the Agreement? If an aspect of a transaction were included in the recitals but not in the next section, "AGREEMENT," is it enforceable?

5. What is this clause for? Why is it here? Is it just unnecessary legalese?

6. Why is this here? Are the recitals not already part of the agreement and thus already agreed to?

161

ARTICLE 1

SALE AND PURCHASE

1.1 *Sale and Purchase of Seller's Assets.* Subject to the terms and conditions below, on the Closing Date (as defined in Section 2.2 below), Seller shall sell, convey, transfer and deliver to Buyer, and Buyer shall purchase from Seller, all of the assets of the Seller, other than those assets specifically excluded under Section 1.2 below (collectively, the "Acquired Assets"). It is expressly understood and agreed that Buyer is purchasing the Acquired Assets subject to all encumbrances thereon existing as of the Close of Escrow.[7]

1.2 *Excluded Assets.* Buyer will not acquire any interest in the following assets of the Debtors ("Excluded Assets"):

(a) all of the Seller's cash on hand, deposits in bank accounts and cash equivalent securities or other similar items (collectively, the "Cash Assets") as of the Closing Date;

(b) tax refunds and insurance policies related to the Acquired Assets; and

(c) equity securities of and in Seller.

1.3 *Purchase Price: Payment.* Seller shall sell and Buyer shall purchase the Acquired Assets for a total purchase price of _____dollars ($_____) (the "Purchase Price").[8]

1.3.1 *Deposit.* Upon execution of this Agreement, Buyer shall deliver to Seller an initial deposit (the "Deposit") of _____ dollars ($_____) in Cash Substitute to be applied towards the Purchase Price. "Cash Substitute" means

(i) a certified or cashier's check, with Buyer as drawer or remitter thereof, drawn and paid through a banking institution acceptable to Seller, currently dated, payable to Seller and honored upon presentation for payment, or

(ii) an amount credited by wire transfer from an account of Buyer into Seller's bank.

The Deposit will be non-refundable to Buyer pursuant to Article 9 below (subject, however, to Sections 2.2 and 3.1 below). Seller will hold the Deposit in a separate, segregated, interest-bearing account to be distributed or released as provided herein. It is understood and agreed that, until the Close of Escrow or a default by Buyer (as described in Article 9), the Deposit is not property of the Seller, and seller shall not commingle the Deposit with any other assets of the Seller until such time.[9]

---

7. Is there any way to buy Assets without encumbrances? How, if at all, do encumbrances on assets differ from Seller's liabilities?

8. The total purchase price is the sum of the amount provided in sections 1.3.1, 1.3.4 and 1.3.5.

9. What is the purpose of this sentence?

1.3.2 *Refunds of Deposit.* Any refund of the Deposit made pursuant to this Agreement will be made to and accepted by Buyer as a corporation.

1.3.3 *Grant of Security Interest.* Buyer hereby grants to Seller a security interest in the Deposit to secure Buyer's contingent obligation to pay Seller liquidated damages, pursuant to Article 9 below, in the event Buyer defaults.[10]

1.3.4 *Additional Cash at Closing.* The additional sum of _____dollars ($_____) in cash or Cash Substitute ("Additional Cash") will be delivered by Buyer to Seller at or prior to the Close of Escrow (as more particularly provided in Section 4.1 below).

1.3.5 *Note.*[11] Prior to the Close of Escrow (as more particularly provided in Section 4.1 below), Buyer shall execute and deliver into Escrow a Promissory Note in the principal amount of _____ Dollars ($_____) in the form of Exhibit A to this Agreement (the "Note") executed by Buyer. Escrow Agent is hereby instructed to, at the Close of Escrow, date the Note as of the Close of Escrow. The Note will be backed by an irrevocable standby letter of credit in the amount of _____ Dollars,[12] ($_____) in the form of Exhibit B to this Agreement (the "Letter of Credit"), issued by [*bank*] and delivered by Buyer into Escrow prior to the Close of Escrow (as more particularly provided in Section 4.1 below).[13] Buyer shall cause the Letter of Credit or a replacement letter of credit to be in effect at all times until Seller has received payment of all amounts payable pursuant to the Note. The Letter of Credit shall not be replaced by a replacement letter of credit more frequently than once every year, i.e., the term of the Letter of Credit and any replacement letter of credit will be a minimum of one (1) year. Any replacement letter of credit must be delivered to Seller at least thirty (30) days prior to the expiration of the then-current letter of credit.[14]

ARTICLE 2

ESCROW

2.1 *Opening of Escrow.*[15] Within five (5) business days of the execution of this Agreement, Buyer and Seller shall open an Escrow

10. Why? Is this perfected? If so, how? Would you recommend that the Deposit be greater than, equal to, or less than the specified liquidated damages?

11. Use this type of provision when some or all of the Purchase Price is to be paid over time, post-closing. This provision features letter of credit support for the Promissory Note, but that may not be appropriate for all transactions featuring deferred payments.

12. What considerations may have gone into the determination of this amount? Why a Letter of Credit? Why not a simple security interest?

13. What does this letter of credit add to the transaction? How is it different from a guaranty or a deposit of the deferred payment amount?

14. Why not provide for a decreasing Letter of Credit?

15. What is an "escrow" really? Is it any different from any arrangement where a third party holds funds or other property for one or more people involved in a transaction? Is it different from a trust? A bailment? An agency relationship? What if the clients want one of their attorneys or law firms to act as the escrow agent in order to save the escrow agent's fee—would it be

account with Escrow Agent and shall deposit with Escrow Agent fully executed counterparts of this Agreement for use as escrow instructions. The parties agree to execute Escrow Agent's usual form of supplemental escrow instructions for transactions of this type provided, however, that such escrow instructions will be for the purpose of implementing this Agreement and will not have the effect of modifying this Agreement unless they expressly so state and are initialed by Buyer and Seller. "Opening of Escrow" as used herein means the date when Escrow Agent (i) has received a counterpart or counterparts of this Agreement executed by both Buyer and Seller, (ii) has received notification from Seller that Seller has received the Deposit from Buyer, and (iii) has executed the Consent of Escrow following the signature page of this Agreement.

2.2 *Close of Escrow.* The closing of the sale and transfer of the Acquired Assets ("Close of Escrow") is to take place on or prior to _____ (the "Closing Date"). If the closing has not occurred by [*date certain*], either party may terminate this Agreement by providing to the other party and to Escrow Agent five (5) days prior written notice thereof, in which case (i) Seller shall return to Buyer the Deposit, minus the amount of Seller's attorneys' fees and any other costs incurred in connection with the transaction contemplated by this Agreement (provided, however, that the total amount of such fees and costs shall not exceed, in the aggregate, _____dollars ($_____)), and (ii) the Parties shall have no further obligations under this Agreement.

ARTICLE 3

CONDITIONS TO THE PARTIES' OBLIGATIONS

3.1 *Conditions to Buyer's Obligation to Purchase.*[16] Buyer's obligation to purchase the Acquired Assets is expressly conditioned upon each of the following:

3.1.1 [List conditions specific to this deal.]

3.1.2 *Seller's Deliveries to Escrow Agent.* Timely delivery of those documents required to be delivered to Escrow Agent by Seller pursuant to Article 5 below.

3.2 *Conditions to Seller's Obligation to Sell.*[17] Seller's obligation to sell the Acquired Assets is expressly conditioned upon each of the following:

3.2.1 *Performance by Buyer.* Timely performance of each obligation and covenant of, and delivery required of, Buyer hereunder.[18]

3.2.2 *Buyer's Deliveries to Seller and Escrow Agent.* Timely delivery of the items required to be delivered to Seller and/or Escrow Agent by Buyer pursuant to Article 4 below including, but not limited to,

---

prudent for the attorney or firm to do so? Why or why not?

16. Who, if anyone, can waive these conditions?

17. Who, if anyone, can waive these conditions?

18. Is this a promise, covenant, representation, or warranty of anyone?

the Deposit, the Additional Cash, the Note, the Letter of Credit, and the Consent.[19]

ARTICLE 4

BUYER'S DELIVERIES

4.1 *Balance of Purchase Price.* Buyer shall, at or prior to the Close of Escrow, deliver to Seller cash or Cash Equivalent in the amount of the Additional Cash. Buyer will, at or prior to the Close of Escrow, deliver to Escrow Agent written confirmation, countersigned by Seller, that Buyer has made the delivery required by this Section 4.1.

4.2 *Note, Letter of Credit and Consent.* Buyer shall, at or prior to the Close of Escrow, deliver to Escrow Agent (i) the Note, in the form attached as Exhibit A and executed by Buyer and (ii) the Letter of Credit, in the form attached as Exhibit B.[20]

4.3 *Transfer Documents.* Buyer shall, at or prior to the Close of Escrow, deliver to Escrow Agent counterparts, executed by Buyer, of those Transfer Documents set forth in Article 5 below which are required to be executed by Buyer.

4.4 *Cash—Prorations.* Buyer shall, at or prior to the Close of Escrow, deliver to Escrow Agent cash in the amount, if any, required of Buyer under Article 7 entitled "Proration, Fees and Costs."

ARTICLE 5

SELLER'S DELIVERIES TO ESCROW AGENT

5.1 *Transfer Documents.* Seller shall, at or prior to the Close of Escrow, deposit into Escrow the following instruments of conveyance and transfer ("Transfer Documents") in order to transfer to Buyer Seller's right, title, and interest in and to the Acquired Assets:

5.1.1 *Real Property.* With respect to each parcel of real property being transferred, a quitclaim deed in the form of Exhibit C to this Agreement ("Quitclaim Deed")[21] executed and acknowledged by Seller;

5.1.2 *Notes.* With respect to each debt owed to Seller which is evidenced by a note in favor of Seller ("Note"), an Allonge in the form of Exhibit D to this Agreement, executed by Seller;

5.1.3 *Deeds of Trust.* With respect to each Note which is secured by a deed of trust under which Seller is the beneficiary, either as original beneficiary or via assignment ("Deed of Trust"), an Assignment of Deed of Trust in the form of Exhibit E to this Agreement, executed and acknowledged by Seller;

19. Is this a promise, covenant, representation, or warranty of anyone?

20. Why is it good practice to have all the subordinate documents agreed to up front? What if your client just wants to hurry through the basic agreement and leave those "basic form documents" for later?

21. Why a quitclaim deed? Why not a general warranty deed or some other deed?

5.1.4 *Vehicles.* With respect to each vehicle owned by Seller, a Department of Motor Vehicles "pink slip" executed by Seller and transferring all of Seller's title in such vehicle to Buyer;

5.1.5 *Stock.* With respect to all stock owned by a Seller, an Assignment Separate from Certificate in the form of Exhibit F to this Agreement, executed and acknowledged by Seller; and

5.1.6 *Personal Property.* With respect to all personal property of Seller (including, but not limited to accounts receivable), a bill of sale in the form of Exhibit G to this Agreement (the "Bill of Sale") executed in counterpart by Seller, pursuant to which Seller will transfer all of the personal property of Seller, other than the Excluded Assets, otherwise not transferred pursuant to Sections 5.1.1 through 5.1.6 above.

5.2 *Availability of Original Documents.*[22] Seller makes no representation or warranty as to the availability of original copies of instruments normally associated with ownership of the Acquired Assets. It is hereby agreed that, except to the extent caused by Seller's gross negligence or willful misconduct, any delay in or ineffectiveness of any transfer of assets contemplated by this Agreement which is caused by the unavailability of such documents shall not constitute a default by Seller hereunder.

ARTICLE 6

BUYER'S REPRESENTATIONS

6.1 *Condition of Acquired Assets.*[23] THEREFORE, BUYER IS TAKING THE ACQUIRED ASSETS IN AN "AS—IS, WHERE—IS, WITH–ALL–FAULTS–AND–ENCUMBRANCES" CONDITION EXISTING AS OF THE CLOSE OF ESCROW, BASED UPON BUYER'S OWN FAMILIARITY THEREWITH AND NOT UPON ANY STATEMENTS, ADVICE, OPINIONS OR REPRESENTATIONS WHICH MAY HAVE BEEN MADE BY SELLER OR SELLER'S AGENTS. THE SALE OF THE ACQUIRED ASSETS IS MADE WITHOUT COVENANT, WARRANTY OR REPRESENTATION, EXPRESS OR IMPLIED IN FACT OR LAW, AND BUYER WILL HAVE FULL RESPONSIBILITY FOR ASCERTAINING ALL MATTERS PERTAINING TO THE ACQUIRED ASSETS. WITHOUT LIMITING THE GENERALITY OF THE FOREGOING, SELLER MAKES NO REPRESENTATIONS OR WARRANTIES REGARDING THE CONDITION OF TITLE OF THE ACQUIRED ASSETS. ALSO WITHOUT LIMITING THE GENERALITY OF THE FOREGOING, WITH RESPECT TO ANY AND ALL REAL PROPERTY TRANSFERRED PURSUANT TO THIS AGREEMENT BUYER WILL HAVE FULL RESPONSIBILITY FOR ASCERTAINING ALL MAT-

---

22. What is this about?

23. Does ALL CAPS really make this easier to read? "Some writers overuse capitalization for emphasis, but that is not good style. All-caps text is less legible than lowercase text, so the message ("read this!") conflicts with the medium ("don't read this!"). Garner at § 2.1, p. 45. Garner also warns to use all-caps "sparingly." He reminds us to find a healthy balance—"A few instances heighten the effect but overuse dulls the impact." Garner at § 2.18(b), p. 55.

TERS PERTAINING TO SUCH REAL PROPERTY, INCLUDING BUT NOT LIMITED TO (I) FINANCIAL, ECONOMIC, MECHANICAL, AR-CHITECTURAL, ENGINEERING, STRUCTURAL, HAZARDOUS MA-TERIALS WASTE CONDITIONS; (II) THE IMPACT OF WATER, SEWER AND UTILITY CHARGES, FEES, TAXES, PERMITS, RE-QUIREMENTS AND BUSINESS LICENSES; (III) ZONING AND SOILS CONDITIONS; (IV) THE USE TO WHICH THE REAL PROP-ERTY CAN BE PUT; (V) THE EXISTENCE OR PRIOR EXISTENCE OF ABOVE OR BELOW–GROUND STORAGE TANK(S); (VI) THE ENVIRONMENTAL CONDITION; (VII) THE EXISTENCE OR PRIOR EXISTENCE ON OR UNDER THE REAL PROPERTY OF ANY HAZ-ARDOUS MATERIAL OR ANY SPILL, DISPOSAL, DISCHARGE, RE-LEASE, LEAK, ACCIDENT OR INCIDENT RELATING TO HAZARD-OUS MATERIAL CONTAMINATION; (VIII) THE EXISTENCE OR PRIOR EXISTENCE ON OR UNDER THE REAL PROPERTY OF ANY ASBESTOS—CONTAINING MATERIALS OR ANY TRANSFORMER, FLUORESCENT LIGHT FIXTURES WITH BALLAST, OR OTHER EQUIPMENT CONTAINING PCB's; (IX) THE CONFORMANCE OF THE REAL PROPERTY TO ANY LAWS, ORDINANCES OR REGULA-TIONS OF ANY GOVERNMENTAL AUTHORITY OR AGENCY; (X) DEED RESTRICTIONS; (XI) THE LEGALITY OF LOT SIZE; (XII) THE CONDITION OF THE REAL PROPERTY; AND (XIII) ANY AND ALL OTHER MATTERS PERTAINING TO SUCH REAL PROPERTY.

SELLER WILL HAVE NO LIABILITY OR RESPONSIBILITY FOR REMEDIATION OR REMOVAL OF ANY SUBSTANCE OR MATERIAL WHICH MAY BE POTENTIALLY INJURIOUS TO PUBLIC HEALTH OR WELFARE AND IS LOCATED ON THE REAL PROPERTY.

WITHOUT LIMITING THE GENERALITY OF THE FOREGOING, BUYER HEREBY EXPRESSLY RELINQUISHES ANY RIGHTS AND REMEDIES BUYER MAY NOW OR HEREAFTER HAVE, WHETHER KNOWN OR UNKNOWN, AGAINST SELLER, WITH RESPECT TO ANY PAST, PRESENT, OR FUTURE PRESENCE OR EXISTENCE OF "HAZARDOUS MATERIALS" (AS HEREIN DEFINED) IN, ON, ABOUT, UNDER OR AFFECTING THE REAL PROPERTY OR WITH RESPECT TO ANY PAST, PRESENT, OR FUTURE VIOLATIONS OF ANY RULES, REGULATIONS, OR LAWS, NOW OR HEREAFTER ENACTED, REGULATING OR GOVERNING THE USE, HANDLING, STORAGE, OR DISPOSAL OF HAZARDOUS MATERIALS, INCLUD-ING, WITHOUT LIMITATION, (I) ANY RIGHTS BUYER MAY NOW OR HEREAFTER HAVE TO SEEK CONTRIBUTION FROM SELLER UNDER SECTION 113(F)(I) OF THE COMPREHENSIVE ENVIRON-MENTAL RESPONSE COMPENSATION AND LIABILITY ACT OF 1980 ("CERCLA"), AS AMENDED BY THE SUPERFUND AMEND-MENTS AND REAUTHORIZATION ACT OF 1986 (42 U.S.C.A. § 9613), AS THE SAME MAY BE FURTHER AMENDED OR RE-PLACED BY ANY SIMILAR LAW, RULE OR REGULATION, AND (II) ANY CLAIMS, WHETHER KNOWN OR UNKNOWN, NOW OR HERE-AFTER EXISTING, WITH RESPECT TO THE REAL PROPERTY UNDER SECTION 107 OF CERCLA (42 U.S.C.A. § 9607). AS USED

HEREIN, THE TERM "HAZARDOUS MATERIAL(S)" INCLUDES, WITHOUT LIMITATION, ANY HAZARDOUS OR TOXIC MATERIALS, SUBSTANCES OR WASTES, SUCH AS (A) ANY MATERIALS, SUBSTANCES OR WASTES WHICH ARE TOXIC, IGNITABLE, CORROSIVE, OR REACTIVE AND WHICH ARE REGULATED BY ANY LOCAL GOVERNMENTAL AUTHORITY, ANY AGENCY OF THE STATE OF _____, OR ANY AGENCY OF THE UNITED STATES GOVERNMENT, (B) ASBESTOS, (C) PETROLEUM AND PETROLEUM BASED PRODUCTS, (D) UREA FORMALDEHYDE FOAM INSULATION, (E) POLYCHLORINATED BIPHENYLS (PCBS), AND (F) FREON AND OTHER CHLOROFLUOROCARBONS.

The acknowledgments, waivers, and releases by Buyer in Section 6.1 survive the Closing and the recordation of the quitclaim deeds, and will not be deemed merged into the quitclaim deeds upon their recordation.

ARTICLE 7
PRORATIONS, FEES AND COSTS

7.1 *Prorations.* All non-delinquent personal and real property taxes, water, gas, electricity and other utilities, local business or other license fees or taxes and other similar periodic charges payable with respect to the Acquired Assets will be prorated between Buyer and Seller as of the Close of Escrow and on the basis of a thirty (30) day month.[24]

7.2 *Seller's Closing Costs.* Seller shall pay (i) Seller's own attorneys' fees, (ii) one-half of Escrow Agent's escrow fee, and (iii) one-half of all documentary transfer taxes payable in connection with the recordation of Quitclaim Deeds and Escrow Agent's customary charges to buyers and sellers for document drafting, recording and miscellaneous charges.

7.3 *Buyer's Closing Costs.* Buyer shall pay (i) Buyer's own attorneys' fees, (ii) one-half of Escrow Agent's escrow fee, and (iii) one-half of all documentary transfer taxes payable in connection with the recordation of Quitclaim Deeds and Escrow Agent's customary charges to buyers and sellers for document drafting, recording and miscellaneous charges, (iv) all sales and use taxes payable as a result of the transactions contemplated by this Agreement, and (v) the cost and expense of any title policies desired by Buyer with respect to the Acquired Assets; provided, however, that Buyer expressly acknowledges and agrees that the acquiring of a title policy or policies with respect to the Acquired Assets is not a condition to Buyer's obligations under this Agreement, nor shall Buyer's efforts to acquire such policy or policies in any way delay the Close of Escrow.

ARTICLE 8
RECORDATION; DISTRIBUTION OF
FUNDS AND DOCUMENTS

8.1 *Form of Disbursements.* All disbursements by Escrow Agent will be made by checks of the Escrow Agent or by wire transfer to the account of the receiving party, as such party may direct.

---

24. What is the "30–day month convention"? How does it work?

8.2 *Recorded Documents.* Escrow Agent shall cause the County Recorder of _____ County (the "County Recorder") to record the Quitclaim Deeds and any other documents which are herein expressed to be, or by general usage are, recorded ("Recorded Documents"). After recordation, Escrow Agent shall cause the County Recorder to mail Recorded Documents to the grantee, beneficiary, or person (i) acquiring rights under the Recorded Documents, or (ii) for whose benefit the Recorded Documents were acquired.

8.3 *Non–Recorded Documents.* Escrow Agent shall, at the Close of Escrow, deliver by United States Mail, (or hold for personal pick-up, if requested), each non-recorded document received hereunder by Escrow Agent to the payee or person (i) acquiring rights under the non-recorded document, or (ii) for whose benefit the non-recorded document was acquired.

8.4 *Cash Disbursements.* Escrow Agent shall, at the Close of Escrow, hold for personal pick-up, or will arrange for wire transfer, (i) to Seller, or order, any excess funds delivered to Escrow Agent by Seller, and (ii) to Buyer, or order, any excess funds theretofore to Escrow Agent by Buyer. Upon Escrow Agent's request, Buyer and Seller shall deposit with Escrow Agent all sums necessary to pay their respective shares of the costs of Closing; provided, however, Buyer and Escrow Agent acknowledge that Seller shall not be required to advance any of its own funds to pay its respective share of the costs of Closing; all such costs will be paid solely out of the Deposit.

8.5 *Copies of Documents.* Escrow agent shall, at the Close of Escrow, deliver to Buyer and to Seller, copies of the Recorded Documents, conformed to show the recording data.

ARTICLE 9

DEFAULT

9.1 *Seller's Remedies.* If Buyer defaults under this Agreement and fails to complete the purchase of the Acquired Assets as herein provided, then Seller will be released from any further obligations under this Agreement and will be entitled to the following:

BECAUSE IT WOULD BE EXTREMELY IMPRACTICABLE AND DIFFICULT TO DETERMINE THE DAMAGE AND HARM WHICH SELLER WOULD SUFFER IN THE EVENT BUYER DEFAULTS HEREUNDER, AND BECAUSE A REASONABLE ESTIMATE OF THE TOTAL NET DETRIMENT THAT SELLER WOULD SUFFER IN THE EVENT OF BUYER'S DEFAULT AND FAILURE TO DULY COMPLETE THE ACQUISITION HEREUNDER IS THE SUM OF $_____ PLUS ANY INTEREST ACCRUED THEREON, SELLER WILL BE ENTITLED TO RETAIN THE DEPOSIT OF $_____ PLUS ANY INTEREST ACCRUED THEREON, AS LIQUIDATED DAMAGES. THE PAYMENT OF SUCH AMOUNT AS LIQUIDATED DAMAGES IS NOT INTENDED AS A FORFEI-

TURE OR PENALTY WITHIN THE MEANING OF [CALI-
FORNIA CIVIL CODE SECTIONS 3275 OR 3369 *OR OTHER
APPLICABLE STATUTE*], BUT IS INTENDED TO CONSTI-
TUTE LIQUIDATED DAMAGES TO SELLER PURSUANT TO
[CALIFORNIA CIVIL CODE SECTIONS 1671, 1676 AND 1677
OR OTHER APPROPRIATE STATUTE].

—————   —————

Buyer's Initials   Seller's Initials

Any fees, costs, or attorneys' fees incurred in the enforcement and
collection of liquidated damages as herein provided will not be included
in the calculation of liquidated damages and shall be recoverable in
addition thereto.

9.2 *Buyer's Remedies*. If the sale contemplated by this Agreement
is not completed according to its terms by reason of any material default
of Seller, Buyer will have the right to pursue any remedy at law;
provided, however, that upon the occurrence of any material default by
Seller, Buyer agrees that it will not (i) record a lis pendens or seek any
provisional remedies including, but limited to, the appointment of a
receiver, any temporary restraining order, any preliminary injunction or
any action for claim and delivery with respect to the Acquired Assets or
(ii) request the specific performance of this Agreement.

ARTICLE 10

GENERAL PROVISIONS

10.1 *Captions*. Captions in this Agreement are asserted for convenience of reference only and do not define, describe, or limit the scope or
the intent of this Agreement or any of the terms of this Agreement.

10.2 *Exhibits*. All exhibits referred to in and attached to this
Agreement are a part of this Agreement.

10.3 *Entire Agreement*. This Agreement contains the entire agreement between the Parties and supersedes all prior or contemporaneous
agreements, understandings, representations, and statements, oral or
written, between the Parties with respect to the subject matter of this
Agreement and the transactions contemplated by this Agreement.

10.4 *Modification*. No modification, waiver, amendment, discharge,
or change of this Agreement shall be valid unless the same is in writing
and signed by the party against which the enforcement of such modification, waiver, amendment, discharge, or change is or may be sought.

10.5 *Attorneys' Fees*. Should any party employ an attorney for the
purpose of enforcing or construing this Agreement, or obtaining any
judgment or court order based on this Agreement, in any legal proceeding whatsoever, including insolvency, bankruptcy, arbitration, declaratory relief, or other litigation, the Prevailing Party (herein defined) shall
be entitled to receive from the other party or parties thereto, reimbursement for all attorneys fees and all costs, including but not limited to

service of process, filing fees, court and court reporter costs, investigative costs, expert witness fees, and the cost of any bonds, whether taxable or not. Such reimbursement shall be included in any judgment or final order issued in that proceeding. The "Prevailing Party" means the party determined to most nearly prevail and not necessarily the one in whose favor a judgment is rendered. As provided in Article 10 herein, Seller may recover its attorneys fees in addition to liquidated damages.

10.6 *Governing Law*. This Agreement is governed by the laws of the State of _____ and federal law, as applicable, without regard to the choice of law provisions of those bodies of law.[25]

10.7 *Successors and Assigns*. All terms of this Agreement shall be binding upon, inure to the benefit of, and be enforceable by the Parties and their respective legal representatives, successors, and assigns.

10.8 *Counterparts*. This Agreement may be executed in any number of counterparts, each of which so executed shall be deemed an original, and all of which shall together constitute but one agreement.

10.9 *Further Assurances*. The Parties shall cooperate with each other and execute any documents reasonably necessary to carry out the intent and purpose of this Agreement.

10.10 *Survival of Warranties and Obligations*. All warranties and representations contained in this Agreement, and all obligations and indemnities referred to in this Agreement that are to be performed at a time or times after the Close of Escrow, survive the Close of Escrow.

10.11 *Construction*. Each party and its counsel have reviewed and revised this Agreement. Any rule of construction to the effect that ambiguities are to be resolved against the drafting party will not apply in the interpretation of this Agreement or any amendments or exhibits hereto.

10.12 *Back-up Agreements*.[26] Buyer acknowledges that Seller has a right to (i) advertise the Acquired Assets to other potential buyers, (ii) furnish any information concerning the Acquired Assets to any person (other than buyer) interested in acquiring the Acquired Assets, and (iii), solicit, negotiate, or engage in any discussions relating to the sale of the Acquired Assets with persons other than Buyer. Buyer acknowledges that Seller may enter into back-up agreements, which are expressly conditioned upon the termination of this Agreement, with potential purchasers of the Acquired Assets, and that Seller may perform under such back-up agreements if this Agreement should be terminated for any reason.

25. What is the effect of choice of law provisions? Does this provision also operate as a choice of forum clause?

26. Is this either a necessary or a good idea? For Whom?

  IN WITNESS WHEREOF, this Agreement has been executed as of the date set forth above.

    SELLER: [*Name*][27]

Signed: _____

Typed: _____

    BUYER: [*Company Name*][28]

By: _____
Name: _____
Title: _____

By: _____
Name: _____
Title: _____

---

27. This is a signature block for an individual, a sole proprietor.

28. These are signature blocks for incorporeal entities such as corporations, partnerships, and limited liability companies. Why are two signatures for officers used here? Clue/Tip: Various states have different rules and requirements for valid actions by incorporeal entities! Local counsel can be *very* helpful in spotting those issues.

CONSENT OF ESCROW AGENT[29]

The undersigned Escrow Agent hereby agrees to (i) accept the foregoing agreement, (ii) be escrow agent under said agreement, and (iii) be bound by said agreement in the performance of its duties as Escrow Agent.

Dated: _____   *[TITLE COMPANY NAME]*

By: _____
Typed: _____
Its: _____

29. Why doesn't the escrow agent just sign with the other parties?

EXHIBIT A

PURCHASE MONEY
PROMISSORY NOTE

[*City, State*]

$_____

_____, 2000

THIS SECURED PURCHASE MONEY PROMISSORY NOTE (the "Note") is executed and effective as of the date set forth above by ("Maker"), for the purpose of evidencing an obligation from Maker to _____ ("Payee").

1. *Promise to Pay.* For value received, Maker promises to pay Payee or order at _____, or at such other place as may be designated in writing by the holder of this Note, the principal sum of ____ Dollars ($____), with interest thereon from the date of this Note.

2. *Interest Rate.* The unpaid principal balance of this Note shall bear simple interest at the rate of ____ percent (__%) per annum, computed on the basis of a 365–day year.[30]

3. *Maturity Date.* The maturity date ("Maturity Date") shall be the date which is two years from the date of this Note. All unpaid amounts under this Note shall be due and payable in full on the Maturity Date; there is no grace period under this Note.

4. *No Offsets.* Maker agrees to make all payments free from any offset, deduction or counterclaim.

5. *Prepayment.* Maker may prepay all or any part of the indebtedness evidenced by this Note at any time without penalty.

6. *Letter of Credit.* This Note is backed by a ____ Dollar ($__) irrevocable standby letter of credit in favor of Payee, issued by _____ (the "Letter of Credit"). Maker hereby agrees to replace the Letter of Credit (or any replacements thereto) by delivering to Trustee (or other holder of the Note), no later than thirty (30) days prior to its expiration, a replacement letter of credit issued by _____, in an equal amount and with substantially identical terms and conditions as the Letter of Credit. Any failure by Maker to so replace the Letter of Credit (or replacements thereto) shall constitute a default under this Note and the entire unpaid balance of this Note and all accrued interest thereon shall become immediately due and payable at the option of the holder of this Note. If Maker (i) has not paid to Payee, on or prior to the Maturity Date, all amounts owed to Payee under this Note, or (ii) Maker defaults on its obligation, pursuant to this paragraph, to replace the Letter of Credit, or (iii) Maker is the subject of a voluntary or involuntary proceeding under

---

30. Do you understand what this means? What if it were compound interest? Would you have all the variables needed to compute compound interest due? If not, what is missing? What happens if this inter-est rate were to be found usurious? Are there any "safety valve" provisions that can be inserted to protect the Payee in that situation?

Title 11 of the United States Code,[31] Payee is authorized to draw upon the Letter of Credit in an amount equal to the entire unpaid balance of this Note and all accrued interest thereon. Anything in this Note to the contrary notwithstanding, Payee's right to draw upon the Letter of Credit pursuant to this Paragraph 6 shall be Payee's sole remedy in the event that Maker defaults on any of its obligations hereunder. Anything in the foregoing to the contrary notwithstanding, Maker's obligation to maintain the Letter of Credit or a replacement letter of credit shall terminate upon Maker's payment in full of all amounts owed under this Note.

7. *Attorneys' Fees.* If an action is instituted on this Note, Maker agrees to pay all costs and attorneys' fees incurred by the holder of this Note in connection therewith.[32]

8 *Application of Payments.* Except as otherwise expressly stated herein, any payments received by the holder of this Note will be applied in the following order: (a) any payments, other than principal and interest, due under this Note or any document securing this Note, (b) accrued interest; and (c) principal.[33]

9. *Lawful Money.* All payments required by this Note shall be payable in lawful money of the United States.

10. *Modification.* This Note may only be modified or amended by a written amendment signed by Maker and the holder of this Note. The holder of this Note shall not be deemed to have waived any rights or remedies hereunder unless such waiver is in writing and signed by the holder of this Note, and then only to the extent specifically set forth in the writing.

11. *Time of Essence.* Time is of the essence in the performance of the obligations under this Note.[34]

12. *Governing Law.* This Note shall be governed and construed in accordance with and pursuant to the laws of the State of _____.

13. *Joint and Several Liability.* All of the obligations of Maker hereunder shall be joint and several obligations of each such person and/or entity.

14. *Miscellaneous.* No single or partial exercise of any power hereunder or under the Agreement shall preclude other or further exercise thereof or the exercise of any other power. No delay or omission on the

---

31. Does this work? Can you trigger a Letter of Credit draw with a bankruptcy proceeding? How about other defaults under contracts? What is an "Ipso Facto" clause?

32. This is a "one way" attorneys' fee clause. What might be the problem with that in some jurisdictions? (*See, e.g.*, Cal. Civ. Code § 1717 (West 2002) ("... where the contract specifically provides that attorney's fees and costs ... shall be awarded either to one of the parties or to the prevailing party, then the party who is determined to be the party prevailing ... whether ... specified in the contract or not, shall be entitled to reasonable attorney's fees in addition to other costs")). Does this conflict with the Purchase Agreement? If so, which trumps which, when, and why?

33. Who does this order of application favor and why?

34. What is this for? What does it do?

part of Holder in exercising any right hereunder or under the Agreement shall operate as a waiver of such right or any other right under this Note. The obligations of each party executing this Promissory Note shall be joint and several. The release of any party liable under this Note shall not operate to release any other party liable hereunder. The Maker of this Note expressly waives presentment, protest and demand, notice of protest, demand and dishonor and nonpayment of this Note and all other notices of any kind, and expressly agrees that this Note, or any payment hereunder, may be extended from time to time without in any way affecting the liability of Maker and endorsers hereof.

15. *Successors and Assigns.* This Note shall be binding upon and shall inure to the benefit of the successors and assigns of the parties hereto.

        "Maker"   [*CORPORATE NAME*]

                                    By: _____
                                    Its: _____

                                    By: _____
                                    Its: _____

EXHIBIT B
IRREVOCABLE STANDBY LETTER OF CREDIT

To Beneficiary: _____

Amount: _____
($___)

Date: _____, 20__

Expiration Date: _____, 20__

We hereby establish our Irrevocable Standby Letter of Credit No. _____ in your favor (or in favor of any person or persons who may succeed, via assignment, transfer, operation of law or otherwise ("Successor-in-Interest")) available by your (or a successor-in-interest's) drafts at sight drawn on _____ **[include address]** and accompanied by the document specified below:

Document Required:

A certificate in the form of Exhibit 1 attached hereto, appropriately completed and signed by you or a Successor-in-Interest. Partial drawings are permitted.

This Letter of Credit is freely transferable by Beneficiary, including, without limitation, to any and all successors to Beneficiary as Trustee for the above-referenced bankruptcy estates, and shall inure to the benefit of and be fully enforceable by such successor Trustees.

We hereby agree with you that all drafts drawn under and in compliance with the terms of this Letter of Credit will be duly honored if drawn and presented for payment at the drawee on or before the Expiration Date of this Letter of Credit.

This Letter of Credit is subject to Division 5 of the _____ **[state-enacted version of the Uniform Commercial Code]**.

[Authorized Signature][35]

35. Who signs this document?

EXHIBIT 1 (TO EXHIBIT B)

CERTIFICATE

The undersigned beneficiary (the "Beneficiary") hereby certifies to _____ (the "Bank"), with reference to Irrevocable Standby Letter of Credit No. _____ issued by the Bank (the "Credit"), that,

1. The Beneficiary is entitled to draw on the Credit under the terms of a Purchase Money Promissory Note (the "Note") dated _____, executed by _____.

2. The amount of the draft accompanying this Certificate does not exceed the amount to which the Beneficiary is entitled under the Note.

3. The amount of the draft accompanying this Certificate does not exceed the amount available to be drawn under the Credit on the date hereof.

IN WITNESS WHEREOF, the undersigned has executed this Certificate as of _____, 2000.

_____
Beneficiary

EXHIBIT C

QUITCLAIM DEED[36]

RECORDING REQUESTED BY
AND WHEN RECORDED MAIL TO:

_____

_____

_____

_____

Attention: _____

_____

(Space Above For Recorder's Use)

<u>QUITCLAIM DEED</u>

Documentary Transfer Tax: $_____
(Computed on full value of property conveyed)

FOR VALUABLE CONSIDERATION, receipt of which is hereby acknowledged, [*insert Seller's name*], hereby remises, releases and forever quitclaims all right, title and interest it may have or acquires during the pendency of the above-referenced cases to [*Buyer's name*], in that certain real property in the City of _____, County of _____, State of _____, more particularly described on Exhibit 1 attached hereto and incorporated herein by this reference.

Dated: _____, 20__   _____

                                                          [*Seller*]

---

36. The form of a deed will vary state to state. It is typical, but check local requirements.

STATE OF _____   )[37]
)   SS:
COUNTY OF _____   )

On _____, before me, _____, a Notary Public in and for said state, personally appeared _____, personally known to me (or proved to me on the basis of satisfactory evidence) to be the person whose name is subscribed to the within instrument and acknowledged to me that he/she executed the same in his/her authorized capacity, and that by his/her signature on the instrument, the person, or the entity upon behalf of which the person acted, executed the instrument.

WITNESS my hand and official seal.

_____
Notary Public in and for said State

(SEAL)

37. This is known as the notary "jurat". The formal text of jurats are generally statutorily prescribed and vary state to state. The "Law Digest" portion of the Martin- dale–Hubble Law Directory contains forms of jurats for various states and territories. Alternatively, a local notary can provide the local form.

EXHIBIT 1 (TO EXHIBIT C)
DESCRIPTION OF REAL PROPERTY

[To be attached]

EXHIBIT D

ALLONGE[38]

Allonge to Promissory Note, dated as of ———, in the original principal amount of $———, made by ———, in favor of ———.

Pay to the order of [*Buyer's name*], without recourse, representation or warranty of any kind express or implied.

_____

[*Seller*]

38. What is an allonge? What is its purpose?

EXHIBIT E

RECORDING REQUESTED BY
AND WHEN RECORDED MAIL TO:

_____

_____

_____

_____

Attention: _____   _____

(Space Above For Recorder's Use)

ASSIGNMENT OF DEEDS OF TRUST
AND COLLATERAL DOCUMENTS

FOR VALUABLE CONSIDERATION, the receipt of which is hereby acknowledged, [*Seller's name*] ("Assignor") hereby grants, assigns, conveys and transfers to [*Buyer's name*] ("Assignee"), and its successors and assigns, without recourse to Assignor, all right, title and interest of Assignor in and to (a) the beneficial interest under the deeds of trust described on Schedule I attached hereto creating a lien on the real properties described in Exhibit "A" attached hereto, together with any and all additions or modifications thereto (the "Deed of Trust"), (b) the promissory notes described on Schedule I attached hereto, and (c) the security agreements, assignments of rents, and other documents described on Schedule I attached hereto together with any and all additions or modifications thereto (collectively, the "Assigned Assets").

The assignment of the Assigned Assets is made without covenant, warranty or representation, expressed or implied in fact or law, regarding any matter pertaining to the Assigned Assets.

EXECUTED this ___ day of _____, 200_.

ASSIGNOR: _____

[*Seller*]

STATE OF _____   )
)   ss:

COUNTY OF _____   )

On _____, before me, _____, a Notary Public in and for said state, personally appeared _____, personally known to me (or proved to me on the basis of satisfactory evidence) to be the person whose name is subscribed to the within instrument and acknowledged to me that he/she executed the same in his/her authorized capacity, and that by his/her signature on the instrument, the person, or the entity upon behalf of which the person acted, executed the instrument.

WITNESS my hand and official seal.

                               _____

                               Notary Public in and for said State

(SEAL)

EXHIBIT F

ASSIGNMENT SEPARATE FROM CERTIFICATE

FOR VALUE RECEIVED, [*Seller's name*] hereby sells, assigns, and transfers unto [*Buyer's name*] all of its right, title and interest in _____ (_____) shares of the capital stock of _____ standing in the name of _____ on the books of _____ (the "Company") represented by Certificate No. _____ herewith and does hereby irrevocably constitute and appoint _____ attorney to transfer the said stock on the books of the Company with full power of substitution in the matters hereinbefore stated.

Dated: _____, 20__

In the presence of:

———————————————

EXHIBIT G

BILL OF SALE

For good and valuable consideration, the receipt and sufficiency of which are hereby acknowledged, [*Seller's name*] (the "Seller"), hereby sells, transfers and conveys to [*Buyer's name*] ("Buyer"), without recourse or warranty, all of Seller's right, title and interest, if any, in and to all of the Acquired Assets, as defined in the Assignment Purchase Agreement and Escrow Instructions dated _____, 200_ between Seller and Buyer, not otherwise conveyed or transferred by Seller pursuant to the Quitclaim Deeds, Assignments Separate From Certificates, Allonges, and Assignment of Deeds of Trust and Collateral Documents dated the date hereof.

Buyer acknowledges that neither Seller nor Seller's agents have made any statements, representations or warranties, written or oral, express or implied, with respect to the physical, legal, economic or other condition of the Acquired Assets or the condition of title to or the suitability of the Acquired Assets for Buyer's purposes. Buyer is familiar with the Acquired Assets, has conducted such Buyer's investigation of the Acquired Assets as it has deemed necessary and appropriate and has obtained the advise of his own legal counsel. Buyer hereby acknowledges that Buyer is relying solely on his own familiarity with the Acquired Assets, his own investigations and inspections of the Acquired Assets and his legal counsel's advice in purchasing the Acquired Assets. Buyer acknowledges and agrees that Buyer has acquired the Acquired Assets in their "AS—IS" condition and Buyer hereby waives any claims against Seller with respect thereto. This Bill of Sale may be executed in counterparts.

Dated: _____, 200_.

[insert proper signature block(s)][39]

39. Who needs to sign a bill of sale? What is the purpose of a bill of sale?

Appendix 3

REAL PROPERTY LEASE

[A relatively simple lease; complex ones run to 100 pages or more]

LEASE

THIS LEASE ("Lease"), made at _____, _____, on the ___ day of_____ _____ _____, 20__, between _____ a _____ _____ _____ (the "Landlord"), and _____, a _____ (the "Tenant") (collectively, the "Parties").

1. *Premises.* Upon the terms and conditions set forth in this Lease, Landlord hereby leases to Tenant, and Tenant hereby takes from Landlord, those certain premises containing approximately _____ square feet located in _____ and outlined in red on Exhibit "A" attached hereto ("Premises"), which are located on the _____ _____ floor(s) of the building ("The Building") located at _____.

2. *Term.* The term of this Lease shall be for _____ _____ (_____) years ("Term") and shall commence on the _____ day of_____, 20__ (the "Commencement Date"), and end on the _____ day of _____ _____ _____, 20__, inclusive. However, in the event Landlord, for reasons beyond Landlord's control or for reasons not created through the negligence or other fault of Landlord, is unable to deliver possession of the Premises to Tenant upon the Commencement Date, neither Landlord nor its agent shall be liable for any damage caused thereby, nor shall this Lease thereby become void or voidable, and the Term shall in such case commence upon the date of delivery of possession of the premises to Tenant and shall terminate _____ (___) years thereafter. In such event, Tenant shall not be liable for any rent until Landlord delivers possession of Premises to Tenant. Notwithstanding the provisions of this Paragraph 2, in the event Landlord is unable to deliver possession of the Premises to Tenant for the above-stated reasons by the _____ day of _____, 20__, then this Lease may be cancelled by Tenant without any liability to Landlord.

In the event that Landlord is unable to deliver possession of the Premises upon the Commencement Date through the negligence or other fault of Landlord, this Lease may be cancelled by Tenant without liability to Landlord by written notice delivered to Landlord within fifteen (15) days of the Commencement Date.

3. *Option to Extend Term.* Landlord grants to Tenant the option to extend the Term on all the provisions contained in this Lease, except for minimum monthly rent, for _____consecutive periods of _____ years (the "Extended Term") following expiration of the initial Term. Tenant

must give notice of exercise of the option ("Option Notice") to Landlord at least two (2) months before the commencement of the Extended Term.

If Tenant is in default on the date of giving the Option Notice, the Option Notice shall be totally ineffective. If Tenant is in default on the date the Extended Term is to commence, the Extended Term shall not commence and this Lease shall expire at the end of the existing Term. The rental rate for any of the Extended Terms shall be the then prevailing market rate (herein defined), which shall be based upon a use substantially similar to that which Tenant is then using the Premises and shall take into consideration all provisions of this Lease to be determined by mutual agreement of the Parties as set forth in Paragraph 4 below.

4. *Determination of Rent.* In any case where the rent to be paid by Tenant is to be at the "then prevailing rate" ("Rental Rate"), the Rental Rate is determined as follows:

The Parties shall have thirty (30) days after Landlord receives the Option Notice in which to agree on monthly rent during the Extended Term ("Extended Term"). If the Parties agree on the Extended Term Rent during that period, they shall immediately execute an amendment to this lease stating the minimum monthly rent. If the Parties are unable to agree on the Extended Term Rent within that period, each party shall appoint one real estate appraiser who is a member of the American Institute of Real Estate Appraisers to act as arbitrators. The two real estate appraisers so appointed shall then appoint a third real estate appraiser who is also a member of the Institute. When all three have been appointed, they shall then appraise the Premises and determine a rental value for the use to which Tenant is then utilizing the Premises. The appraisal and determination shall be made within fifteen (15) days prior to expiration of the Term and in writing and signed by the arbitrators in duplicate. Each party to this Lease shall pay the charges of the arbitrators appointed by him and the expenses incurred by such arbitrator. The charges and expenses of the third arbitrator shall be paid by the Parties in equal shares. The Parties will be bound by the decision of the appraisers. If at least two of the three arbitrators appointed do not agree on a rental figure on or before the ___th day prior to the expiration of the Term or Extended Term, the reasonable Rental Rate shall be determined by computing the average of the reasonable rental figure determined by each arbitrator.

If the Parties fail to mutually agree on an Extended Term Rate and if either or both fail to appoint an appraiser, or if the two appraisers appointed fail to appoint a third appraiser, the reasonable Rental Rate of the Premises shall be determined by the _____ Court of the State of _____ for the County of _____ _____ in a declaratory relief or other action brought therein for that purpose. In any such action, each party shall bear his own attorney's fees and costs and each will be bound by the Rental Rate as determined by the judgment of the Court.

5. *Rent.* Tenant shall pay to Landlord as rent for the Premises the annual sum of _____ ($_____), payable in equal monthly installments of _____ ($_____) per month[1] ("Rent") in advance on the 1st day of the Term of this Lease and on the 1st day of each calendar month thereafter during the Term. If the 1st day of the Term is not the 1st day of the month, the Rent for the portion of the Term occurring in the first and last calendar months of the Term shall be appropriately prorated. All installments of rent shall be paid at the office of Landlord, or at such other place as may be designated in writing from time to time by Landlord, in lawful money of the United States. The Rent shall be subject to adjustment as provided in Paragraph ___ in this Lease, or other covenants and conditions set forth in this Lease.

6. *Use.* The Premises may be used for any lawful purpose. No use shall be made or permitted to be made of the Premises, nor acts done in or about the Premises, which will in any way conflict with any law, ordinance, rule, or regulation affecting the occupancy or use of the Premises which are or may hereafter be enacted or promulgated by any public authority. Tenant shall not sell, or permit to be kept, used, or sold in or about the Premises any article which may be prohibited by the standard form of fire insurance policy. Tenant shall not commit, or suffer to be committed, any waste upon the Premises, or any public or private nuisance, or other act or thing which may disturb the quiet enjoyment of any other tenant in the Building. Tenant shall not to connect with electric wires or water or other pipes any apparatus, machinery, or device without the consent of Landlord, except that Tenant may install the usual office machines and equipment, such as electric typewriters, adding machines, teletypewriters, and similar equipment.

7. *Assignment and Subletting.* Tenant may assign, mortgage, or pledge this Lease, or any interest therein, or sublet the Premises or any part thereof, or any right or privilege appurtenant thereto. Upon any assignment of the Premises, Tenant shall not be relieved of further obligation under this Lease for the portion of the Premises assigned without the consent of Landlord, which consent shall not unreasonably be withheld.

8. *Repairs.* Throughout Tenant's occupancy, Tenant shall use the Premises in a reasonable manner and shall be responsible for the repair of any damage caused by the misuse or negligence of Tenant, its employees or agents, (except that Tenant shall not be liable or responsible for loss or damage ordinarily covered by fire and/or extended coverage insurance). Aside only from damage named in this Lease to be repaired by Tenant, the Premises and the fixtures and equipment thereof (other than Tenant's trade fixtures) and those portions of the

---

1. Why is this formulation used? Why give rent in annual and monthly amounts? In commercial lease negotiations, brokers and other real estate professionals quote rates in terms of annual square foot rents. This is useful for business purposes but does not help those that must pay the monthly rent. The dual format is used to address both audiences in this Lease.

Building outside the Premises but affecting the Tenant's use and enjoyment of the premises, shall be kept in good repair by and at the expense of Landlord, including the repair of damage occasioned by action of the elements or accident or by matter ordinarily covered by fire and extended coverage insurance. Compliance with all requirements made by any public authority or insurance rating body with respect to the Premises shall be the responsibility of the Landlord, with the exception only of any requirement having to do with actions of Tenant as distinguished from physical aspects of the Premises.

At the termination of this lease by the expiration of time or otherwise, Tenant shall surrender the Premises to Landlord in as good condition as when received by Tenant from Landlord, reasonable wear, tear, and casualty excepted. Tenant shall pay for all damage to the Building, as well as all damage to tenants or occupants of the Building, caused by Tenant's misuse or neglect of the Premises or the appurtenances to the Premises.

9. *Alterations.* Tenant may make any alteration, modification, or improvement ("Alterations") in and to the Premises not affecting structural portions of the Building, without Landlord's consent, which when viewed as a whole does not adversely affect the fair market value of the premises. As to all Alterations made by Tenant to the premises, Tenant shall use its best efforts to minimize the effect of any such remodeling on the operations of the Building and the rights of other tenants with respect to their respective space in the Building, and all such Alterations shall be at the sole cost and expense of Tenant, and all of same will be of a standard of construction and finish comparable to that now existing and will in no way, without the consent of Landlord, affect the structural integrity of the Building. For purposes of this paragraph, the reference to "Structural Portions" shall mean the roof, exterior walls, foundation, and weight-bearing walls or other supporting members. Improvements made at any time on the Premises during the Terms of this Lease shall be and remain the property of Tenant during the Term of the Lease. Tenant shall not have the right upon expiration of the Term of the Lease or other termination of this Lease to remove Tenant's Alterations other than Tenant's movable furniture, business machines, and vault doors, and trade fixtures purchased or installed at Tenant's expense. Any damage to the Premises caused by the removal of such machines or trade fixtures shall be repaired by Tenant at its sole expense.

10. *Destruction.* If the Premises or the Building shall be destroyed by fire or other cause, or be so damaged that they are untenantable and cannot be rendered tenantable within one hundred and twenty (120) days from the date of such destruction or damage ("Damage Date"), this Lease may be terminated by Tenant by written notice. Within forty-five (45) days from Damage Date, Landlord shall give written notice to Tenant as to whether or not the premises will be rendered tenantable within one hundred twenty (120) days from the Damage Date. In the event this Lease is not terminated, Landlord shall with due diligence render Premises tenantable, and a proportionate reduction shall be made

in the Rent corresponding to the time during which and to the portion of the Premises of which Tenant shall be deprived of possession.

11. *Services.* Landlord shall furnish the Premises with services generally provided for first-class office buildings, which services shall include the following:

During reasonable and usual business hours and subject to the regulations of the Building, Landlord shall furnish the Premises with a reasonable amount of water and electricity suitable for the intended use of the Premises, daily janitor service (except on Sundays and public holidays), window washing with reasonable frequency, replacement of fluorescent tubes and light bulbs, toilet room supplies, and elevator service consisting either of non-attended automatic elevators or elevators with attendants at the option of Landlord. Such heat and air-conditioning as may be required for the comfortable occupation of the Premises will be provided during the hours of 8:00 a.m. to 6:00 p.m. daily except Saturdays, Sundays and public holidays. During other hours, Landlord shall provide reasonable heat and air-conditioning upon twenty-four (24) hours notice by Tenant to Landlord, and Tenant, upon presentation of a bill, shall pay Landlord for such service on an hourly basis at the then prevailing rate as agreed upon by Landlord and Tenant.

12. *Insurance.* Tenant shall maintain in full force during the Term of the Lease, at its own expense, a policy or policies of comprehensive liability insurance, including property damage coverage, with respect to any liability for injury to persons or property or death of persons occurring in or about the Premises. Such liability coverage shall be issued by an insurer(s) and in a form reasonably satisfactory to Landlord and shall name Landlord as an additional insured.

13. *Notices.* As an alternative to personal service, all notices which Landlord or Tenant may be required, or may desire, to serve on the other may be served, by mailing the notice, postage prepaid, addressed to Landlord at its office located at _____, and to Tenant at _____, or addressed to such other address or addresses as either Landlord or Tenant may from time to time designate to the other in writing.

14. *Insolvency or Receivership.* Tenant shall be in breach of this Lease if one of the following occurs: (i) the appointment of a receiver to take possession of all, or substantially all, of the assets of Tenant or (ii) a general assignment by Tenant for the benefit of creditors, or (iii) any action taken or suffered by Tenant under any insolvency or bankruptcy act. However, that so long as Tenant continues to pay Rent pursuant to this Lease, this Lease may not be terminated pursuant to this Section.

15. *Default and Re-entry; Right to Cure.*

(a) After notice from Landlord of a breach of this Lease by Tenant, Tenant shall have a period of thirty (30) days in which to cure any breach which is curable by the payment of money, and shall have a reasonable period of time not less than sixty (60) days after notice to cure any other breach of this Lease. In the event of any breach of this

Lease by Tenant not cured within the above time periods, or if Tenant vacates or abandons the Premises for a period of more than sixty (60) days, then Landlord, besides other rights or remedies it may have, shall have the immediate right of re-entry and may remove all persons and property from the Premises and may store such property at the cost of and for the account and risk of Tenant. Should Landlord elect to reenter, or should Landlord take possession pursuant to legal proceedings or pursuant to any notice provided by law, it may either terminate this Lease or it may from time to time, without terminating this Lease, re-let the Premises, or any part thereof, for such Term or terms (which may be for a term extending beyond the Term of this Lease) and at a rental and upon other terms and conditions as Landlord, in its sole discretion, may deem advisable with the right to make alterations and repairs to the Premises. Rents received by Landlord from such re-letting shall be applied as follows: first, to the payment of any costs and expenses of such re-letting, including a reasonable attorney's fee and any real estate commission actually paid, and any costs and expenses of such alterations and repairs; second, to the payment of rent due and unpaid under this Lease and the residue, if any, shall be held by Landlord and applied in payment of future rent or other obligations as the same may become due and payable hereunder. If rent received from such re-letting during any month be less than that to be paid during that month by Tenant, Tenant shall pay any deficiency to Landlord, and a deficiency shall be calculated and paid monthly. No such re-entry or taking possession of Premises by Landlord shall be construed as an election on its part to terminate this Lease unless a written notice of such intention is given to Tenant or unless the termination thereof be decreed by a court of competent jurisdiction.

(b) Notwithstanding any such re-letting without termination, Landlord may at any time thereafter elect to terminate this Lease for previous breach. Should Landlord at any time terminate this Lease for any breach, interest shall be allowed upon unpaid rent at 10% per annum or the maximum rate permitted by law, whichever is greater. Any proof by Tenant as to the amount of rental loss that could be reasonably avoided, shall be made in the following manner:

(c) Landlord and Tenant shall each select a licensed real estate broker in the business of renting property of the same type and use as the leased Premises and in the same geographic vicinity. The two real estate brokers shall select a third licensed real estate broker and the three licensed real estate brokers shall determine the amount of the rental loss that could be reasonably avoided for the balance of the Term of this Lease after the time of award. The decision of the majority of the licensed real estate brokers shall be final and binding upon the Parties.

16. *Waiver.* The waiver by Landlord or Tenant of any breach of any term, covenant, or condition ("Condition") contained in this Lease shall not be deemed to be a waiver of Conditions of any subsequent breach of the same or any other term, covenant, or condition herein contained. The acceptance of Rent by Landlord shall not be deemed to be a waiver

of any preceding breach by Tenant of any Condition of this Lease, other than the failure of Tenant to pay the particular rental so accepted, regardless of Landlord's knowledge of the preceding breach at the time of acceptance of Rent.

17. *Removal of Property.* Whenever Landlord removes any property of Tenant ("Property") from the Premises and stores the Property elsewhere for the account, and at the expense and risk of Tenant, as provided in Paragraph 15 hereof, and if Tenant fails to pay the cost of storing any Property after it has been stored for a period of ninety (90) days or more, Landlord may sell any or all such property at public or private sale, in a manner and at times and places as Landlord in its sole discretion, may deem proper, without notice to Tenant, for the payment of any part of charges or the removal of any Property, Landlord shall apply the proceeds of the sale:

First, to the cost and expenses of the sale, including reasonable attorney's fees actually incurred; second, to the payment of the cost of or charges for storing any Property; third, to the payment of any other sums of money which may then or thereafter be due to Landlord from Tenant under any of the terms of this Lease; and fourth, the balance, if any, to Tenant.

18. *Costs of Suit.* If Tenant or Landlord bring any action for any relief against the other, declaratory or otherwise, arising out of this Lease, including any suit by Landlord for the recovery of Rent or possession of the Premises, the losing party shall pay the successful party a reasonable sum for attorneys' fees in such suit, and such attorneys' fees shall be deemed to have accrued on the commencement of the action and shall be paid whether or not the action is prosecuted to judgment.

19. *Tax on Tenant's Property.* Tenant shall be liable for all taxes levied against any personal property or trade fixtures placed by Tenant in or about the Premises ("Taxes"). If any Taxes are levied against Landlord or Landlord's property, and if Landlord pays the Taxes, which Landlord shall have the right to do regardless of the validity of such levy, or if the assessed value of Landlord's premises is increased by the inclusion of a value placed upon such personal property or trade fixtures of Tenant, and if Landlord pays the taxes based upon increased assessments which Landlord shall have the right to do regardless of the validity, Tenant shall, upon demand, repay to Landlord the taxes levied against Landlord, or the proportion of the taxes resulting from the increase in the assessment.

20. *Liens.* Tenant shall keep the Premises and building, and the property on which the Premises are situated, free from any liens arising out of any work performed, materials furnished, or obligations incurred by Tenant.

21. *Rental Adjustment.*

(a) If the Operating Expenses for the calendar year first following the Base Year, or for any subsequent calendar year, are higher than the Operating Expenses for the Base Year, then Tenant shall pay additional Rental in the first following calendar year and continuing as adjusted for each subsequent calendar year the Tenant's share of such increase.

(b) Landlord shall furnish Tenant with written notice as to any Rental adjustment, detailing any increases in Operating Expenses, as soon as practicable after the commencement of each calendar year. The payment of any additional rent shall then be made as follows:

(i) On the day for payment of Rent under Paragraph 3 first following the receipt of such Rent adjustment notice, Tenant shall pay a sum equal to the additional rent for the entire prior calendar year for which the additional rent is due (less a credit for prepayments, if any) plus one-twelfth (1/12) of such additional annual rent for each month of the then current calendar year, and each succeeding month Tenant shall continue to pay one-twelfth (1/12th) of such additional annual rent until a new rent adjustment notice, if any, is furnished to Tenant as provided above.

(ii) For the purposes of subparagraph 21(b)(i):

"Base Year" means the calendar year in which this Lease Term commenced, which is the calendar year _____ _____. "Operating Expenses" means the annual maintenance, repair and operating charges (including, but not limited to repairs, maintenance, utility charges, cleaning and janitorial services, servicing of equipment, and license, permit, and inspection fees), real estate taxes and assessments, and insurance premiums attributable to the Building with Operating Expenses for the Base Year to be calculated by projection as if the building were substantially completed and 95% occupied for the entire calendar year if such improvements were not in fact substantially completed prior to commencement of the Base Year.

"Tenant's Share" means the ratio borne by the number of square feet in the Premises to the total number of rentable square feet in the entire Building (exclusive of the parking area), which ratio is agreed to be ___%, based on _____ square foot of leased space, to be increased for changes in amount of leased space.

(c) As a precondition to the payment of any additional rent, Landlord shall in the case of additional Rent based on tax increases, furnish Tenant with certified copies of the receipted tax bills for the Base Year and any subsequent year for which the Landlord claims a contribution; and in the case of additional Rent based on increased operating expenses of the Building, furnish the Tenant with a certificate by a certified public accountant itemizing and substantiating increases in operating costs computed in accordance with standard accounting principles and showing in reasonable detail the nature of the manner of computing the costs.

(d) In no event will the total of such additional Rent in any one lease year exceed a sum equal to ___% of the initial fixed annual Rent called for by this Lease.

22. *Subordination.* This Lease shall be subject and subordinate to any first mortgage, first deed of trust, or like encumbrance ("Encumbrances") hereafter placed upon Premises by Landlord or Owner, or their successors in interest, to secure the payment of moneys loaned, interest thereon, and other obligations. However, this Lease shall not be made subject and subordinate to Encumbrances unless Landlord procures from such mortgagee, trustee, or secured party holding an interest to which this Lease is to be subject and subordinated (and deliver to Tenant) an agreement of such party that so long as Tenant is not in default under this Lease so as to permit the termination of it pursuant to its terms, this Lease shall not be terminated nor Tenant's possession under this Lease be disturbed by such party or any successor in interest. The agreement shall be delivered to Tenant in recordable form. Tenant shall execute and deliver, upon demand of Landlord or Owner, any instruments desired by Landlord or Owner subordinating in the manner requested by Landlord or Owner this Lease to Encumbrances.

23. *Subrogation.* Each party waives its legal right of recovery against the other for any insured losses, provided this is permitted by its insurance policies, or by endorsement which it may obtain at no extra cost and without invalidation of the policies.

24. *Condemnation.* Should the whole or any part of the Premises be condemned and taken by any competent authority for any public or quasi-public use or purpose, all awards payable on account of such condemnation and taking shall be payable to Landlord and Tenant in proportion to the value of their respective interests in the Premises. The value of Tenant's interest shall be determined as if the Lease continued for the entire Term, including all extensions. If the whole of the Premises shall be so condemned and taken, then this Lease shall terminate. If a part only of the Premises is condemned and taken and the remaining portion is not suitable in Tenant's opinion for the purposes to which Tenant had leased Premises, Tenant shall have the right to terminate this Lease. If by such condemnation and taking only a part of the Premises is taken and the remaining part is suitable for the purposes for which Tenant has leased Premises, this Lease shall continue, but the Rent shall be reduced in an amount proportionate to the value of the portion taken as it related to the total value of the Premises.

25. *Holding Over.* If Tenant holds over after the Term of the Lease, with or without the express or implied consent of Landlord, such tenancy shall be from month to month only, and not a renewal or an

extension for any further term. In such case Rent shall be payable in the amount and at the time specified in Paragraphs 3 and 21, and such month to month tenancy shall be subject to every other term, covenant, and agreement contained in this Lease.

26. *Entry and Inspection.* Tenant will permit Landlord and its agents to enter into the Premises at all reasonable times for the purpose of inspecting the Premises, or for the purpose of protecting the interest of Landlord or the Owner, or to post notices of non-responsibility, or to make alterations or additions to the Premises or to any other portion of the Building, including the erection of scaffolding, props or other mechanical devices, or to provide any service provided by Landlord to Tenant under this Lease, including window cleaning and janitor service.

27. *Successors and Assigns.* Subject to the provisions of this Lease relating to assignment, mortgaging, pledging, and subletting, this Lease is intended to and does bind the heirs, executors, administrators, successors, and assigns of any of the Parties.

28. *Time.* Time is of the essence of this Lease.

IN WITNESS WHEREOF, Landlord and Tenant have executed these presents the day and year first above written.

[proper signature blocks]

EXHIBIT "A"

Suite Improvements

Landlord agrees to furnish and install, at its own cost and expense, suite improvements as follows:

(1) Up to a total of _____ lineal feet non-rated and ___ lineal feet rated of Building Standard office partitions (measured through door openings).

(2) Up to a total of ___ Building Standard interior doors and ___ Building Standard corridor entrance doors. Entrance doors shall have locksets and interior doors shall have latchsets.

(3) Up to a total of ___ duplex electrical outlets to be located in partitions wherever possible and ___ duplex electrical outlets to be located in the floor and ___ light switches.

(4) Up to a total of ___ telephone outlets to be located in partitions wherever possible and ___ floor-mounted telephone outlets.

(5) Building Standard carpeting.

(6) Building Standard exterior window drapes.

(7) Paint all perimeter wall surfaces and interior walls, specified herein, in colors to be selected by Tenant from Building Standard paints and colors.

(8) _____ square feet of ceiling grid.

(9) Heating, ventilation, and air conditioning system.

(10) ___ light fixtures.

Any additional partitioning, doors, telephone or electrical outlets, or other interior improvements, alterations, additions, or other electrical, or other suite improvements necessary to meet the occupancy requirements of Tenant shall be furnished and installed in the Premises during regular working hours and under the control of Landlord's contractor, at the expense of Tenant and Tenant shall be liable for all Taxes levied against such suite improvements in the manner set forth in Paragraph 20.

Notwithstanding the provisions of Paragraph 2 of this lease, the commencement of the Term of this Lease shall not be delayed because of (1) construction to be furnished by Landlord hereunder has not been completed if such Landlord's construction has been delayed at the instruction of Tenant, or (2) such Landlord's construction has been appropriately delayed by Tenant's trade fixtures, equipment or improvements or (3) additional improvements ordered by Tenant subsequent to the execution of this Lease.

Landlord's obligation to pay for Tenant improvements shall not exceed a total cost of $_____ per square foot of lease space. The excess of such Tenant improvement allowance over the actual Tenant improvement cost incurred by Landlord shall be credited to Tenant's first month's Rent under this Lease.

*

Appendix 4
SETTLEMENT AGREEMENT

This appendix features three versions of a settlement agreement relating to a lease dispute to which California law applies.[1] The first is a copy of a settlement agreement, drafted by the litigator handling the matter for the Landlord. Note the use of archaic forms and use of contractual terms with less than precision. The second version is a black-lined revision of the document, correcting and improving it as well as making it generic for use as an exemplar. The third version is a "clean" copy of the revised settlement agreement.

---

1. The *cognovit* or "confession of judgment" and waiver of California Civil Code Section 1542 provisions are the specific sections that implicate California law. Other jurisdictions may have similar provisions; others may not permit waivers or *cognovit* arrangements.

SETTLEMENT AGREEMENT AND MUTUAL RELEASE

This SETTLEMENT AGREEMENT AND MUTUAL RELEASE ("Agreement") is entered into by and between _____ ("_____"),on the one hand, and _____ ("_____"), on the other hand, and is intended to extinguish the claims, obligations, disputes and differences hereinafter described.

W I T N E S S E T H:

WHEREAS, on or about December 20, 1991, _____'s predecessor in interest, _____ and _____, entered into an Office Lease (the "Lease"), for certain premises located at __ West Broadway, Suite _____, San Diego, California (the "Premises");

WHEREAS, _____ contends that _____ is in breach of the Lease for failure to pay all rent and additional rent due and as of December 8, 200_ is in arrears in the sum of $_____;

WHEREAS, on _____, _____ served _____ with a Three–Day Notice to Pay Rent or Quit;

WHEREAS, _____ failed to pay the rent demanded within the three-day notice period, and has failed to deliver possession of the Premises to _____;

WHEREAS, as a result of the foregoing breaches, _____ is entitled to commence an unlawful detainer action and/or breach of lease action against _____;

WHEREAS, _____ and _____wish to avoid the disruption, inconvenience, uncertainty and costs associated with further processing or litigation of the above disputes and desire to amicably resolve the above disputes;

NOW, THEREFORE, for mutual consideration receipt of which is hereby acknowledged (including the terms, provisions, conditions, agreements, payments, releases, warranties and representations herein contained), _____ and _____ agree as follows:

1. Vacation of Premises. On or before December __, 200_, _____ shall vacate the Premises and deliver possession of the Premises to _____ or its agent.

2. Payment of $ _____ by _____ to _____. _____ shall pay to _____ the total sum of $_____ [with/without] interest, in the following manner:

(a) $_____ per month for the period of _____;

201

(b) thereafter, and commencing on _____, 200_, $_____ per month for the period of _____ years;

(c) thereafter, and commencing on _____, 200_, $_____ per month for the period of _____ year, with an additional $_____ to be paid at or before the end of that year.

3. <u>Confession of Judgment by _____</u>. Concurrently with the execution of this Agreement, _____ shall execute, or cause to be executed, and/or approve and deliver to _____ all documents (described below) necessary to enable _____ to obtain a judgment against _____ by a confession of judgment, pursuant to California Code of Civil Procedure Section 1132 *et seq.*, in favor of _____, in the amount of $_____ plus _____ percent interest accruing from _____, less any amounts paid pursuant to paragraph 2 of this Agreement. Said documents include "Defendant's Statement re Confession of Judgment", "Attorney's Declaration in Support of Statement Confessing Judgment", "Judgment by Confession" and "Judgment", copies of which are attached hereto as Exhibits "A", "B", "C" and "D", respectively. The originals of such documents, when executed and/or approved (by the execution of this Agreement) by or on behalf of _____ and delivered to _____, shall be held in trust by _____, or its counsel, and will not be filed or entered with the Court except as set forth in paragraph 4, below.

4. <u>Default.</u> In the event _____ fails to timely vacate the Premises, as described in paragraph 1, above, or fails to make one or more payments described in paragraph 2, above, in full and when due, _____ shall be entitled to file and have entered the above-mentioned Judgment by Confession and related documents in any court of competent jurisdiction, and to execute thereon or engage in other legitimate post-judgment activities in an effort to obtain possession of the Premises and/or be paid the amounts owed thereunder by _____ to _____ provided, however, that such Judgment by Confession and/or Judgment may be filed only after the 5th day from the mailing of the notice of such default via the United States Post Office, certified mail to:

[INSERT ADDRESS]

Such default may be cured by payment of all sums then owing, said sums to be paid <u>only</u> by cash or cashier's check made payable to _____ prior to the expiration of the above notice period. If the required funds are not received by the end of business on the 5th day after the above mailing of notice, said Judgment by Confession and/or Judgment may be entered forthwith and the concomitant post-judgment remedies may be pursued by _____. In such event, _____ hereby expressly waives any right he may have to a hearing prior to the entry of said Judgment by Confession and/or Judgment. _____ also agrees that Exhibits "A", "B", "C" and "D" may be modified after execution/approval without further consent by _____, before filing with the Court, to the extent necessary for _____ to identify its representative in the upper left-hand corner of the front page of each Exhibit.

5. <u>Mutual Release.</u> Except as to the obligations created by this Agreement, the parties hereby release and forever discharge each other and their respective successors, heirs, spouses, assigns, employees, shareholders, officers, directors, agents, attorneys, insurance carriers, corporations, and their subsidiaries, divisions, or affiliated corporations, organizations or entities, whether previously or hereinafter affiliated in any manner, jointly and severally, from any and all claims, demands, causes of action, obligations, damages, attorneys' fees, costs and liabilities of any nature whatsoever, whether or not now known, suspected or claimed, which the parties ever had, now have or may claim to have as of the date of this Agreement which arise out of, or are connected to, or are related, in any fashion, to the Lease and the Premises.

6. <u>Later Discovered Facts.</u> The parties hereto acknowledge that they may hereafter discover facts different from or in addition to those they now know or believe to be true with respect to the claims, demands, causes of action, obligations and liabilities that are the subject of the releases set forth in paragraph 5, above, and the parties expressly agree to assume the risk of the possible discovery of additional or different facts, and agree that this Agreement shall be and remain effective in all respects regardless of such additional or different facts.

7. <u>Waiver of Civil Code Section 1542.</u> Except as provided by this Agreement, and with respect only to the claims that are the subject of the releases set forth in paragraph 5, the parties hereto expressly waive and relinquish all rights and benefits they may have under Section 1542 of the Civil Code of the State of California. Civil Code, Section 1542 reads as follows:

"§ 1542 [<u>CERTAIN CLAIMS NOT AFFECTED BY GENERAL RELEASE.</u>] A GENERAL RELEASE DOES NOT EXTEND TO CLAIMS WHICH THE CREDITOR DOES NOT KNOW OR SUSPECT TO EXIST IN HIS FAVOR AT THE TIME OF EXECUTING THE RELEASE, WHICH IF KNOWN BY HIM MUST HAVE MATERIALLY AFFECTED HIS SETTLEMENT WITH THE DEBTOR."

8. <u>Representations and Warranties.</u> The parties represent and warrant to and agree with each other as follows:

(a) This Agreement in all respects has been voluntarily and knowingly executed by the parties hereto.

(b) Each party has had an opportunity to seek independent legal advice from attorneys of its choice with respect to the advisability of executing this Agreement.

(c) All parties hereto have made such investigation of the facts pertaining to this Agreement as they deem necessary.

(d) The terms of this Agreement are contractual and are the result of negotiation between the parties.

(e) This Agreement has been carefully read by each of the parties and the contents hereof are known and understood by each of the parties.

(f) Each party covenants and agrees not to bring any action, claim, suit or proceeding against any party hereto, directly or indirectly, regarding or relating to the matters released hereby, and further covenants and agrees that this Agreement is a bar to any such claim, action, suit or proceeding except as provided herein.

9. Covenant Re Assignment. The parties hereto, and each of them, represent and warrant to each other that each is the sole and lawful owner of all right, title and interest in and to every claim and other matter which each purports to release herein, and that they have not heretofore assigned or transferred, or purported to assign or transfer, to any person, firm, association, corporation or other entity, any right, title or interest in any such claim or other matter. In the event that such representation is false, any such claim or matter is asserted against any party hereto (and/or the successor of such party, including without limitation, any of the parties released hereby) by any party or entity who is the assignee or transferee of such claim or matter, then the party hereto who assigned or transferred such claim or matter shall fully indemnify, defend and hold harmless the party against whom such claim or matter is asserted (and its successors, including without limitation, any of the parties released hereby) from and against such claim or matter and from all actual costs, fees, expenses, liabilities, and damages which that party (and its successors, including without limitation, any of the parties released hereby) incurs as a result of the assertion of such claim or matter.

10. Attorneys' Fees. Except as otherwise provided by this Agreement, the parties hereto agree to bear their own costs and attorneys' fees in connection with the Lease, the Premises, the Three–Day Notice and the preparation and negotiation of this Agreement. In the event that any action, suit or other proceeding is instituted to remedy, prevent or obtain relief from a breach of this Agreement, arising out of a breach of this Agreement, or pertaining to a declaration of rights under this Agreement, the prevailing party shall recover all of such party's attorneys' fees incurred in each and every such action, suit or other proceeding, including any and all appeals or petitions therefrom. Such attorneys' fees shall be deemed to mean the full and actual costs of any legal services actually performed in connection with the matters involved, calculated on the basis of the usual fee charged by the attorneys performing such services, and shall not be limited to "reasonable attorneys' fees" as defined in any statute or rule of court.

11. Agreement Binding on Successors. This Agreement, and all the terms and provisions hereof, shall be binding upon and shall inure to the benefit of the parties and their respective heirs, legal representatives, successors and assigns.

12. Governing Law. This Agreement shall be construed in accordance with and be governed by the laws of the State of California.

13. <u>Severability</u>. Should any portion, word, clause, phrase, sentence or paragraph of this Agreement be declared void or unenforceable, such portion shall be considered independent and severable from the remainder, the validity of which shall remain unaffected.

14. <u>Gender.</u> Whenever required by the context, as used in this Agreement, the singular number shall include the plural, and the masculine gender shall include the feminine and the neuter and vice versa.

15. <u>Counterparts.</u> This Agreement may be executed in multiple counterparts, each of which shall be considered an original but all of which shall constitute one agreement.

16. <u>Entire Agreement.</u> This Agreement constitutes the entire agreement between _____ and _____ and supersedes any and all other agreements, understandings, negotiations, or discussions, either oral or in writing, express or implied, relative to the matters which are the subject of this Agreement. The parties hereto acknowledge that no representations, inducements, promises, agreements or warranties, oral or otherwise, have been made by any party hereto, or anyone acting on their behalf, which are not embodied in this Agreement, that they have not executed this Agreement in reliance on any such representation, inducement, promise, agreement or warranty, and that no representation, inducement, promise, agreement or warranty not contained in this Agreement including, but not limited to, any purported supplements, modifications, waivers or terminations of this Agreement shall be valid or binding unless executed in writing by all of the parties.

17. <u>No Implied Waiver.</u> Failure to insist on compliance with any term, covenant or condition contained in this Agreement shall not be deemed a waiver of that term, covenant or condition, nor shall any waiver or relinquishment of any right or power contained in this Agreement at any one time or more times be deemed a waiver or relinquishment of any right or power at any other time or times.

18. <u>Construction.</u> The parties to this Agreement, and each of them, acknowledge (i) this Agreement and its reduction to final written form is the result of extensive good faith negotiations between the parties through their respective counsel, (ii) said counsel have carefully reviewed and examined this Agreement before execution by said parties, or any of them, and (iii) any statute or rule of construction that ambiguities are to be resolved against the drafting party shall not be employed in the interpretation of this Agreement.

IN WITNESS WHEREOF, the undersigned have executed this Agreement on the dates set forth hereinafter.

DATED: December ___, 20___

                 By: _____

                 Its: _____

DATED: December ___, 20___

                 By: _____

SETTLEMENT AGREEMENT AND MUTUAL RELEASE

This SETTLEMENT AGREEMENT AND MUTUAL RELEASE (the "Agreement") is entered into by and between _____ (" ~~_____~~ "), ~~on the one hand,~~ Landlord") and _____ (" _____ Tenant"), on the other hand, and is intended to extinguish the claims, obligations, disputes and differences ~~hereinafter described.~~

~~W I T N E S S E T H:~~

~~WHEREAS, on or about December 20, 1991,~~ _____ ~~'s predecessor in interest,~~ _____ ~~and~~ _____, described below.

R E C I T A L S:

A. On or about _____, ____, Landlord and Tenant entered into an Office Lease (the "Lease"), for certain premises located at ~~West Broadway~~ _____, ~~Suite~~ _____ _____ ~~%, San Diego, California~~ _____ (the "Premises") ~~;~~ .

~~WHEREAS,~~ _____ ~~contends that~~ _____ B. Tenant is in breach of the Lease for failure to pay all rent and additional rent due and as of ~~December 8~~ _____, ~~200~~ ____ is in arrears in the sum of $_____ ~~;~~ .

~~WHEREAS, o~~C. On _____, _____ ~~Landlord~~ served _____ ~~Tenant~~ with a Three–Day Notice to Pay Rent or Quit ~~;~~ .

~~WHEREAS,~~ _____ D. Tenant failed to pay the rent demanded within the three-day notice period, and has failed to deliver possession of the Premises to _____ ~~;~~ Landlord.

~~WHEREAS, as~~E. As a result ~~of the foregoing breaches,~~ _____, Landlord is entitled to commence an unlawful detainer action and/or breach of lease action against _____ ~~;~~ Tenant.

~~WHEREAS,~~ _____ F. Landlord and _____ ~~wish~~Tenant wish to avoid the ~~disruption,~~ inconvenience, uncertainty, and costs ~~associated with further processing or~~of litigation ~~of the above disputes~~ and desire to amicably resolve ~~the above disputes;~~this matter.

A G R E E M E N T

~~NOW, THEREFORE, for~~For mutual consideration, receipt of which is hereby acknowledged ~~(including the terms, provisions, conditions, agreements, payments, releases, warranties and representations herein contained),~~ _____ ~~and~~ _____ ~~agree as follows.~~, Landlord and Tenant agree that the recitals above are true in all respects and further agree:

1. **Vacation of Premises.** On or before ~~December~~ ____, ~~200~~ _____, _____ ____, Tenant shall vacate the Premises and deliver possession of the Premises to _____ Landlord or its agent.

2. Payment of $_____ by _____Tenant to _____Landlord.- _____Tenant shall pay to _____Landlord the total sum of $_____ [with/without] interest [What rate? Compound or not?], in the following manner:

(a) $_____ per month for the period of _____;

(b) thereafter, and commencing on _____, 200-____, $_____ per month for the period of _____ years;

(c) thereafter, and commencing on _____, 200-____, $_____ per month for the period of _____ year, with an additional $_____ to be paid at or before the end of that year.

3. Confession of Judgment by _____Tenant. Concurrently with the execution of this Agreement, _____Tenant shall execute, or cause to be executed, and/or approve and deliver to _____Landlord all the documents (described below) necessary to enable _____Landlord to obtain a judgment against _____Tenant by a confession of judgment, pursuant to California Code of Civil Procedure Section 1132 et seq., in favor of _____, in the amount of $_____ plus _____ percent interest accruing from _____, less any amounts paid pursuant to paragraph 2 of this Agreement. SaidThose documents include "Defendant's Statement re Confession of Judgment", "Attorney's Declaration in Support of Statement Confessing Judgment", "Judgment by Confession," and "Judgment", copies of which are attached hereto as Exhibits "A", "B", "C" and "D", respectivelyexhibits. The originals of such documents, when executed and/or approved (by the execution of this Agreement) by or on behalf of _____by Tenant and delivered to _____Landlord, shall be held in trust by _____Landlord, or its counsel, and willmay not be filed or entered with the Ccourt except as set forth in paragraph 4, below.

4. Default. In the event _____Tenant fails to timely vacate the Premises, as described in paragraph 1, above, or fails to make oneany or moref the payments described in paragraph 2, above, in full and when due, _____ shall be entitled to file and have entered the above-mentioned Judgment by Confession and related documents in any court of competent jurisdiction, and to execute thereon or engage in other legitimate post-judgment activities in an effort to obtain possession of the Premises and/or be paid the amounts owed thereunder by _____ to _____ provided, however, that such Judgment by Confession and/or Judgment may be filed only after the 5th day from theLandlord may provide Tenant with notice of default under this Agreement by mailing of the notice of such default via the United States Post Office, certified mail to:

[INSERT ADDRESS]

SuchThe default may only be cured by payment of all sums then owing, said sums to be paid only by cash or cashier's check made payable to _____Landlord prior to the expiration of the above5–day notice period. If Landlord does not receive the required funds are not received by ~~the end of business~~5:00 p.m. on the 5th day after the ~~above~~ mailing of the notice of default, ~~said~~Landlord may immediately file and have entered the Judgment by Confession ~~and/or~~and Judgment and Landlord may ~~be entered forthwith and the concomitant~~pursue its post-judgment remedies ~~may be pursued by _____. In such event, _____~~Tenant hereby ~~expressly~~ waives any right ~~he~~it may have to a hearing prior to the entry of ~~said~~the Judgment by Confession ~~and/or~~or Judgment. ~~_____~~Tenant also agrees that ~~Exhibits "A", "B", "C" and "D"~~the exhibits to this Agreement may be modified after ~~execution/approval~~execution of this Agreement without further consent by ~~_____, before filing with the Court, to the extent necessary for _____ to identify its~~Tenant before they are filed with the court to identify Landlord's representative in the upper left-hand corner of the front page of each Exhibit.

5. <u>Mutual Release.</u> Except as to the obligations created by this Agreement, the parties hereby release and forever discharge each other and their respective successors, heirs, spouses, assigns, employees, shareholders, officers, directors, agents, attorneys, insurance carriers, corporations, and their subsidiaries, divisions, or affiliated corporations, organizations or entities, whether previously or hereinafter affiliated in any manner, jointly and severally, from any and all claims, demands, causes of action, obligations, damages, attorneys' fees, costs and liabilities of any nature whatsoever, whether or not now known, suspected or claimed, which the parties ever had, now have or may claim to have as of the date of this Agreement which arise out of, or are connected to, or are related, in any fashion, to the Lease and the Premises (the "Claims").

6. <u>Later Discovered Facts.</u> The parties hereto acknowledge that they may ~~hereafter~~ discover facts in the future that are different from or in addition to those they now know or believe to be true with respect to the ~~claims, demands, causes of action, obligations and liabilities that are the subject of the releases set forth in paragraph 5, above, and the parties expressly agree to assume the risk of the possible discovery of additional or different facts, and~~Claims and the Parties agree that this Agreement shall be ~~and remain~~ effective in all respects regardless of such additional or different facts.

7. <u>Waiver of Civil Code Section 1542.</u> Except as provided by this Agreement, and with respect only to the ~~c~~Claims ~~that are the subject of the releases set forth in paragraph 5~~, the parties hereto expressly waive and relinquish all rights and benefits they may have under Section 1542 of the Civil Code of the State of California~~. Civil Code, Section 1542~~which reads as follows:

"§ 1542 [CERTAIN CLAIMS NOT AFFECTED BY GENERAL RELEASE.] A GENERAL RELEASE DOES NOT EXTEND TO CLAIMS WHICH THE CREDITOR DOES NOT KNOW OR SUSPECT TO EXIST IN HIS FAVOR AT THE TIME OF EXECUTING THE RELEASE, WHICH IF KNOWN BY HIM

MUST HAVE MATERIALLY AFFECTED HIS SETTLEMENT WITH THE DEBTOR."

8. ~~Representations and Warranties~~Fundamental Fairness. The parties ~~represent and warrant to and agree with each other as follows:~~

~~(a)This Agreement in all respects has been voluntarily and knowingly executed by the parties hereto.~~

~~(b)Each party has had an opportunity to seek independent legal advice from attorneys of its choice with respect to the advisability of executing this Agreement.~~

~~(c)All parties hereto have made such investigation of the facts pertaining to this Agreement as they deem necessary.~~

~~(d)The terms of this Agreement are contractual and are the result of negotiation between the parties.~~

~~(e)This~~agree that this Agreement has been ~~carefully read by each of the parties and the contents hereof are known and understood by each of the parties.~~

~~(f)Each party covenants and agrees not to bring any action, claim, suit or proceeding against any party hereto, directly or indirectly, regarding or relating to the matters released hereby, and further covenants and agrees that this Agreement is a bar to any such claim, action, suit or proceeding except as provided herein.~~

~~9.~~Covenant ~~Re~~entered into by each of them voluntarily and with the assistance of counsel after both have read, understood, and negotiated each of its provisions. They further agree that any rule of construction that ambiguities are to be resolved against the drafter shall have no application to this Agreement.

9. No Prior Assignment. The parties hereto, and each of them, represent and warrant to each other that each is the sole and lawful owner of ~~all right, title and interest in and to~~ every ~~c~~Claim ~~and other matter which~~that each purports to release by this Agreement herein, and that they have not ~~heretofore~~previously assigned or transferred,~~ or purported to assign or transfer, to any person, firm, association, corporation or other entity, any right, title or interest in any such claim or other matter~~ any Claim or portion of a Claim to any entity. In the event that ~~such~~the representation and warranty is false, and any such claim ~~or matter~~ is asserted against any party ~~hereto (and/or the successor of such party, including without limitation, any of the parties released hereby) by any party or entity who is the assignee or transferee of such claim or matter~~, then the party ~~hereto~~ who assigned or transferred ~~such c~~the Claim or matter shall ~~fully~~ indemnify, defend, and hold harmless the party against whom such claim or matter is asserted ~~(and its successors, including without limitation, any of the parties released hereby) from and against such claim or matter and from all actual costs, fees, expenses, liabilities, and damages which that party (and its successors, including without limitation, any of the parties released hereby) incurs as a result of the assertion of such claim or matter.~~

10. Attorneys' Fees. ~~Except as otherwise provided by this Agreement, t~~The parties hereto agree to bear their own costs and attorneys' fees in connection with the Lease, the Premises, the Three–Day Notice, and the preparation and negotiation of this Agreement. In the event that any action~~, suit or other proceeding is instituted to remedy, prevent or obtain relief from a breach of this Agreement, arising out of a breach of this Agreement, or pertaining to a declaration of rights under~~ is taken to enforce or interpret this Agreement, the prevailing party shall recover all ~~of such party's~~attorneys' fees involved. Those attorneys' fees ~~incurred in each and every such action, suit or other proceeding, including any and all appeals or petitions therefrom. Such attorneys' fees shall be deemed to mean~~include the full and actual costs of any ~~legal~~ services ~~actually~~ performed in connection with the matters involved, calculated on the basis of the usual fee charged by the attorneys or others performing ~~such~~these services, and shall not be limited to "reasonable attorneys' fees" as defined in any statute or rule of court.

11. Agreement Binding on Successors. ~~This Agreement, and a~~All the terms and provisions ~~hereof,~~of this Agreement shall be binding upon and shall inure to the benefit of the parties and their respective ~~heirs, legal representatives,~~ successors and assigns.

12. Governing Law. This Agreement ~~shall~~will be construed in accordance with and ~~be~~is governed by the laws of the State of ~~California~~_____.

13. Severability. Should any portion~~, word, clause, phrase, sentence or paragraph~~ of this Agreement be declared void or unenforceable, ~~such~~that portion ~~shall~~will be considered independent and severable from the remainder, the validity of which shall remain unaffected~~.~~

~~14. Gender. Whenever required by the context, as used in this Agreement, the singular number shall include the plural, and the masculine gender shall include the feminine and the neuter and vice versa.~~

~~15.~~ provided that this provision shall not be applied so as to defeat the primary intent of the parties: The waiver of the Claims in exchange for delivery of the premises and payments as outlined in paragraphs 1 and 2.

14. Counterparts. This Agreement may be executed in multiple counterparts, each of which shall be considered an original but all of which shall constitute one agreement.

1~~6~~5. Entire Agreement. This Agreement constitutes the entire agreement between _____Landlord and _____Tenant and supersedes any and all other agreements, understandings, negotiations, or discussions, either oral or in writing, express or implied, ~~relative to~~regarding the matters ~~which~~that are the subject of this Agreement. The parties ~~hereto~~ acknowledge (a) that no ~~representations, inducements, promises, agreements~~statements or ~~warranties~~promises, oral or otherwise, have been made ~~by any party hereto, or anyone acting on their behalf,~~ ~~which~~that are not embodied in this Agreement, (b) that they have not executed this Agreement in reliance on any such ~~representation, induce-ment, promise, agreement or warranty, and that no representation, inducement, promise, agreement or warranty~~statement or promise, and (c) that no statement or promise not contained in this Agreement including, ~~but not limited to,~~ any purported supplements, modifications, waivers or terminations of this Agreement shall be valid or binding unless executed in writing by all of the parties.

17. No Implied Waiver. ~~F~~The failure of any party, at any time, to insist on compliance with any term, covenant or condition contained in this Agreement shall not be deemed a waiver of that term, covenant or condition, nor shall any waiver or relinquishment of any right or power ~~contained in this Agreement~~ at any one time ~~or more times~~ be deemed a waiver or relinquishment of any right or power at any other time ~~or times.~~

~~18. Construction. The parties to this Agreement, and each of them, acknowledge (i) this Agreement and its reduction to final written form is the result of extensive good faith negotiations between the parties through their respective counsel, (ii) said counsel have carefully reviewed and examined this Agreement before execution by said parties, or any of them, and (iii) any statute or rule of construction that ambiguities are to be resolved against the drafting party shall not be employed in the interpretation of this Agreement.~~

~~IN WITNESS WHEREOF, the undersigned have executed this Agreement on the dates set forth hereinafter.~~

~~DATED: December ___, 200_~~

By: ~~_____~~

~~_____ Its: _____~~

~~DATED: December ___, 200_~~

~~By:~~

~~:~~

AGREED:

DATED: _____, 20___

By: _____

Its:_____

DATED: _____, 20___

By: _____

SETTLEMENT AGREEMENT AND MUTUAL RELEASE

This SETTLEMENT AGREEMENT AND MUTUAL RELEASE (the "Agreement") is entered into by and between _____ ("Landlord") and _____ ("Tenant"), on the other hand, and is intended to extinguish the claims, obligations, disputes and differences described below.

R E C I T A L S:

A. On or about _____, ____, Landlord and Tenant entered into an Office Lease (the "Lease"), for certain premises located at _____, _____, _____ (the "Premises").

B. Tenant is in breach of the Lease for failure to pay all rent and additional rent due and as of _____, ____ is in arrears in the sum of $_____.

C. On _____, Landlord served Tenant with a Three–Day Notice to Pay Rent or Quit.

D. Tenant failed to pay the rent demanded within the three-day notice period, and has failed to deliver possession of the Premises to Landlord.

E. As a result, Landlord is entitled to commence an unlawful detainer action and/or breach of lease action against Tenant.

F. Landlord and Tenant wish to avoid the inconvenience, uncertainty, and costs of litigation and desire to amicably resolve this matter.

A G R E E M E N T

For mutual consideration, receipt of which is hereby acknowledged, Landlord and Tenant agree that the recitals above are true in all respects and further agree:

1. Vacation of Premises. On or before _____, ____, Tenant shall vacate the Premises and deliver possession of the Premises to Landlord or its agent.

2. Payment of $ _____ by Tenant to Landlord. Tenant shall pay to Landlord the total sum of $_____ [with/without] interest [What rate? Compound or not?], in the following manner:

(a) $_____ per month for the period of _____;

(b) thereafter, and commencing on _____, ____, $_____ per month for the period of _____ years;

(c) thereafter, and commencing on _____, ___, $_____ per month for the period of _____ year, with an additional $_____ to be paid at or before the end of that year.

3. <u>Confession of Judgment by Tenant</u>. Concurrently with the execution of this Agreement, Tenant shall execute and deliver to Landlord all the documents described below to enable Landlord to obtain a judgment against Tenant by a confession of judgment pursuant to California Code of Civil Procedure Section 1132 et seq., in the amount of $_____ plus _____ percent interest accruing from _____, less any amounts paid pursuant to paragraph 2 of this Agreement. Those documents include "Defendant's Statement re Confession of Judgment", "Attorney's Declaration in Support of Statement Confessing Judgment", "Judgment by Confession," and "Judgment", copies of which are attached hereto as exhibits. The originals of such documents, when executed by Tenant and delivered to Landlord, shall be held in trust by Landlord, or its counsel, and may not be filed or entered with the court except as set forth in paragraph 4, below.

4. <u>Default</u>. In the event Tenant fails to timely vacate the Premises as described in paragraph 1, or fails to make any of the payments described in paragraph 2 in full and when due, Landlord may provide Tenant with notice of default under this Agreement by mailing of the notice of such default via the United States Post Office, certified mail to:

[INSERT ADDRESS]

The default may only be cured by payment of all sums then owing by cash or cashier's check made payable to Landlord prior to the expiration of the 5–day notice period. If Landlord does not receive the required funds by 5:00 p.m. on the 5th day after the mailing of the notice of default, Landlord may immediately file and have entered the Judgment by Confession and Judgment and Landlord may pursue its post-judgment remedies. Tenant hereby waives any right it may have to a hearing prior to the entry of the Judgment by Confession or Judgment. Tenant also agrees that the exhibits to this Agreement may be modified after execution of this Agreement without further consent by Tenant before they are filed with the court to identify Landlord's representative in the upper left-hand corner of the front page of each Exhibit.

5. <u>Mutual Release.</u> Except as to the obligations created by this Agreement, the parties hereby release and forever discharge each other and their respective successors, heirs, spouses, assigns, employees, shareholders, officers, directors, agents, attorneys, insurance carriers, corporations, and their subsidiaries, divisions, or affiliated corporations, organizations or entities, whether previously or hereinafter affiliated in any manner, jointly and severally, from any and all claims, demands, causes of action, obligations, damages, attorneys' fees, costs and liabilities of any nature whatsoever, whether or not now known, suspected or claimed, which the parties ever had, now have or may claim to have as of the date of this Agreement which arise out of, or are connected to, or are related, in any fashion, to the Lease and the Premises (the "Claims").

6. <u>Later Discovered Facts.</u> The parties hereto acknowledge that they may discover facts in the future that are different from or in

addition to those they now know or believe to be true with respect to the Claims and the Parties agree that this Agreement shall be effective in all respects regardless of such additional or different facts.

7. <u>Waiver of Civil Code Section 1542.</u> Except as provided by this Agreement, and with respect only to the Claims, the parties hereto expressly waive and relinquish all rights and benefits they may have under Section 1542 of the Civil Code of the State of California, which reads as follows:

§ 1542 [CERTAIN CLAIMS NOT AFFECTED BY GENERAL RELEASE.] A GENERAL RELEASE DOES NOT EXTEND TO CLAIMS WHICH THE CREDITOR DOES NOT KNOW OR SUSPECT TO EXIST IN HIS FAVOR AT THE TIME OF EXECUTING THE RELEASE, WHICH IF KNOWN BY HIM MUST HAVE MATERIALLY AFFECTED HIS SETTLEMENT WITH THE DEBTOR.

8. <u>Fundamental Fairness.</u> The parties agree that this Agreement has been entered into by each of them voluntarily and with the assistance of counsel after both have read, understood, and negotiated each of its provisions. They further agree that any rule of construction that ambiguities are to be resolved against the drafter shall have no application to this Agreement.

9. <u>No Prior Assignment.</u> The parties hereto, and each of them, represent and warrant to each other that each is the sole and lawful owner of every Claim that each purports to release by this Agreement herein, and that they have not previously assigned or transferred any Claim or portion of a Claim to any entity. In the event that the representation and warranty is false, and any such claim is asserted against any party, then the party who assigned or transferred the Claim or matter shall indemnify, defend, and hold harmless the party against whom such claim or matter is asserted.

10. <u>Attorneys' Fees.</u> The parties hereto agree to bear their own costs and attorneys' fees in connection with the Lease, the Premises, the Three–Day Notice, and the preparation and negotiation of this Agreement. In the event that any action is taken to enforce or interpret this Agreement, the prevailing party shall recover all attorneys' fees involved. Those attorneys' fees include the full and actual costs of any services performed in connection with the matters involved, calculated on the basis of the usual fee charged by the attorneys or others performing these services, and shall not be limited to "reasonable attorneys' fees" as defined in any statute or rule of court.

11. <u>Agreement Binding on Successors.</u> All the terms and provisions of this Agreement shall be binding upon and shall inure to the benefit of the parties and their respective successors and assigns.

12. <u>Governing Law.</u> This Agreement will be construed in accordance with and is governed by the laws of the State of _____.

13. <u>Severability.</u> Should any portion of this Agreement be declared void or unenforceable, that portion will be considered independent and

severable from the remainder, the validity of which shall remain unaffected, provided that this provision shall not be applied so as to defeat the primary intent of the parties: The waiver of the Claims in exchange for delivery of the premises and payments as outlined in paragraphs 1 and 2.

14. <u>Counterparts.</u> This Agreement may be executed in multiple counterparts, each of which shall be considered an original but all of which shall constitute one agreement.

15. <u>Entire Agreement.</u> This Agreement constitutes the entire agreement between Landlord and Tenant and supersedes any and all other agreements, understandings, negotiations, or discussions, either oral or in writing, express or implied, regarding the matters that are the subject of this Agreement. The parties acknowledge (a) that no statements or promises, oral or otherwise, have been made that are not embodied in this Agreement, (b) that they have not executed this Agreement in reliance on any such statement or promise, and (c) that no statement or promise not contained in this Agreement including any purported supplements, modifications, waivers or terminations of this Agreement shall be valid or binding unless executed in writing by all of the parties.

17. <u>No Implied Waiver.</u> The failure of any party, at any time, to insist on compliance with any term, covenant or condition contained in this Agreement shall not be deemed a waiver of that term, covenant or condition, nor shall any waiver or relinquishment of any right or power at any one time be deemed a waiver or relinquishment of any right or power at any other time.

AGREED:

DATED: _____, 20___

By:_____

Its:_____

DATED: _____, 20___

By:_____

†